T0350621

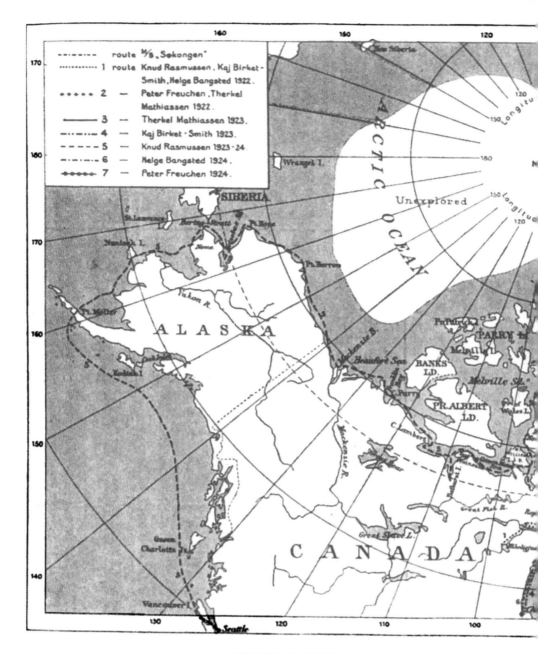

Legend:

- —·—·— route M/S „Søkongen"
- ·········· 1 route Knud Rasmussen, Kaj Birket-Smith, Helge Bangsted 1922.
- ·•·•·• 2 — Peter Freuchen, Therkel Mathiassen 1922.
- ———— 3 — Therkel Mathiassen 1923.
- —··—··— 4 — Kaj Birket-Smith 1923.
- — — — 5 — Knud Rasmussen 1923-24.
- —·—·— 6 — Helge Bangsted 1924.
- ◆•◆•◆ 7 — Peter Freuchen 1924.

AN EPIC ROUTE

When ancient man migrated from Siberia to America one branch went south and became Indians; the other branch went east across the top edge of the continent, winding through the American archipelago to Greenland and down the Greenland coast, around Cape Farewell and up to the Angmagsalik on its eastern side. Starting from Greenland Knud Rasmussen sledged backwards over this epic highway. En route he visited the little tribes of Eskimos, left like pools of water after rain by that great ancient human migration.

ROUTES OF THE
FIFTH THULE EXPEDITION
1921-24

A STONE AGE PEOPLE

In the sumptuousness of our Temperate Zone we live quite ignorant of the terrific struggle that goes on among a little human unit that inhabits the icy shores of our upper continental edge. Beyond the treeline, beyond the crop line, far into the area of eternal ice and snow are buried a score of nomadic Eskimo tribes. These tribes eke out an existence by hunting and fishing. They have no business, no work, no real interests in life save preservation thereof. Their struggles and sacrifices, while tragic, make one of the great stories of the human race.

[endpaper reproduced from original edition, 1927]

ACROSS ARCTIC AMERICA

Knud Rasmussen.

ACROSS
ARCTIC AMERICA

Narrative of the Fifth Thule Expedition

By
KNUD RASMUSSEN

With Introduction By
TERRENCE COLE

UNIVERSITY OF ALASKA PRESS
FAIRBANKS, ALASKA

Library of Congress Cataloging-in-Publication Data

Rasmussen, Knud, 1879–1933.
    [Fra Grønland til Stillehavet. English]
    Across Arctic America: narrative of the Fifth Thule Expedition /
by Knud Rasmussen; with introduction to the 1999 edition by
Terrence Cole.
       p. cm. -- (Classic reprint series; no. 6)
    Originally published: New York: G.P. Putnam's Sons, 1927.
    Includes index.
    ISBN 0-912006-93-5 (cloth: alk. paper). -- ISBN 0-912006-94-3
(pbk.: alk. paper)
    1. Thule Expedition (5th: 1921–1924) 2. Arctic regions-
-Discovery and exploration. 3. Eskimos. I. Title. II. Series:
Classic reprint series (Fairbanks, Alaska); no. 6.
G700 1921.R3813   1999
919.8--dc21   98-32117
                                                CIP

Originally published in 1927 by G. P. Putnam's Sons, New York—
    London.
Introduction to the 1999 Edition by Terrence Cole © 1999 University of
    Alaska Press

International Standard Book Number: cloth 0-912006-93-5
                                         paper 0-912006-94-3
Library of Congress Catalog Number: 98-32117

Printed in the United States.

This publication was printed on acid-free paper that meets the minimum
    requirements of American National Standard for Information
    Sciences-Permanence of Paper for Printed Library Materials, ANSI
    Z39.48-1984.

Publication coordination by Deborah Gonzalez, University of Alaska
    Press
Cover design by Dixon Jones, Rasmuson Library Graphics, University of
    Alaska Fairbanks
Index prepared by Kish Indexing Service
Across Arctic America is volume No. 6 of the University of Alaska
    Press's Classic Reprint Series. This series brings back into print
    highly regarded, classic works of enduring excellence. For more
    information contact the University of Alaska Press, P.O. Box 756240,
    University of Alaska Fairbanks, Fairbanks, Alaska, 99775-6240.

CONTENTS

ILLUSTRATIONS

ILLUSTRATIONS

MAPS

INTRODUCTION TO THE 1999 EDITION

Across Arctic America tells the tale of one of the epic voyages of world history, Knud Rasmussen's trek from Greenland to Siberia in 1921–1924. Like Captain Cook's exploration of the Pacific, or Lewis and Clark's march across the Rockies, Rasmussen's Fifth Thule Expedition set the standard by which all future explorers would be judged. In three and a half years he and his companions traveled nearly 20,000 miles by dog team, collected 20,000 artifacts, and compiled thousands of pages of information about arctic natural history, Eskimo folklore, culture, and customs.* On his journeys Rasmussen explored both the visible world of ice and snow and the invisible world of mind and spirit, recording an incomparable wealth of data about Eskimo intellectual and spiritual life. It was a rich, new dimension which previous explorers had largely missed. "I have not sounded all the depths," Rasmussen wrote. "One can never finish exploring a people."[1]

Rasmussen has been called "the founder of Eskimology."[2] Fellow scientist and explorer Vilhjalmur Stefansson claimed Rasmussen "excelled all others" in the study of the Eskimo and was "supreme in the field of northern folklore."[3] Like

---

*During the age of exploration, "Eskimo" was the term commonly used by outsiders to describe the people of the far north, who generally prefer today to be called Inuit, their word for people. For consistency with Rasmussen's work, the term Eskimo is used in this introduction.

xi

Charles Darwin, Rasmussen had revolutionary insights that created an entirely new way of understanding the history of the world. The ten-volume *Report of the Fifth Thule Expedition* by Rasmussen and his colleagues rivals the *Encyclopedia Britannica* in size and scope and is one of the great treasures of anthropological literature; it is a foundation for virtually every substantial work written about the Eskimo since the 1920s.[4] *Across Arctic America* is a one-volume English translation of the explorer's popular account of his most memorable journey. The University of Alaska Press is pleased to reissue this classic work of arctic literature in commemoration of the seventy-fifth anniversary of the completion of the Fifth Thule Expedition.

As a child Knud Johan Victor Rasmussen probably received the finest training of any European polar explorer in history.[5] The oldest of three children, he was born June 7, 1879, in Jacobshavn (present-day Ilulissat) on the west coast of Greenland, and grew up equally adept at driving dogs and speaking *Kalaallisut*, or Greenlandic Eskimo. In fact he spoke *Kalaallisut* before he learned Danish. Knud's Eskimo name was *Kununguaq* ("Little Knud"). His mother, Sofie Louise Fleischer, was one-quarter Eskimo, and his father, Christian Rasmussen, was a Danish missionary who compiled a Greenlandic grammar, co-authored a Danish-Greenlandic dictionary, and later taught the language at the University of Copenhagen. From his grandmother and both his parents he inherited a deep appreciation for Native language and culture, and enormous pride in his Greenlandic heritage. Famed Danish anthropologist Kaj Birket-Smith later wrote that Rasmussen's "drop of native blood in his veins" undoubtedly strengthened "his feeling of kinship with the Eskimos and even to some extent left its traces in his appearance, although...his features were more like those of an American Indian than of

KNUD
RASMUSSEN
Photograph courtesy of
Dartmouth College Library

an Eskimo."[6] A Native elder in central Canada once praised Rasmussen as "the first white man he had ever seen who was also an Eskimo."[7]

His Greenland childhood gave him a unique perspective. For Rasmussen, the Arctic was naturally not the foreign wasteland that so terrified many European explorers; for him, going to Greenland was going home. "From the very nature of things," Rasmussen wrote, "I was endowed with attributes for Polar work which outlanders have to acquire through painful experience." His arctic journeys invariably brought back memories of his childhood on the shore of Disko Bay. In his mind the "expeditions of later years were like happy continuations of the experiences of my childhood and youth," such that even "the most strenuous sledge-trips became pleasant routine for me."[8]

Rasmussen claimed that his interest in exploring the remote reaches of the Eskimo world also started in childhood. By the age of twelve he believed he knew what his destiny would be. "When I was a child I used often to hear an old Greenlandic woman tell how, far away North at the end of the world, there lived a people who dressed in bearskins and ate raw flesh.... Even before I knew what traveling meant, I determined that one day I would go and find these people...."[9]

After finishing school in Denmark—where he nearly failed due to his poor grades in mathematics—he experimented briefly with a career as an actor and opera singer. He abandoned the stage when a famed soloist told him he was "not exactly a world-shaking baritone," but Rasmussen never lost his passion for fine music. He seldom traveled in the Arctic without a phonograph.[10] Rebuffed as a singer, he then decided to become a writer; it was a serendipitous choice, for his skill with words and his love of language would bring him back to the Arctic and back to Greenland.

At age twenty-one in 1900–1901 he seized the opportunity to visit Iceland and Scandinavia as an apprentice newspaper correspondent. In 1902–1904 his arctic explorations began in earnest when he returned to Greenland as the interpreter for the ill-fated Danish Literary Expedition. In 1902 L. Mylius-Erichsen, a Danish investigative reporter and friend of Rasmussen's, was determined to crack the great wall of secrecy around Greenland and expose official corruption and ineptitude. Since the 18th century the Danish government had attempted to isolate Greenland and its people from the outside world, prohibiting access to the island except for government officials and missionaries. Apparently Mylius-Erichsen planned to publish articles contrasting living conditions in the established Danish settlements in West Greenland with those of the isolated Polar Eskimo in the far north of Greenland, whom Rasmussen had dreamed of visiting as a small child.[11] Reluctantly the government approved the expedition, which arrived in Godthaab in 1902.

Though poorly funded and haphazardly conceived, Mylius-Erichsen's expedition would alter the course of Danish rule in Greenland by prompting a series of government reforms, but even more important, it would launch Knud Rasmussen's career as one of history's foremost arctic explorers. "Rarely has an expedition been founded on so slender a basis," one of Rasmussen's colleagues later explained, "and still obtained such far-reaching results."[12]

The Literary Expedition traveled far north up the coast of Greenland and across Melville Bay to the land of the Polar Eskimo north of Cape York in 1903–1904. These were the northernmost inhabitants on the planet, who lived north of everywhere and everyone. They were the so-called new people or natural people, who had lived in isolation from the Eskimo of West Greenland for at least a century. Cut off from the south by the inland ice cap, which reaches the sea at Melville Bay and forms an ice barrier nearly 200 miles long, the Polar Eskimo were literally a world apart from Danish Greenland, as the government had yet to establish sovereignty over the area. Even for someone who had grown up in Greenland like Rasmussen, his first encounter with the "new people" proved to be a shock.

"Never in my life," Rasmussen wrote, "have I felt myself to be in such wild, unaccustomed surroundings, never so far, so very far away from home, as when I stood in the midst of the tribe of noisy Polar Eskimos on the beach at Agpat."[13]

The winter of 1903–1904 was the first of many that Rasmussen would spend in the Cape York District; over the course of the next three decades he would virtually become a member of the Polar Eskimo band himself. "No hunter exists up there with whom I have not hunted," he later wrote, "and there is hardly a child whose name I do not know...."[14]

The account he published of his first Greenland expedition, *Nye Mennesker* (1905) or "New People," established his reputation as an insightful and sympathetic observer of the Eskimo and a delightful travel writer who relished the wonders of life in the open. Birket-Smith called Rasmussen's "dazzling little book" the story of a journey on which Rasmussen had "found his way back and in to the Eskimo and into himself."[15] Like most of Rasmussen's writings, the book was half ethnology and half poetry.[16]

"It is good sometimes to feel the power of Nature over one," Rasmussen wrote. "You bend in silence and accept the beauty, without words."[17] Facing the hardships of the north, he learned to enjoy the pleasures of what life offered at the present moment, whether it be feasting on "a few cups of tea and a little moldy bread," or camping in a hillside cave out of the wind. "Our tiny winter lair was of cold stones," Rasmussen wrote, "and we had no stove to warm ourselves with, and no firing. And we should have to procure our food from day to day. And yet—I felt a warming wave of joy rush through my body, the joy which those who live on their travels feel most keenly: excitement at the rich possibilities of life!"[18]

Some of his most pleasant memories were the days he was "weatherbound on a desolate coast, far from the conveniences of the overheated huts. There grows up within you a feeling that you have just defeated the malice of the storm nicely when...you have been able to reach a satisfactory shelter, and you can rest at ease with a good friend, wrapped in soft skins— with well-filled stomachs and delicacies to eat—and laugh at everything."[19]

At night he recalled a "quite extraordinary feeling of well-being in the heavy, dozing satisfaction that leads to sleep and dreams. You take your rest when it offers itself, and you take it thoroughly, and drink it in in deep draughts; that storm and misfortune must be slept through, is the sound principle of the Eskimos.... The chance and hazard of existence brings many surprises, and you soon learn to seize and enjoy what offers."[20]

On all of his expeditions Rasmussen seemed to take his greatest pleasure in recording Eskimo legends and tales. What always distinguished him from other explorers like American naval officer Robert E. Peary and Norwegian Roald Amundsen was his fluent command of the Eskimo tongue and the focus and complexity of his investigations. The intellectual and spiritual life of the people themselves were his primary interests, not simply geographical discovery, and thus even when following the tracks of previous explorers, he found uncharted territory.

His basic principle was first to earn the trust of the local people by showing understanding and patience: living with the people and not apart from them, sharing their work and their food, even when it was not the most palatable. "Rotten meat I like," Rasmussen once admitted, "but rotten fish I have never been able to get used to."[21] Nothing of value could be learned by forcing the issue, or asking too many questions too soon. "So I determined to begin by doing nothing," he once described his method, "but simply to live amongst them, be as communicative as possible myself, and wait for an opportunity when the desire to narrate should overmaster their reserve."[22]

When the stories and songs finally started to flow he studied them intently, like an actor preparing to take the stage. In memorizing and writing down what he heard, his rule was "never to repeat any story until I myself had learnt it and told it. In this way I made the whole manner of the story-telling my own, and I have endeavored, as far as possible, to give literal translations."[23]

Listening to the tales of epic travels, he often found himself transfixed by the story-tellers and could imagine he was in the presence of ancient Greek heroes like Odysseus or Achilles.[24] "The Greenlanders love this wandering life," Rasmussen wrote, "and when the conversation turns on their adventures, their tales run on apace. The narrator is fired by the many eyes directed upon him; he gesticulates in illustration of his story, which is now listened to in breathless silence, now accompanied by laughter and shouts of acclamation. It is no read-up knowledge that the Greenlander spins out, but it is a fragment of his own restless life that he is retailing to his comrades...."[25]

As early as 1906, inspired by the Polar Eskimos and his own restless spirit and love of travel, Rasmussen started planning what became his life-long quest: a multiyear scientific expedition by dog team from Greenland to Siberia, which might solve the riddles of northern prehistory, and for the first time give a comprehensive picture of the Eskimo world.[26] But his long-range plans had to be placed on hold due to a more immediate concern: the threat to the Polar Eskimos in the face of encroaching western civilization, largely due to the race to the North Pole.

The passage between Greenland and Ellesmere Island had become the main highway to the North Pole, thanks to the efforts of the indomitable Peary, who had chosen the Greenland route for his repeated unsuccessful attempts at the pole. The Polar Eskimos of the Cape York District were the backbone of Peary's expeditions, and he relied upon them to drive his sledges and pack his supplies in exchange for a wide variety of trade goods, especially guns and ammunition. "There was not a rifle in the tribe when I first went there," Peary wrote about his first expedition in 1891, and he subsequently provided the local people who worked for him with plentiful supplies of breech-loading shotguns, repeating rifles, and boxes of ammunition. Peary likened himself to a millionaire coming upon a small country town and offering every man a "Brownstone mansion and an unlimited bank account." He literally brought these northernmost people gifts from another world, "as far beyond their own unaided efforts as the moon and Mars are beyond the dwellers on this planet."[27]

In reality the supplies which Peary, other explorers, and occasional whaling parties traded with this small band of northernmost Eskimos were of little or modest value by outside standards. Furthermore, all too often alcohol and venereal disease were part of the bargain. Where the Danish flag flew in precincts farther south, the colonial government insulated the Eskimos from unscrupulous traders, but despite Rasmussen's repeated pleas the Danish authorities had never extended their administrative control to the judicial no-man's land north of Melville Bay.

By 1909 the affairs of the Polar Eskimos and the future of northernmost Greenland had reached a critical stage. Peary claimed he had conquered the North Pole and thus would not be returning with his regular supply of guns and ammunition upon which they had come to depend. In addition, Rasmussen learned that traders from three other nations—the United States, Germany, and Norway—were each considering establishing a trading post in the Cape York District. The Danish government refused to take any action, and thus in order to keep out these foreign competitors, and to ensure that the Greenlanders' welfare be protected, Rasmussen decided to take matters into his own hands; he would bring quasi-Danish rule to northwestern Greenland himself.

In the tradition of the 18th century missionary Hans Egede, the "Apostle of Greenland" who initiated Danish colonization and established the paternalistic principles under which the Greenlanders lived, Rasmussen assisted with the founding of a mission outpost at North Star Bay in 1909. The following year, backed by a group of concerned Danish citizens, he and Peter Freuchen established a privately financed trading station for the Cape York District with an inspired dual mission: to provide for the welfare of the local people, and to serve as a base of operations for scientific exploration. As Rasmussen explained, his post was both "bigger and cheaper than a common tradesplace, meant to be like a gentle preparer for civilization and the white man," in which "cultural purposes" would always take precedence over profit.[28] Any money that was made would be used to finance scientific expeditions. Rasmussen gave this unique enterprise, the farthest north trading post in the entire world, the fittingly poetic and legendary name of Thule, after the mystical land that the ancients believed was the end of the earth. Henceforth the world's northernmost inhabitants would be known as the Thule Eskimos, and the seven major arctic expeditions the post sponsored from 1912 to 1933 would be called the Thule Expeditions.[29]

The first four Thule Expeditions (1912–1919) were devoted to northern and eastern Greenland. Not until shortly after his 42nd birthday in 1921 was Rasmussen finally ready to depart on his long-awaited ethnographic and archaeological expedition from Greenland to the Pacific with a goal of solving "the great primary problem of the origin of the Eskimo race."[30] Among Rasmussen's companions on the Fifth Thule Expedition were seven Polar Eskimos, who did the invaluable work of driving dogs, mending clothes, and hunting for food.[31] They included *Iggianguaq* and his wife

Anarulunguaq and her cousin *Miteq*; *Arqioq* and his wife *Anaranguaq*; *Nasaitordluarsuk* and his wife *Aqatsaq*. In addition, the expedition team included Thule Station manager Peter Freuchen, destined to become a world-famous author for his books on polar exploration, and two young Danish scientists in their late 20s who became founding fathers of arctic anthropology: ethnographer Kaj Birket-Smith and archaeologist Therkel Mathiassen.

The Fifth Thule Expedition would not solve the question of the origin of the Eskimo race—indeed the theory of H. P. Steensby endorsed by Rasmussen in this book, that the ancient Eskimo homeland lay inland in central Canada, and that the Eskimos were an offshoot of an Indian tribe, has been discounted by modern researchers.[32] Nevertheless the expedition revolutionized the world's view of the Eskimo, providing for the first time a comparative look at the most widely scattered people on earth, who shared the same basic language and culture.

Though completely sympathetic to the Eskimo, and understanding of the hardships they endured daily, Rasmussen's account in *Across Arctic America* is a powerful antidote to anyone who imagines the Eskimo world of pre-European contact was an idyllic paradise. Without condemnation he writes of habitual female infanticide, abandonment of the aged, disease, murder, cannibalism, starvation and war, and the harsh conditions which engendered such practices. Overshadowing everything else was the constant struggle for survival, and the enveloping fear that he believed inspired most Eskimo religious practices, superstitions, taboos, stories, and folktales. A shaman and skilled poet in central Canada named *Orpingalik,* who was "always singing when not otherwise employed, and called his songs his 'comrades in loneliness,'" told Rasmussen he had no idea how many songs he had made up. "Only I know that they are many, and that all in me is song. I sing as I draw breath."[33] Much of the rich oral literature Rasmussen recorded might otherwise have been lost forever.

Repeatedly Rasmussen was astonished at how well the various Eskimo groups he encountered all across Canada and Alaska could understand his Greenlandic dialect. As University of Alaska Fairbanks linguist Dr. Michael E. Krauss explains, Rasmussen adjusted to the varying dialects he encountered, "village-hopping, milk-train style," across the Arctic. Similarities in language, folklore, ethnographic implements, and archaeological artifacts, from locations thousands of miles distant, demonstrated the unity of the sea-mammal hunting, maritime culture, henceforth known as the Thule Culture after Rasmussen's Fifth Thule Expedition. The Thule Culture had expanded across the Arctic from Alaska to Greenland about a thousand years ago, with the ancestral population of the modern Eskimo people.

At the end of the Fifth Thule Expedition in 1924, Rasmussen wrote that he imagined he could "see our sledge tracks in the white snow out over the edge of the earth's circumference," and like a mirage he could also see "the thousand little native villages which gave substance to the journey."[34] A whole new world, stretching from the rocky shores of Greenland to the east coast of Asia "has all become alive to me. And the Greenland language has opened all hearts, so that I have gone from settlement to settlement like a man picking wild mountain flowers and getting armful after armful...."[35]

"When I think of all this," Rasmussen wrote, "I enjoy again the sweetness of the work...."[36]

Rasmussen's original popular account of the Fifth Thule Expedition was a two-volume work in Danish called *From Greenland to the Pacific*. *Across Arctic America*, the one-volume English translation, appeared in 1927; it was

RASMUSSEN AT BARROW, 1924
Photograph courtesy of Dartmouth College Library

Rasmussen's first book to be widely available in the United States. His poetic style and sure knowledge of the subject captivated readers. "This is in every respect a great book," praised the *Geographical Journal*. "I believe that this book will become one of the primary sources of our knowledge of the Eskimos," William Thalbitzer wrote in the *Geographical Review*. In the *New York Times* Vilhjalmur Stefansson claimed that while other explorers had approached the Eskimos from the outside, Rasmussen had provided a look at the "inner meaning" of Eskimo life. Stefansson's only regret was that the one-volume English version was so drastically shortened from the two-volume Danish original. Nevertheless, he found much in the English edition to praise. In fact Stefansson claimed that Rasmussen had essentially "composed afresh" in English, and hence *Across Arctic America* was not really a translation at

RASMUSSEN MEMORIAL STONE
near Thule, from his friends among the Polar Eskimos, August 1957.
Photograph courtesy of Dartmouth College Library

all, but an original composition that was "not only a work of literary charm but also one of the deepest and soundest interpretations of primitive life and thought that has ever been put into a book."[37]

In the seventy-five years since the conclusion of the Fifth Thule Expedition in 1924, the library of scientific reports it has generated has established Rasmussen's famed expedition as the single most important scientific venture in the history of the Arctic. Rasmussen never lived to see the publication of more than a fraction of the Fifth Thule's findings. He died of complications from food poisoning and pneumonia in December 1933, after the Seventh (and final) Thule Expedition to East Greenland. He was only 54. The *Polar Record* said his sudden death had "robbed the Eskimo of Greenland of their greatest friend," but his books "will long serve to remind us of a genial traveler, a scholar and a poet."[38]

One of Rasmussen's greatest legacies, beyond the volumes of folklore and the rooms of ethnographic and archaeological specimens he collected, may have been his vision of a unified Eskimo culture and oral literature, stretching from the shores of Siberia to the east coast of Greenland. With the Fifth Thule Expedition he was the first to demonstrate the unity of the Eskimo world. In the 1970s, when the Inuit people of Alaska, Canada, and Greenland decided to form the Inuit Circumpolar Conference (ICC) in order to make their common concerns heard more clearly in Washington, Ottawa, Copenhagen, and elsewhere, Knud Rasmussen was clearly the spiritual god-father of the movement. A Danish journalist, one of many travelers in recent years inspired by the Fifth Thule Expedition, subtitled his account of the organization of the ICC, "In the Sledgetracks of Rasmussen."[39]

In *Across Arctic America* Rasmussen captured the pleasure of his life on the trail, and the spirit of his famous expedition which has left such a lasting impression on the history of the Arctic.

—Terrence Cole
History Department
University of Alaska Fairbanks

NOTES

1. See page xxxix.

2. Jean Malaurie, *The Last Kings of Thule* (Chicago: University of Chicago Press, 1985), p. 324.

3. Vilhjalmur Stefansson to Knud Rasmussen, 12/1/30; 1/20/30, Stefansson Collection, Dartmouth College Library.

4. Rasmussen's 1925 article in *The Geographical Review*, "The Danish Ethnographic and Geographic Expedition to Arctic America: Preliminary Report of the Fifth Thule Expedition," (Vol. 15, No. 4, October 1925, pp. 521–562), is a brief summary of the work of the Fifth Thule Expedition. See also Therkel Mathiassen, *Report on the Expedition*, in *Report of the Fifth Thule Expedition 1921–1924*, Vol. 2, No. 1 (Copenhagen: Gyldendal, Nordisk Forlag, 1945).

The literature by and about Rasmussen and his expeditions is enormous. A bibliography compiled by Rasmussen's daughter and his son-in-law contains 3,567 entries through the year 1975. See Inge Kleivan, et. al. "Selected Works by Knud Rasmussen," in *Inuit Studies: The Work of Knud Rasmussen*, Vol. 12, No. 1–2 (1988). The special 1988 issue of *Inuit Studies* entirely devoted to Rasmussen's career is the best overview of his contributions to northern folklore, ethnography, and linguistics.

5. For biographical details about Rasmussen's life see: Rolf Gilberg, "Profile: Knud Rasmussen, 1879–1933," *Polar Record*, Vol. 22, No. 137 (1984), pp. 169–171; E. Cruwys, "Profile: Knud Rasmussen," *Polar Record*, Vol. 26, No. 156 (1990), pp. 27–33. An interesting personal view of Rasmussen can be found in the works of his friend, explorer Peter Freuchen, who wrote several versions of his life with Rasmussen in the Arctic. See: *Arctic Adventure: My Life in the Frozen North* (New York: Farrar and Rinehart, 1935); *Vagrant Viking: My Life and Adventures* (New York: Julian Messner, Inc., 1953); *I Sailed with Rasmussen* (New York: Julian Messner, Inc., 1958).

6. Kaj Birket-Smith, "Knud Rasmussen Biographical Sketch," p. 1, Stefansson Collection, Dartmouth College Library.

7. See p. 64.

8. See p. xxxii.

9. Knud Rasmussen, *The People of the Polar North: A Record* (London: Kegan Paul, Trench, Trubner and Co., 1908), p. xix.

10. Freuchen, *I Sailed With Rasmussen*, p. 38.

11. Birket-Smith, "Knud Rasmussen Biographical Sketch," p. 2.

12. Rev. H. Ostermann, "The Trade From 1870 to the Present Time: A Historical Review," p. 196, in M. Vahl et. al., *Greenland: The Colonization of Greenland and Its History Until 1929*, Vol. III (London: Oxford University Press, 1929).

13. Rasmussen, *The People of the Polar North*, p. 9.

14. Knud Rasmussen, *Greenland by the Polar Sea: The Story of the Thule Expedition from Melville Bay to Cape Morris Jesup* (London: Willian Heinemann, 1921), p. 4.

15. Birket-Smith, "Knud Rasmussen Biographical Sketch," p. 22.

16. H. P. Steensby, "The Polar Eskimos and the Polar Expedition," *The Fortnightly Review*, Vol. 92 (November 1909), p. 894.

17. Rasmussen, *The People of the Polar North*, p. 91.

18. *Ibid.*, pp. 78–79.

19. *Ibid.*, p. 88.

20. *Ibid.,* p. 87.

21. *Ibid.*, p. 338.

22. *Ibid.*, p. 288.

23. *Ibid.*, p. 159.

24. *Ibid.*, p. 260.

25. *Ibid.*, pp. 259–260.

26. *Ibid.*, pp. vii, x–xi.

27. Robert E. Peary, *The North Pole* (New York: Dover Publications, 1986), p. 48.

28. Knud Rasmussen to Vilhjalmur Stefansson, 5/11/1920, Stefansson Collection, Dartmouth College Library; Knud Rasmussen, "The Arctic Station at Thule, North Star Bay, N. Greenland," *Meddelelser om Grønland*, Vol. 51 (1915), pp. 285–286.

29. Rolf Gilberg, "Thule," *Arctic* (June 1976), pp. 83-86; Malaurie, *The Last Kings of Thule*, p. 431.

30. See p. xxxiii.

31. See page xxxiv.

32. Knud Rasmussen, *Observations on the Intellectual Culture of the Caribou Eskimos,* in *Report of the Fifth Thule Expedition 1921–1924,* Vol. 7, No. 2 (Copenhagen: Gyldendal, Nordisk Forlag, 1930), p. 7; Robert McGhee, *Canadian Arctic Prehistory* (Toronto: Van Nostrand Reinhold, Ltd., 1978), pp. 13–25.

33. See pp. 163–164.

34. See p. xxx.

35. Regitze Margrethe Søby, "Some of the Works of Knud Rasmussen as yet Unpublished," p. 201, in *Inuit Studies,* Vol. 12, No. 1–2 (1988), p. 201.

36. H. Ostermann, ed., *The Alaskan Eskimos: As Decribed in the Posthumous Notes of Dr. Knud Rasmussen,* in *Report of the Fifth Thule Expedition 1921–1924,* Vol. 10, No. 3, (Copenhagen: Gyldendal, Nordisk Forlag, 1952), p. 266.

37. *The Geographical Journal,* November 1927, p. 496; *Geographical Review,* April 1927, p. 342; *New York Times Book Review,* April 10, 1927, p. 3; *Canadian Historical Review,* September 1927, p. 251.

38. *New York Times,* December 22, 1993, p. 21; *Geographical Review,* Vol. 24, No. 2, pp. 336–337; *Polar Record,* July 1934, p. 3.

39. Philip Lauritzen, *Oil and Amulets* (Canada: Breakwater Books, 1983). For various other expeditions in recent years intended to retrace Rasmussen's steps see: "Greenland Eskimo Attempt to Retrace Rasmussen Arctic Journey," *Qausagniq: A New Dawn* (North Slope Borough, February 1992), p. 1; *Anchorage Times,* April 11, 1992, p. F9; *Fairbanks Daily News-Miner,* January 3–4, 1992, p. C1; Lew Freedman, "The Long Cold Journey," *We Alaskans (Anchorage Daily News),* February 20, 1994, pp. H7–H14; *Polar Star* (University of Alaska Fairbanks), October 15, 1971, p. 10.

DOGS WHICH MADE THE WHOLE JOURNEY FROM HUDSON BAY TO POINT HOPE, ALASKA

INTRODUCTION

IT is early morning on the summit of East Cape, the
steep headland that forms the eastern extremity of
Siberia.

The first snow has already settled on the heights, giving
one's thoughts the first cool touch of autumn. The air is
keen and clear; not a breeze ruffles the waters of Bering
Strait, where the pack ice glides slowly northward with
the current.

The landscape has a calm grandeur all its own; far away
in the sun-haze of the horizon rises Great Diomede Island,
here forming the boundary between America and Asia.

From where I stand, I look from one continent to
another; for beyond Great Diomede lies, like a bank of
blue fog, another island, the Little Diomede, which belongs
to Alaska.

All before me lies bathed in the strong light of sun and
sea, forming a dazzling contrast to the land behind me.
Here lies the flat, marshy tundra, apparently a land of
dead monotony, but in reality a plain-realm, with the life
of the plain in game and sounds; a lowland which, un-
broken by any range of hills, extends through a world of
rivers and lakes to places with a distant ring, to the
Lena Delta, and, farther, farther on, beyond Cape
Chelyushkin, to regions that lie not far from my own land.

At the foot of the hill I have just ascended I see a crowd
of Tchukchi women on foot, dressed in skins of curious
cut; they have on their backs bags made of reindeer skin
which they are filling with berries and herbs. They fit,

as an item of detail, so picturesquely into the great expanse that I continue to gaze at them until they are lost to sight among the green slopes of the valley.

On a narrow spit of land, with pack ice to the one side and the smooth waters of the lagoon on the other, lies the village or township of Wahlen. It is only now beginning to wake; and one by one the cooking-fires are lighted in the dome-shaped tents of walrus hide.

Not far from the coast town, clearly silhouetted on the skyline, a flock of tame reindeer move slowly along the crest of a hill, nibbling the moss as they go, while herdsmen, uttering quaint far-sounding cries, surround them and drive them down to the new feeding grounds.

To all these people, this is an ordinary day, a part of their everyday life; to me, an adventure in which I hardly dare believe. For this landscape and these people mean, to me, that I am in Siberia, west of the last Eskimo tribe, and that the Expedition has now been carried to its close.

The height on which I stand, and the pure air which surrounds me, give me a wide outlook, and I see our sledge tracks in the white snow out over the edge of the earth's circumference, through the uttermost lands of men to the North. I see, as in a mirage, the thousand little native villages which gave substance to the journey. And I am filled with a great joy; we have met the great adventure which always awaits him who knows how to grasp it, and that adventure was made up of all our manifold experiences among the most remarkable people in the world!

Slowly we have worked our way forward by unbeaten tracks, and everywhere we have increased our knowledge.

How long have those sledge journeys been?—counting our road straight ahead together with the side excursions up inland and out over frozen seas, now hunting game,

and now seeking out some isolated and remote people?
Say, 20,000 miles; more or less,—nearly the circumference of the earth.   Yet how little that matters, for it
was not the distances that meant anything to us!   One
forgets to count miles after three and a half years of
constant go, go, go,—and tries only to keep in mind the
accumulating experiences.

In my joy in having been permitted to take this long
sledge journey, my thoughts turn involuntarily to a
contrasting enterprise ending also in Alaska, where last
Spring, people were awaiting the visit of daring aviators
from the other side of the globe.   And from my heart I
bless the fate that allowed me to be born at a time when
Arctic exploration by dog sledge was not yet a thing of
the past.   In this sudden retrospect, kindled by the great
backward view from East Cape, indeed, I bless the whole
journey, forgetting hardship and chance misfortune by
the way, in the exultation I feel in the successful conclusion of a high adventure!

A calmer and more deliberate mental review of that long
journey brings almost as much regret as pleasure.   For
I find that to tell of my observations on the trip, in a book
of proper length, compels me to omit more than I can include; and, often, things of great interest.

Particularly painful is it to leave out a statement of the
accomplishments of my associates on the Expedition.
At the beginning I was merely the leader of a whole group,
which included some Danish scientists of note.   During
the first year, we worked together out of a base on the
eastern coast of Canada, going out in small parties to
various stations, and returning from time to time to
collate our material.   Our work had mainly to do with
ethnography; my associates were concerned also with

archeology, geology, botany and cartography. They did notable work in mapping territory known before only in a vague way. We did much excavating in ruins of former Eskimo cultures. The work of my colleagues in this field, especially, contributed much to knowledge of the past. Full reports of their findings have been published in books, monographs, and papers under their own names before learned societies. This allusion here must stand as the chief acknowledgment, in the present book, of their work. They enter hereafter only in passing.

For, here, I am constrained by limitations of subject to confine myself to a portion of the material I gathered personally, both while I was with them, and later, when I set out on my visit alone to all the tribes of Arctic North America.

It was my privilege, as one born in Greenland, and speaking the Eskimo language as my native tongue, to know these people in an intimate way. My life's course led inevitably toward Arctic exploration, for my father, a missionary among the Eskimos, married one who was proud of some portion of Eskimo blood. From the very nature of things, I was endowed with attributes for Polar work which outlanders have to acquire through painful experience. My playmates were native Greenlanders; from the earliest boyhood I played and worked with the hunters, so that even the hardships of the most strenuous sledge-trips became pleasant routine for me.

I was eight years old when I drove my own team of dogs, and at ten I had a rifle of my own. No wonder, therefore, that the expeditions of later years were like happy continuations of the experiences of my childhood and youth.

Later, when I became aware of the interest which the culture and history of the Eskimo hold for science, I was able to spend eighteen years in Greenland again, laying down the foundation, by the long study of one tribe, for a more comprehensive study of all the tribes.

In 1902, I began my active ethnographical and geographical work with the Eskimos, which has continued pretty steadily since. In 1910 I established, in collaboration with M. Ib Nyeboe, a station for trading and for study in North Greenland, and to it I gave the name of "Thule," because it was the most northerly post in the world,—literally, the Ultima Thule. This became the base of my subsequent expeditions, four major efforts in ten years, and all called "Thule Expeditions."

By 1920 I had completed my program of work in Greenland, and the time had come to attack the great primary problem of the origin of the Eskimo race. The latter enterprise took definite shape in the summer of 1921, in the organization of an expedition which went from Greenland all the way to the Pacific. At the beginning we worked from a headquarters on Danish Island, west of Baffinland, excavating among the ruins of a former Eskimo civilization, and studying the primitive inland Eskimo of what are known as the Barren Grounds.

Later, with two Eskimo companions, I travelled by dog sledge clear across the continent to the Bering Sea. I visited all the tribes on the way, living on the country, and sharing the life of the people. What I observed on that trip constitutes my story.

The Eskimo is the hero of this book. His history, his present culture, his daily hardships, and his spiritual life constitute the theme and the narrative. Only in form of telling, and as a means of binding together the various incidents is it even a record of my long trip by dog sledge. Whatever is merely personal in my adventures must be cut out, along with the record of the scientific achievements of my associates.

Even the Eskimo will suffer some omissions,—for it is obvious that only a portion of the story can be told, when the selection has to be made from thirty note-books, and 20,000 items of illustrative material.

Yet I think it due my companions, before so summarily disposing of them, to point out that the first year of joint effort with them helped greatly to shape my own work and to spur me to enthusiasm sufficient to carry over the long pull alone. In enumerating the rest of the party, I am in one sense naming co-authors.

With me, then, were Peter Freuchen, cartographer and naturalist; Therkel Mathiassen, archeologist and cartographer; Kaj Birket-Smith, ethnographer and geographer; Helge Bangsted, scientific assistant; Jacob Olsen, assistant and interpreter; and Peder Pedersen, Captain of the Expedition's motor schooner, *Sea-King*.

The official title of the Expedition was: "The Fifth Thule Expedition,—Danish Ethnographical Expedition to Arctic North America, 1921–24."

It was honored by the patronage of King Christian X. of Denmark, and advised by a committee consisting of M. Ib Nyeboe, chairman, and Chr. Erichssen, Col. J. P. Koch, Professors O. B. Boeggild, Ad Jensen, C. H. Ostenfeld, of Copenhagen University, and Th. Thomsen, Inspector of the National Museum at Copenhagen.

Hardly less important to the comfort and success of the Expedition than the work of these scientists was the contribution of our Eskimo assistants from Greenland, and those we added locally from time to time. We brought with us Iggianguaq and his wife, Anarulunguaq; Arqioq and his wife Anaranguaq; Nasaitordluarsuk, hereinafter known as "Bosun," together with his wife, Aqatsaq; and finally, a young man, known as Miteq,—a cousin of Anarulunguaq.

Iggianguaq died of influenza after we were far from home, and his wife continued with me to the end of the long trip, along with Miteq. It was her duty, as that of the other women, to keep the fur clothing mended, to cook, and, on the journey, to help drive the dogs. The men drove, hunted food for men and dogs, and built snow huts wherever we set up new camps.

Anarulunguaq is the first Eskimo woman to travel widely, and along with Miteq, the only one to visit all the tribes of her kinsmen. She has received a medal from the King of Denmark for her fine work. After the first year, I struck out with one team of dogs and these two Eskimos for the trip across to Nome. Considering the rigors they endured, I don't know which is the more remarkable, that I came through the three and a half years with the same team of dogs, or with the same Eskimos. Surely, however, it is no mere sentimental gesture to point out that they had a bigger share in the outcome of the trip than I have space to show.

One omission likely to be welcomed, at least by the reader, is the almost total excision of theories about the origins of the Eskimos. This being one of the chief assignments of our research, I think it a mark of strict literary discipline to have succeeded in keeping it so nearly completely out of the story,—at least in the manner approved by scientists. As an outlet to suppressed dogmatizing, therefore, I am going to make a compact little statement, at this point, of some of our conclusions, and hereafter allow the facts to point to their own conclusions.

The Eskimos are widely scattered from Greenland to Siberia, along the Arctic Circle, about one-third of the way around the globe. They total in all no more than 33,000 souls, which represents, perhaps, the outside number of persons who can gain their livelihood by hunting in a country so forbidding. They have a wide range in following the seasonal movement of game, but in so vast a territory the different tribes are scattered and isolated from each other. Good evidence leads us to believe that a period of at least 1500 years has elapsed since the various tribes broke off from one original stock.

In so prolonged a separation, it would be natural for the language and traditions of the various tribes to have lost all homogeneity. Yet the remarkable thing I found was that my Greenland dialect served to get me into complete understanding with all the tribes. Two great divisions appeared in the customs,—a land culture and a coastal culture. The most primitive Eskimos, a nomadic tribe who lived in the interior and hunted caribou, had almost no knowledge of the sea, and their customs and tabus were limited accordingly. Nothing in their traditions or implements indicated that they had ever been acquainted with marine pursuits. But the folklore of the sea-people, in addition to being unique in its references to ocean life, was in many other respects identical with that of the tribes that had never been down to sea. The conclusion was inevitable that originally all the Eskimos were land hunters, and that a portion of them later turned to hunting sea-mammals. The latter people retained all their old vocabulary and myths, and added thereto a nomenclature and a folklore growing out of their experience on the water.

As for what happened before that, in the remote past, the theory I came to accept was that long, long ago, the Eskimos and the Indians were of common root. But different conditions developed different customs, to such a degree that now there seems to be no resemblance between the Indians and the Eskimos. But the likenesses are there, not obvious to the wayfarer, but sufficiently plain to the microscopic eye of the scientist.

The aboriginal Eskimos developed a special culture around the big rivers and lakes of the northernmost part of Canada. From here, they moved down to the coast, either because they were driven by hostile tribes or because they had to follow the caribou in their migrations. They developed the first phases of a coastal culture at the Arctic Coast of Canada, most probably between Coronation Gulf and the Magnetic North Pole.

From here they wandered over to Labrador, Baffinland, and Greenland, to the east, and westward, reached Alaska and the Bering Sea. Around the Bering, with its abundance of sea-animals, they had their Golden Age, as a coastal people.

From here a new migration took place, for what reason we cannot know, but this time from the West to the East, and here we find the explanation for all the ruins of permanent winter houses we discovered along the Arctic Coast between Greenland and Alaska. The present Eskimos do not construct such houses, which were built in rather recent times by people known as the Tunit. The Greenlanders, however, do, and they are undoubtedly the original Tunit.

During all these years of migration, some tribes kept to their old places in the interior, which explains why we were able to find aboriginal Eskimos in the Barren Grounds. These facts, together, explain why the spiritual culture exhibited a certain continuity between all the tribes.

The foregoing was the theory advanced by Prof. H. P. Steensby, of the University of Copenhagen, and all of our researches lent support to it.

There is another general theory with regard to the

Eskimos which has but slight relation to the question of American origins, for it goes back to much more ancient times,—not less than 25,000 years ago. This theory traces the Eskimo back to a time when our own ancestors of the Glacial Period lived under similar arctic conditions, and, presumably, resembled the Eskimo of today. All remains of the material culture of the Glacial, or Stone Age are exactly comparable with that of the Arctic dwellers, and the theory assumes that a similar spiritual resemblance can be inferred. This grows naturally out of the discovery that the Eskimos, intimately studied, are much more spiritual-minded, much more intelligent, much more likeable than the average man has been led to expect. They prove to be human beings just like ourselves,—so like, indeed, that we cannot avoid drawing them into the fold, and saying, "These people belong to our race!"

For they do, certainly, react to the suffering, the sacrifices, the hardships and the mysteries of evil which they face, much as we do. Their philosophy, even when untouched by any influences of civilization, has many curiously modern slants, including such ideas as auto-suggestion, spirit seances, and cataleptcy. Their poetry has many resemblances to ours, their religion and folklore often resemble, even in phrasing, as well as in content, our earlier religious literature.

Some archeologists have made bold to assert that the Eskimos are surviving remnants of the Stone Age we know, and are, therefore, our contemporary ancestors. We don't have to go so far to claim kinship with them, however, for we *recognize* them as brothers.

I believe that the following pages will bear out this statement. Even so, I do not dare to feel that the whole story of the Eskimo, or his whole appeal to our sympathies will be found here.

"THE SEA-KING" AT DANE ISLAND

In the foreground, preparations for our winter quarters.

THE BLOW-HOLE

Headquarters of the Expedition on Dane Island. As soon as the snow had formed in good firm drifts round the wooden house, we laid a covering of thick snow blocks over all. A whole system of snow huts was also built close by, to serve as sheds and store rooms.

I have not sounded all the depths. One can never finish exploring a people.

The Expedition started from Copenhagen on the 17th of June, 1921, and proceeded via Greenland, in order to pick up additional members of the party, and arctic equipment. The vessel employed was one built especially for the trip,—the schooner *Sea-King*, of something over 100 tons.

Since the scientific members of the Expedition would be so occupied with their tasks that they would hardly have time for hunting, and procuring food for the dogs, this important task was to be entrusted to the Greenlanders from Thule, who are at once skilful travellers and notable hunters.

After a favorable passage across the dreaded and ice-filled Melville Bay, we arrived at Thule on the 3rd of August, and engaged our native assistants. Leaving Greenland through Fox Channel in mid-September, forcing a passage through heavy ice around to the north of Southampton Island, we found a harbor on a little, unknown and uninhabited island. A whole month was spent in building a house for our winter quarters,—we called it the "Blow-hole," by reason of the prevalent winds—and in sledge trips in various directions with a view to ascertaining our position. Our observations gave this as 65° 54′ N, 85° 50′ W, but the old maps were so inadequate that we could not at first mark the locality on any existing chart.

The place was afterward called Danish Island. Here in a smiling valley opening seaward upon a shelving beach, and landward, sheltered by a great crescent of guardian hills, we erected what was to be our home for months to come.

Scarcely were we ashore when we found fresh bear tracks in the sand immediately below the location we had chosen for our home. On our first brief reconnaissance to the top of a neighboring hill, we encountered a hare so amazingly tame that we were tempted actually to essay his capture with our bare hands. Soon afterward we spied a lonely caribou who at once was all curiosity and came running toward us to investigate these strange visitors. The confidence of the game showed well enough how little disturbed the region had been. Never before had I encountered from animals such a friendly greeting.

From the top of the hills we had a fine view of a neighboring fjord, and out in the open water were seen glistening dark backs of walrus curving along the surface as they fed. Such was our first impression of this new country, truly a land hospitable in its promise of game.

By October, the ground was covered with snow, and a narrow channel behind the house frozen over. The first thing now was to get into touch with the nearest natives as soon as possible; but as the mouth of Gore Bay was open water we were unable to travel far, and by the end of October all we had found was a few old cairns and rough stone shelters built by the Eskimo of earlier days for the purpose of caribou hunting with bow and arrow. The first meeting with the Eskimos of the new world was yet before us.

ACROSS ARCTIC AMERICA

THE FIRST MAN TO GREET US IN THESE NEW LANDS

His face and hair were thick with icicles.

ACROSS ARCTIC AMERICA

CHAPTER I

OLD FRIENDS IN NEW SKINS

I HAD halted to thaw my frozen cheeks when a
sound and a sudden movement among the dogs
made me start.

There could be no mistake as to the sound,—it
was a shot. I glanced round along the way we had
come, fancying for a moment that it might be the
party behind signalling for assistance; but I saw
them coming along in fine style. Then I turned to
look ahead.

I had often imagined the first meeting with the
Eskimos of the American Continent, and wondered
what it would be like. With a calmness that surprised myself, I realized that it had come.

Three or four miles ahead a line of black objects
stood out against the ice of the fjord. I got out
my glass; it might, after all, be only a reef of rock.
But the glass showed plainly: a whole line of sledges
with their teams, halted to watch the traveller approaching from the South. One man detached himself from the party and came running across the ice

3

in a direction that would bring him athwart my course. Evidently, they intended to stop me, whether I would or no. From time to time, a shot was fired by the party with the sledges.

Whether the shots fired and the messenger hurrying toward me with his harpoon were evidence or not of hostile intent, I did not stop to think. These were the men I had come so far to seek from Denmark and from my familiar haunts in Greenland. Without waiting for my companions to come up, I sprang to the sledge, and urged on the dogs, pointing out the runner as one would a quarry in the chase. The beasts made straight for him, tearing along at top speed. When we came up with him, their excitement increased; his clothes were of unfamiliar cut, the very smell of him was strange to them; and his antics in endeavoring to avoid their twelve gaping maws only made them worse.

"Stand still!" I cried; and, taking a flying leap out among the dogs, embraced the stranger after the Eskimo fashion. At this evidence of friendship the animals were quiet in a moment, and sneaked off shamefacedly behind the sledge.

I had yelled at the dogs in the language of the Greenland Eskimo. And, from the expression of the stranger's face, in a flash I realized that he had understood what I said.

He was a tall, well-built fellow, with face and hair covered with rime, and large, gleaming white teeth showing, as he stood smiling and gasping, still breathless with exertion and excitement. It had all come about in a moment,—and here we were!

As soon as my comrades behind had come within hail, we moved on toward the party ahead, who had been watching us all the time. Our new friend informed me that his name was Papik and that he had come from the neighborhood of Lyon Inlet,— the next large inlet to the North of our recently established headquarters camp on Danish Island. There was not time for much talk, before we came up with the others; and I was anxious this time to check the dogs before they became too excited. As we approached, the men came out to meet us, the women and children remaining with the sledges.

These men, then, were the Akilinermiut,—the "men from behind the Great Sea," of whom I had heard in my earliest youth in Greenland, when I first began to study the Eskimo legends. The meeting could hardly be more effectively staged; a whole caravan of them suddenly appearing out of the desert of ice, men, women and children, dressed up in their fantastic costumes, like living illustrations of the Greenland stories of the famous "inland-dwellers." They were clad throughout in caribou skin; the fine short haired animals shot in the early autumn. The women wore great fur hoods and long, flapping "coat-tails" falling down over the breeches back and front. The curious dress of the men was as if designed especially for running; cut short in front, but with a long tail out behind. All was so unlike the fashions I had previously met with that I felt myself transported to another age; an age of legends of the past, yet with abundant promise for the future, so far as my own task of comparing the various tribes

of Eskimos was concerned.   I was delighted to find
that the difference in language was so slight that
we had not the least difficulty in understanding one
another.   Indeed, they took us at first for tribes-
men of kindred race from somewhere up in Baffin
Island.

So far as I thought they would understand, I
explained our purposes to my new friends.   The
white men, Peter Freuchen and myself, were part
of a larger party who had come out of the white
man's country to study all the tribes of the Eskimo,
—how they lived, what language they talked, how
they hunted, how they amused themselves, what
things they feared, and believed about the future
life—every manner of thing.   We were going to buy
and carry back to our own country souvenirs of the
daily life of the Eskimo, in order that the white man
might better understand, from these objects, the
different way the people of the northern ice country
had to live.   And we were going to make maps and
pictures of parts of this country in which no white
man had ever been.

I introduced, then, my Eskimo companion (Bosun),
—a man from Greenland who was almost as strange
to the Akilinermiut as I.   He had come along to
hunt and to drive sledges, and do other work for
the white man, while we gave our time to these
studies.

My new friends were greatly pleased and impressed.   They had just set out for their autumn
camp up country at the back of Lyon Inlet, taking
with them all their worldly goods.   Being, however,

like Eskimos generally, creatures of the moment, they at once abandoned the journey on meeting us, and we decided to set off all together for some big snowdrifts close at hand, where we could build snow huts and celebrate the meeting.

Accustomed as we were ourselves to making snow huts, we were astonished at the ease and rapidity with which these natives worked. The Cape York Eskimos, in Greenland, reckon two men to the task of erecting a hut; one cutting the blocks and handing them to the other, who builds them up. Here, however, it was a one-man job; the builder starts with a few cuts in the drift where he proposes to site his house, and then proceeds to slice out the blocks and lay them in place, all with a speed that left us staring open-mouthed. Meantime one of the women brought out a remarkable type of snow-shovel, with an extra handle on the blade, or business end, and strewed a layer of fine snow over the wall as it rose, thus caulking any chinks or crevices, and making all thoroughly weather-proof. Two technical points which particularly impressed our Cape York man, as an expert, were firstly the way these men managed to build with loose snow—some degree of firmness being generally considered essential—and further, the very slight arch of the roof, which has ordinarily to be domed pretty roundly for the blocks to hold, whereas here, it was almost flat. In less than three quarters of an hour, three large huts were ready for occupation; then, while the finishing touches were given to the interior, the blubber lamps were lighted and the whole made warm and cosy.

I and my two companions distributed ourselves among the three huts, so as to make the most of our new acquaintances. Caribou meat was put on to boil; but we found also, that our hosts had both tea and flour among their stores, which they had purchased from a white man down at Repulse Bay, not far from the camp. This was news of importance to us, for it meant we might have a chance of sending letters home in the spring.

In the course of the meal, I obtained some valuable information as to the neighborhood and neighbors. There were native villages, it appeared, in almost every direction round about our headquarters. They were not numerous, but the more interesting in their varied composition. There were the Igdlulik from Fury and Hecla Strait, the Aivilik between Repulse Bay and Lyon Inlet, and a party of Netsilik from the region of the North-west Passage. Only half a day's journey from the camp there was a family from Ponds Inlet, on the north coast of Baffin Land.

Conversation was for the most part general, as it mostly is on first acquaintance. Speaking the same tongue, however, we were not regarded altogether as strangers, and I was able even to touch on questions of religion. And I soon learned that these people, despite their tea and flour and incipient enamel-ware culture, were, as regards their view of life and habit of thought, still but little changed from their ancestors of ages past.

Plainly, here was work for us in plenty, and an interesting task it promised to be. We had, moreover, been well received, and I anticipated little difficulty in gathering information. First of all, however, we must go on to seek the nearest Hudson's Bay Company station, and find out whether there really would be any opportunity of postal communication in the spring.

We started accordingly, on the following morning. On the 5th of December, while it was still daylight, we reached the spot where, according to the Eskimo accounts, the white man had his quarters. At the base of a little creek, behind huge piles of twisted and tumbled ice, stood a modest looking building, dark against the colony of snow huts which surrounded it. This, we found, was the extreme advanced post of the Hudson's Bay Company of Adventurers, one of the oldest and greatest trading companies in the world.

We had hardly drawn up in front of the house before the station manager, Captain Cleveland, came out and greeted us with the most cordial welcome. He proved, also, to be a remarkably quick and efficient cook, and had a meal ready for us in no time; a steaming dish of juicy caribou steaks and a Californian bouquet of canned fruit in all varieties.

George Washington Cleveland was an old whaler who had been stranded on the coast here over a generation before, and made himself so comfortable among the Eskimos that he had never been able to tear himself away. Nevertheless, he was more of an American than one would expect from his isolated life, and was proud of having been born on the very shore where the *Mayflower* had first landed. He had been through all manner of adventures, but neither shipwreck nor starvation, not to speak of the other forms of adversity that had fallen to his lot, could sour his cheery temper or impair his steady, seaman-like assurance of manner.

We knew really very little about this arctic region of Canada, and Captain Cleveland's information was most valuable to us later on.   We learned now that one of the Hudson's Bay Company's schooners, commanded by a French Canadian, Captain Jean Berthie, was wintering at Wager Bay, five days' journey farther to the south.   There was a chance that we might be able to send letters home in the course of the winter by this route, and it was at once decided that Freuchen should set out for the spot and bring back news.

There was a dance that evening, to celebrate the visitors' arrival.   The Eskimo men and women had learned, from the whalers, American country dances. Music was provided by the inevitable gramophone which seems to follow on the heels of the white man to most parts of the world.   And the women were decked out in ball dresses hastily contrived for the occasion from material supplied by Captain Cleveland.

Later on, we made a round of the huts, which were refreshingly cool after the heat of the ballroom.   We were anxious to get more information as to the country round, but being unacquainted with the Eskimo names of places near, we could only go by the old English maps, and were rather at a deadlock when aid arrived from an unexpected quarter.   An old fellow with a long white beard, and eyes reddened with the strain of many a blizzard, revealed himself as a geographical expert.

We brought out paper and pencil, and to my astonishment, this "savage" drew, without hesitation, a map of the coastline for a distance of some hundreds of miles, from Repulse Bay right up to Baffin Land. The map completed, he told me all the Eskimo place names, and at last we are able to get a real idea as to the population of the district and the position of the settlements. I was elated here to note that the majority of these names; Naujarmiut, Pitorqermiut, Nagssugtormiut and many others, were identical with some of the familiar place names from that part of Greenland where I was born. And when I began telling of the Greenland folk tales to the company here, it turned out that they knew them already; and were, moreover, themselves astonished to find that a stranger should be acquainted with what they regarded as their own particular legends.

I was looking forward to closer acquaintance with these people and their history and traditions; Ivaluartjuk, who had drawn the map, would, I foresaw, be particularly useful as a source of information. But we could not now remain longer than the one whole day, and on the 7th of December, we took leave of our new friends, Freuchen going down as arranged to meet Captain Berthie at Wager Bay, while Bosun and I drove back to our winter quarters. After passing Haviland Bay, however, we came upon some old sledge tracks, and decided to follow and see whither they led.

CHAPTER II

IN the middle of a big lake an old Eskimo woman
stood fishing for trout. In spite of the fact that
the winter was yet young the ice had already become
so thick that all her strength must have been needed
in cutting the hole for her line. Now and then she
took a piece of drift-wood shaped like a shovel and
pushed away the fragments of ice that were in her
way. Then stretching out on her stomach she thrust
half her body so far into the hole that all that remained visible was a pair of bent, skin-covered legs
waving in the air.

Suddenly a puppy that had lain buried in the snow
scrambled to his feet and started to bark wildly.
Tumbling out of the hole, the old woman crouched,
bewildered at seeing Bosun and myself so near her.
At full speed our dogs dashed down on the odd pair.

Uttering a sharp cry, she seized the pup by the
scruff of the neck and set out in the direction of the
village as fast as her ancient legs would carry her.
The panic of her flight only served to increase the
wildness of our dogs, already excited by the scent
of the village, and such was their speed that, in passing the fugitive, I had barely time to seize her and
fling her on top of the flying sledge. There she lay

with horror in her eyes, while I burst out laughing at the absurdity of the scene. At length, through her tears of fright, she started to smile, too, realizing that I was a human, and a friendly human being, at that.

It was old Takornaoq. She now sat with arms convulsively clutching the whimpering pup. Then above the noise of the frightened dog I suddenly heard a sound that startled me in turn. Bending over her and cautiously lifting her skin kolitah I discovered far down inside her peltry clothing a small infant clinging to her naked back and whimpering in unison with the mother and the terrified puppy.

Such was my meeting with Takornaoq. Soon we were friends. We raced merrily along to her village, which consisted of three snow huts. Here we were introduced to the notables of the place.

Inernerunassuaq was an old angakoq, or wizard, from the neighborhood of the Magnetic Pole. He screwed up his eyes to a couple of slits on being introduced, and was careful to draw my attention to his magic belt, which was hung about with zoological preparations. His wife was a simple soul, fat and comfortable, as befits one married to a specialist in the secret arts. They had a large family of small children who hung about getting in the way; none of them had reached the age when a child is reckoned worthy of a name, and their parents simply pointed at this one or that when telling them to be quiet.

Then there was Talerortalik, son-in-law to the foregoing, having married Uvtukitsoq, the wizard's daughter. They looked an insignificant pair; but we found out afterwards that it was they who made ends meet for the wizard and his flock. Finally, there was Peqingassoq, the cripple, who was said to be specially clever at catching trout. Others were briefly introduced, and Takornaoq carried me off to her own hut. It was clean and decent as such places go, but chilly, until we got the blubber lamp well alight.

Bosun and I settled down comfortably on the sleeping place among the cosy caribou skins. And as soon as the meat was put on to boil, Takornaoq sat down between us with the unexpected observation that she was "married to both of us now," her husband, whom she loved, being away on a journey. Then taking a tiny infant from her amaut, she laid it proudly in a hareskin bag. The child was named Qasitsoq, after a mountain spirit, the mother explained. It was not her own child, but one of twins born to a certain Nagsuk; she had bought it for a dog and a frying pan. It was too much really, for such a pitiful little creature, nothing but skin and bone; Takornaoq complained bitterly that Nagsuk had cheated, and given her the poorer of the two.

Our hostess told us a great deal about herself and her family. She was of the Igdlulik, from Fury and Hecla Strait, a tribe noted for clever hunters and good women; and she was proud of her origin, as being superior to that of her fellow-villagers here. Our visit was most welcome, she assured us, and even went to the length of voicing her appreciation in an improvised song, which she delivered sitting between us on the bench. Her voice, it is true, was somewhat over-mellowed by her sixty odd winters, but its quavering earnestness fitted the kindly, frank, simplicity of the words:

> Aya iya, aya ya-iya,
> The lands about my dwelling
> Are grown fairer this day
> Since it was given me to see
> The face of strangers never seen.
> All is fairer,
> All is fairer,
> And life is thankfulness itself.
>
> Aya, these guests of mine
> Bring greatness to my house,
> Aya iya, aya ya-iya.

Immediately after the song, dinner was served. Our hostess, however, did not join us at the meal; a sacrifice enjoined by consideration for the welfare of the child. Among her tribe, it appeared, women with infant children were not allowed to share cooking utensils with others, but had their own, which were kept strictly apart.

Not content with feeding us, however, she then opened a small storehouse at the side of the hut, and dragged forth the whole carcase of a caribou. This, the good old soul explained, was for our dogs. And with rare tact, she tried to make the gift appear as a matter of course. "It is only what my husband would do if he were at home. Take it, and feed them." And she smiled at us with her honest old eyes as if really glad to be of use.

Bosun and I agreed that it was the first time in our lives a woman had given us food for our dogs.

We enquired politely after her husband, Patdloq, and learned that she had been married several times before.   One of her former husbands, a certain Quivapik, was a wizard of great reputation, and a notable fighter.   On one occasion, at Southampton Island, he was struck by a harpoon in the eye, while another pierced his thigh.   "But he was so great a wizard that he did not die of it after all."   He was an expert at finding lost property, and had a recipe of his own for catching fish.

"Once we were out fishing for salmon, but I caught nothing.   Then came Quivapik and taking the line from me, swallowed it himself, hook and all, and pulled it out through his navel.   After that I caught plenty."

Another of Takornaoq's adventures shows something of the dreadful reality of life in these regions.

"I once met a woman who saved her own life by eating her husband and her children.

"My husband and I were on a journey from Igdlulik to Ponds Inlet.   On the way he had a dream; in which it seemed that a friend of his was being eaten by his own kin.   Two days after, we came to a spot where strange sounds hovered in the air.   At first we could not make out what it was, but coming nearer it was like the ghost of words; as it were one trying to speak without a voice.   And at last it said:

"*'I am one who can no longer live among humankind, for I have eaten my own kin.'*

"We could hear now that it was a woman.   And we looked at each other, and spoke in a whisper,

WOMAN'S DRESS, FRONT VIEW

The sleeves are made so loose in the shoulder that when travelling in a blizzard the arms can be drawn up out of the sleeves altogether, and crossed on the breast inside to warm them. The band across the forehead, a woman's principal ornament, is here made from a piece of brass that had formed part of a telescope. The woman here shown, Ataguvtaluk, is one of the survivors of a famine, when she lived on the bodies of her husband and children. Blue veins show up prominently round her mouth, said to be due to her having eaten her own flesh and blood.

LANCASTER SOUND

BRODEUR PENINSULA

COCKBURN LAND

BAFFIN ISLAND

GULF OF BOOTHIA

FRANKLIN STRAIT

BOOTHIA PENINSULA

KING WILLIAM ISLAND

Simpson Pen.

COMMITTEE BAY

MELVILLE PENINSULA

FOX CHANNEL

FOX LAND

HUDSON STRAIT

CHESTERFIELD INLET

SOUTHAMPTON ISLAND

Frozen Strait

Coats I.

HUDSON BAY

PRELIMINARY MAP
of the Territories mapped by
5ᵗ THULE EXPEDITION
by
Peter Freuchen and Therkel Mathiassen
1925

Mapped by 5th Thule Expedition
Glaciers
Hudson Bay Company Posts
Heights in metres
Scale on Latitude 64°0′ N.
1:6,600,000

fearing what might happen to us now. Then searching round, we found a little shelter built of snow and a fragment of caribou skin. Close by was a thing standing up; we thought at first it was a human being, but saw it was only a rifle stuck in the snow. But all this time the voice was muttering. And going nearer again we found a human head, with the flesh gnawed away. And at last, entering into the shelter, we found the woman seated on the floor. Her face was turned towards us and we saw that blood was trickling from the corners of her eyes; so greatly had she wept.

"'Kikaq' (a gnawed bone) she said, 'I have eaten my husband and my children!'

"She was but skin and bone herself, and seemed to have no life in her. And she was almost naked, having eaten most of her clothing. My husband bent down over her, and she said:

"'I have eaten him who was your comrade when he lived.'

"And my husband answered: 'You had the will to live, and so you are still alive.'

"Then we put up our tent close by, cutting off a piece of the fore-curtain to make a shelter for the woman; for she was unclean, and might not be in the same tent with us. And we gave her frozen caribou meat to eat, but when she had eaten a mouthful or so, she fell to trembling all over, and could eat no more.

"We ceased from our journey then, and turned back to Igdlulik, taking her with us, for she had a brother there. She is still alive to this day and married to a great hunter, named Igtussarssua, and she is his favorite wife, though he had one before.

"But that is the most terrible thing I have known in all my life."

CHAPTER III

A WIZARD AND HIS HOUSEHOLD

I RETURNED to headquarters on Danish Island full of excitement over the promise of my first reconnoitring expedition. Contact with these shore tribes convinced me that farther back, in the "Barren Grounds" of the American Continent I should find people still more interesting, and that our expedition would be able not only to bear to the world the first intimate picture of the life of a little known people, but also to produce evidence of the origin and migrations of all the Eskimo Tribes.

The key to these mysteries would be found in hitherto unexplored ruins of former civilizations on the shores adjacent to the Barren Grounds, and in the present-day customs of isolated aborigines who were themselves strangers alike to the white man and to the Greenland Eskimos I knew so well.

The "Barren Grounds," as they have long been called, are great tracts of bare, untimbered land between Hudson Bay and the Arctic Coast. Though forming part of the great continent of America, they are among the most isolated and inaccessible portions of the globe. It is for this reason that the most primitive and uncivilized tribes are still to be found there. Despite the zeal with which hunters and traders ever seek to penetrate into unknown regions, the natural obstacles here have hitherto proved an effective barrier, and the territory is known only in the barest outline. On the north, there are the ramifications of the Arctic Ocean, permanently filled with ice, to bar the way. On the south, and to some extent also on the west, lie great trackless forests, where travelling is slow and difficult, the only practicable route being along the little known rivers. Only from Hudson Bay has the east coast of the Barren Grounds been accessible for modern forms of transport. And even here the waters are so hampered with ice that they are reckoned to be navigable for only two or three months a year. These natural obstacles, however, which have kept others away, were all to our advantage, because they have kept the tribes of Eskimos I intended to visit uncontaminated by white civilization, imprisoned within their swampy tundras, unaltered in all their primitive character.

We were now able to plan our first year's work in these regions. Near our headquarters we found a few old cairns and rough stone shelters built by the Eskimos of earlier days for the purpose of hunting caribou with bow and arrow. We were convinced that the excavation of these ruins would be well worth while. The natives we had now met explained that these ruins originated with a mysterious race of "giants," called Tunit.

We divided up our work as follows: Mathiassen, with Kaj Birket-Smith was first to visit Captain Cleveland, to acquire preliminary information, and

then Birket-Smith would travel on south, to investigate the problem of the early relations between the
Indians and the Eskimos.   Mathiassen's first assign-
ment was to go with Peter Freuchen to the north,
to map shores of Baffinland, and study people on
whom no reliable information existed.   Then, on
his return, he was to excavate among the ruins we
had found.

I was to study the inland Eskimos, with special
reference to the spiritual side of their culture.   The
Eskimo members of the party were divided among
the several sub-expeditions as needed, and two of
them would remain on guard at the headquarters
camp.

We had a pretty good supply of pemmican, both
for ourselves and for the dogs, as well as canned goods,
which would form the basis of our provisions.   We
had to supplement it, however, with fresh meat.
We were told that Cape Elizabeth, toward the north,
was a good spot for walrus at this time of year, and
I therefore went off with Miteq and two of the local
natives to try our luck.   We set out on the 11th of
January.   Despite some difficulty, owing to snow,
which drifted thickly at times, we had some exciting
caribou hunting on the ice during the first two days.
The thermometer stood at about minus 50 C. (63
F.) and every time we picked up our guns with the
naked hand the cold steel took the skin off.

We purchased some stores of meat at Lyon Inlet,
and devoted a few days to fetching these, after which
we set out again to the Northward to find the village.
None of us knew exactly where it was, as the natives

had not yet moved down to the coast, but were encamped some way inland where they had been engaged on their autumn caribou hunting.

The 27th of January was fine, but cold; it was
bright starlight towards the close of the journey,
but we had had a long and tiring day, and wished
for nothing better than to find shelter without having
to build it ourselves.

Suddenly out of the darkness ahead shot a long
sledge with the wildest team I have ever seen.
Fifteen white dogs racing down at full speed, with
six men on the sledge. They came down on us at
such a pace that we felt the wind of them as they
drew alongside. A little man with a large beard,
completely covered with ice, leapt out and came towards me, holding out his hand white man's fashion.
Then halting, he pointed inland to some snow huts.
His keen eyes were alight with vitality as he uttered
the ringing greeting: "Qujangnamik" (thanks to
the coming guests).

This was Aua, the angakoq.

Observing that my dogs were tired after their
day's run, he invited me to change over to his sledge,
and quietly, but with authority, told off one of the
young men in his party to attend to mine. Aua's
dogs gave tongue violently, eager to be off again and
get home to their meal; and soon we were racing
away towards the village. A brief dash at break-
neck speed, and we arrived at the verge of a big lake,
where snow huts with gut windows sent out a warm
glow of welcome.

The women came out to greet us, and Aua's wife,

Orulo, led me into the house. It was, indeed, a group of houses, cleverly built together, a real piece of architecture in snow, such as I had never yet seen. Five huts, boldly arched, joined in a long passage with numerous storehouses built out separately, minor passages uniting one chamber with another, so that one could go all over the place without exposure to the weather. The various huts thus united served to house sixteen people in all. Orulo took me from one to another, introducing the occupants. They had been living here for some time now, and the heat had thawed the inner surface of the walls, forming icicles that hung down gleaming in the soft light of the blubber lamp. It looked more like a cave of stalactites than an ordinary snow hut, and would have looked chilly but for the masses of thick, heavy caribou skin spread about.

Through these winding passages, all lit with tiny blubber lamps, we went from room to room, shaking hands with one after another of the whole large family. There was Aua's eldest son Nataq, with his wife, and the youngest son Ijarak who lived with his fifteen-year-old sweetheart; there was Aua's aged sister Natseq with her son, son-in-law and a flock of children; and finally, out in the farthest end of the main passage, the genial Kuvdlo with his wife and a newborn infant.

It was the first time I had visited so large a household, and I was much impressed by the patriarchal aspect of the whole. Aua was unquestioned master in his own house, ordering the comings and goings and doings of all, but he and his wife addressed each

AUA'S ENCAMPMENT OF SNOW HUTS

other and the rest with the greatest kindness, and not a little fun; an atmosphere of genial good humor was evident throughout.

Hot tea, in unlimited quantity, was welcome after our long hours in the cold, and this being followed by a large, fat freshly cooked hare, it was not long before appetite gave way to ease, and we settled ourselves comfortably among the soft and pleasant smelling caribou skins.

We explained that we had come down to hunt walrus, and the news was greeted with acclamation by our host and his party. They had been thinking of doing the same themselves, and it was now suggested that the whole village should move down to some snowdrifts on the lowlying land at Cape Elizabeth. They had been hunting inland all the summer, and there were numerous good meat depots established in the neighborhood. There was oil enough to warm up the houses for a while, but the last bag of blubber had already been opened. We decided therefore to go hunting on the ice. It was necessary first of all, however, to spend one day in fetching in stores of caribou meat from the depots, as there was no saying how long it might be before we procured any other.

On the day of the final move, all were up betimes and busily at work. Pots and dishes and kitchen utensils generally were trundled out through the passages, with great bales of caribou skins, some new and untouched, others more or less prepared, and huge unwieldly bundles of clothing, men's, women's and children's. The things had not seemed to take up much room within doors, where everything had its place and use, but the whole collection stacked outside in the open air looked as cumbrous and chaotic, as unmistakably "moving" as the worldly goods of any city and surburban family waiting on the pavement for the furniture van.

Just at the last moment, when the sledges were loaded up to the full, and the teams ready to start, I had the good fortune to witness a characteristic little ceremony; the initiation of an infant setting out on its first journey into the world.

An opening appeared somewhere at the back of Kuvdlo's house, and through it came crawling Mrs. Kuvdlo with the little new-born infant in her arms. She planted herself in front of the hut and stood waiting until Aua appeared. Aua, of course, was the spiritual shepherd of the flock. He stepped forward towards the child, bared its head, and placing his lips close to its face, uttered the following heathen equivalent of a morning prayer:

"I rise up from rest,
Moving swiftly as the raven's wing
I rise up to meet the day—
Wa-wa.

"My face is turned from the dark of night
My gaze toward the dawn,
Toward the whitening dawn."

It was the child's first journey, and the morning hymn was a magic formula to bring it luck through life.

The winter ice extends some miles out from the shore, to all intents and purposes as firm as land. Then comes the water, with pack ice drifting this way and that according to wind and current. When the wind is blowing off shore, holes appear in the ice just at the edge, and the walrus follow these, diving down to the bottom to feed.

Aua and I had settled ourselves, like the others, in comparative shelter behind a hummock of ice, with a good view all round. The vigil was by no means monotonous; there was something going on all the time, calling up memories of past hunting. The pack ice was in constant movement, surging and straining and groaning at every check. Now and then a gap would appear, and the naked water sent up a freezing mist like blue smoke, through which we could just discern the black shapes of the walrus rising to breathe. We could hear their long, slow gasp—and then down they went to their feeding grounds below.

We had both experienced it all many a time before; and the familiar sights and sounds loosened our tongues in recollection.

"Men and the beasts are much alike," said Aua sagely. "And so it was our fathers believed that men could be animals for a time, then men again." So he told the story of a bear he had once observed, hunting walrus like a human being, creeping up and taking cover, till it got within range, when it flung a huge block of ice that struck its victim senseless.

Then suddenly Aua himself gave a start—he had been keeping a good look out all the time—and

pointed to where Miteq was standing with his harpoon raised. Just ahead of him was a tiny gap in
the ice, the merest puddle, with barely room for the
broad back of a walrus that now appeared. Miteq
waited till the head came up, and then, before the
creature had time to breathe, drove his harpoon deep
into the blubber of its flank. There was a gurgle
of salt water, a fountain of spray flung out over the
ice, and the walrus disappeared. But Miteq had
already thrust his ice-axe through the loop at the
end of his harpoon line, and the walrus was held.

We hurried up and helped to haul it in, despatched
it, and set about the work of cutting up. This was
completed before dark, and when we drove in that
night to the new snow palace at Itibleriang, I was
proud to feel that one of my own party had given
these professionals a lead on their own ground.

There was great rejoicing at our arrival; a full-
grown walrus means meat and blubber for many
days, and this was the first day we had been out.
There was no longer any need to stint the blubber
for the lamps, and there was food in plenty for ourselves and the dogs.

A well-stocked larder sets one's mind at rest, and
one feels more at liberty to consider higher things.
Also, our surroundings generally were comfortable
enough. The new snow hut was not quite as large
as the former, and lacked the fantastic icicle adorn-
ment within; but it was easier to make it warm and
cosy. The main portion, the residence of Aua and
his wife, was large enough to sleep twenty with ease.
Opening out of this, through a lofty portal, was a

kind of entrance hall, where you brush off the snow before coming in to the warmth of the inner apartment. On the opposite side again was a large, light annex, accommodating two families. As long as there was blubber enough, seven or eight lamps were kept burning, and the place was so warm that one could go about half naked and enjoy it.

Which shows what can be made out of a snowdrift when you know how to go about it.

Aua gave me leave to ask questions, and promised to answer them. And I questioned him accordingly, chiefly upon matters of religion, having already perceived that the religious ideas of these people must be in the main identical with those of the Greenland Eskimo.

A prominent character in the Greenland mythology is the Mistress of the Sea, who lives on the floor of the ocean. I asked Aua to tell me all he could about her. Nothing loath, he settled himself to the task, and with eloquent gestures and a voice that rose and fell in accord with the tenor of his theme, he told the story of the goddess of meat from the sea.

Briefly, it is as follows: There was once a girl who refused all offers of marriage, until at last she was enticed away by a petrel disguised as a handsome young man. After living with him for some time, she was rescued by her father, but the petrel, setting out in pursuit, raised a violent storm, and the father, in terror, threw the girl overboard to lighten the boat. She clung to the side, and he chopped off, first the tips of her fingers, then the other joints, and finally the

wrists.   And the joints turned into seal and walrus
as they fell into the sea.   But the girl sank to the
bottom, and lives there now, and rules over all the
creatures of the sea.   She is called Takanaluk Arna-
luk; and it is her father who is charged with the
punishment of those who have sinned on earth, and
are not yet allowed to enter the land of the dead.

I enquired then as to this land of the dead, and
the general arrangements for their after-life.   This
falls mainly into two parts.

When a human being dies, the soul leaves the earth,
and goes to one or the other of two distinct regions.
Some souls go up into heaven and become Uvdlor-
miut, the People of Day.   Their country lies over
towards the dawn.   Others again go down under
the sea, where there is a narrow belt of land with
water on either side.   These are called Qimiujarmiut,
the People of the Narrow Land.   But in either place
they are happy and at ease, and there is always plenty
to eat.

Those who pass to the Land of Day are people who
have been drowned, or murdered.   It is said that
the Land of Day is the land of glad and happy souls.
It is a great country, with many caribou, and the
people there live only for pleasure.   They play ball
most of the time, playing at football with the skull
of a walrus, and laughing and singing as they play.
It is this game of the souls playing at ball that we
can see in the sky as the northern lights.

The greater among the angakoqs, or wizards, often
go up on a visit to the People of Day, just for pleasure.
Such are called Pavungnartut, which means, those

who rise up to heaven. The wizard preparing to set out on such a journey is placed at the back of the bench in his hut, with a curtain of skin to hide him from view. His hands must be tied behind his back, and his head lashed fast to his knees; he wears breeches, but nothing more, the upper part of his body being bare. When he is thus tied up, the men who have tied him take fire from the lamp on the point of a knife and pass it over his head, drawing rings in the air, and saying at the same time: "Nior-ruarniartoq aifale" (Let him who is going on a visit now be carried away).

Then all the lamps are extinquished, and all those present close their eyes. So they sit for a long while in deep silence. But after a time strange sounds are heard about the place; throbbing and whispering sounds; and then suddenly comes the voice of the wizard himself crying loudly:

"Halala—halalale halala—halalale!"

And those present then must answer "ale—ale—ale." Then there is a rushing sound, and all know that an opening has been made, like the blowhole of a seal, through which the soul of the wizard can fly up into heaven, aided by all the stars that once were men.

Often the wizard will remain away for some time, and in that case, the guests will entertain themselves meanwhile by singing old songs, but keeping their eyes closed all the time. It is said that there is great rejoicing in the Land of Day when a wizard comes on a visit. The people there come rushing out of their houses all at once; but the houses have no

doors for going in or out, the souls just pass through
the walls where they please, or through the roof,
coming out without making even a hole. And
though they can be seen, yet they are as if made of
nothing. They hurry towards the newcomer, glad
to greet him and make him welcome, thinking that
it is the soul of a dead man that comes, and one of
themselves. But when he says "Putdlaliuvunga"
(I am still a creature of flesh and blood) they turn
sorrowfully away.

He stays there awhile, and then returns to earth,
where his fellows are awaiting him, and tells of all
he has seen.

The souls that pass to the Narrow Land are those
of people who died of sickness in house or tent. They
are not allowed to go straight up into the land of
souls, because they have not been purified by violent
death; they must first go down to Takanalukarnaluk
under the sea, and do penance for their sins. When
all their penance is completed, then they go either
to the Land of Day or stay in the Narrow Land, and
live there as happily as those who are without sin.

The Narrow Land is not like the Land of Day; it
is a coast land, with all manner of sea creatures in
abundance, and there is much hunting, and all delight in it.

I enquired whether the wizards did not make other
excursions into the supernatural, for some special
purpose. Aua informed me that this was the case,
and kindly gave me further details.

Should the hunting fail at any season, causing a
dearth of meat, then it is the business of the Angakoq

to seek out the Mistress of the Sea and persuade her
to release some of the creatures she is holding back.
The preparations for such a journey are exactly the
same as in the case of a visit to the Land of Day,
already described. The wizard sits, if in winter, on
the bare snow, in summer, on the bare earth. He
remains in meditation for a while, and then invokes
his helping spirits, crying again and again:

"Tagfa arqutinilerpoq—tagfa neruvtulerpoq!"
(The way is made ready for me; the way is opening
before me.)

Whereupon all those present answer in chorus:
"Taimalilerdle" (let it be so).

Then, when the helping spirits have arrived, the
earth opens beneath the wizard where he sits; often,
however, only to close again; and he may have to
strive long with hidden forces before he can finally
cry that the way is open. When this is announced,
those present cry together: Let the way be open,
let there be way for him! Then comes a voice close
under the ground: "halala—he—he—he" and again
farther off under the passage, and again still farther
and ever farther away until at last it is no longer
heard; and then all know that the wizard is on his
way to the Mistress of the Sea.

Meantime, those in the house sing spirit songs in
chorus to pass the time. It may happen that the
clothes which the wizard has taken off come to life
of themselves, and fly about over the heads of the
singers, who must keep their eyes closed all the time.
And one can hear the sighing and breathing of souls
long dead. All the lamps have been put out, and the

sighing and breathing of the departed souls is as the voice of spirits moving deep in the sea; like the breathing of sea-beasts far below.

One of the songs is a standing item on these occasions; it is only to be sung by the elders of the tribe, and the text runs thus:

"We stretch forth our hands
To lift thee up.
We are without food,
Without fruits of our hunting.
Come up then from below,
From the hollow place
Force a way through.
We are without food,
And here we lie down
We stretch forth our hands
To lift thee up."

Great wizards find a passage opening of itself for their journey down under the earth to the sea, and meet with no obstacles on the way. On reaching the house of Takanalukarnaluk, they find a wall has been built in front of the entrance; this shows that she is hostile towards men for the time being. The wizard must then break down the wall and level it to the earth. The house itself is like an ordinary human dwelling, but without a roof, being open at the top so that the woman seated by her lamp can keep an eye on the dwellings of men. The only other difficulty which the wizard has to encounter is a big dog which lies stretched across the passage, barring the way. It shows its teeth and growls, impatient at being disturbed at its meal—for it

will often be found gnawing the bones of a still
living human being. The wizard must show no sign
of fear or hesitation, but thrust the dog aside and
hurry into the house. Here he meets the guardian
of the souls in purgatory, who endeavors to seize
him and place him with the rest, but on stating that
he is still alive: "I am flesh and blood," he is
allowed to pass. The Mother of the Sea is then
discovered seated with her back to the lamp and to
the animals gathered round it—this being a sign of
anger—her hair falls loose and dishevelled over her
face. The wizard must at once take her by the
shoulder and turn her face the other way, at the
same time, stroking her hair and smoothing it out.
He then says:

"Those above can no longer help the seal up out
of the sea."

To which she replies: "It is your own sins and
ill doing that bar the way."

The wizard then exerts all his powers of persuasion,
and when at last her anger is appeased, she takes the
animals one by one and drops them on the floor.
And now a violent commotion arises, and the animals
disappear out into the sea; this is a sign of rich
hunting and plenty to come.

As soon as the wizard returns to earth, all those
in the house are called upon to confess any breach
of tabu which they may have committed.

All cry out in chorus, each eager to confess his
fault lest it should be the cause of famine and disaster
to all. And in this way "much is made known
which had otherwise been hidden; many secrets are

told." But when the sinners come forward weeping
and confess, then all is well, for in confession lies
forgiveness. All rejoice that disaster has been
averted, and a plentiful supply of food assured;
"there is even something like a feeling of gratitude
towards the "sinners" added Aua naïvely.

I enquired whether all wizards were able to accomplish such an errand, and was informed that only
the greatest of them could do so. One of the greatest
angakoqs Aua had known was a woman. And he
told us the story of Uvavnuk, the woman who was
filled with magic power all in a moment. A ball of
fire came down from the sky and struck her senseless;
but when she came to herself again, the spirit of
light was within her. And all her power was used
to help her fellows. When she sang, all those
present were loosed from their burden of sin and
wrong; evil and deceit vanished as a speck of dust
blown from the hand.

And this was her song:

> "The great sea has set me in motion,
> Set me adrift,
> Moving me as the weed moves in a river.
>
> The arch of sky and mightiness of storms
> Have moved the spirit within me,
> Till I am carried away
> Trembling with joy."

All had listened so intently to Aua's stories of the
supernatural that none noticed the women had neglected their duty, and the lamps were almost out. It
was indeed an impressive scene; men and women sat

in silence, hushed and overwhelmed by the glimpses of a spirit world revealed by one of its priests.

By the 14th of February, our whole party was assembled at Itibleriang. The Baffin Land party were to stay on for a few days more, walrus hunting; the rest of us, who were going south, split up into detachments; Miteq and Anarulunguaq went with me. Birket-Smith and Bangsted were also with us most of the way.

On a fine sunny morning then—February 16—we waved goodbye to our comrades and set off homewards. This is the first time since leaving Denmark that we have been separated for any long or indefinite period, and there is much important work to be done in the eight months which must elapse before we meet again.

After three cold days on the road, and warm nights in comfortable snow huts, we reached home in a gale of wind that is no discredit to this windy region. So dense was the whirling snow that the whole of the last day's journey was accomplished with bent backs and bowed heads; we had literally to creep along, following the well-worn sledge track with our noses almost to the ground. It was the only way we could be sure of crossing Gore Bay from Qajugfit without missing the little island that was our goal. When at last we got in, our faces were completely coated with ice, all save two small gaps round the eyes that just enabled us to see. Oddly enough, however, we had no feeling of cold; possibly the exertion, with our heavy skin garments, had kept us warm, or perhaps the Eskimos are right in declaring that "heat comes out of the earth" in a blizzard.

CHAPTER IV

FINGER-TIPS OF CIVILIZATION

OUR route lay southward, to the country of the inland Eskimos of the Barren Grounds, with Chesterfield, the "Capital" of Hudson Bay, as our first objective.

A last farewell, and off we went, the dogs giving tongue gaily as they raced away. We followed the old familiar high road down to Repulse Bay. We were anxious to make the most of each day's run while the dogs were still fresh, and intended therefore to make but a short stay at Captain Cleveland's. Actually, however, matters turned out otherwise. A blizzard from the north-west whirled us down to his place, and kept on for three days in a flurry of snow that made it impossible to see an arm's length ahead.

At last, when the storm had thrashed itself out, we made ready to push on. Our loads weighed something like 500 kilos per sledge, and ran heavily. We had reckoned, at starting, to make do with the iron runners, as generally used in Greenland, but the first day's journey showed that they dragged in the snow to such a degree that the pace was of the slowest, and would soon spoil the temper of the dogs. We had therefore, while at Cleveland's, had recourse to ice-shoeing, a great improvement on the naked iron, and a triumph of Eskimo invention. The process is complicated, and should be described in detail.

As long as the snow is moist, and the air not too cold, iron or steel runners make quite good going. But as soon as the thermometer falls below 20° C, they begin to stick, and the colder it gets, the worse it is. The cold makes the snow dry and powdery, until it is like driving through sand, the runners screeching and whining with the friction, so that even light loads are troublesome to move. The Eskimos of earlier days of course knew nothing of iron runners, but made shift with a patchwork of walrus tooth, whalebone or horn, cut and smoothed to fit, and lashed under the sledge. These runners acted then exactly as does the iron.

It had, of course, been observed that ice ran easiest over snow, and obviously it would be an advantage to give the runners a coating of ice. But this was not so easy to begin with. Ice would not hold on iron or steel, bone or wood. Ultimately, someone hit on the idea of coating the runners first of all with a paste made from peat softened in water, and laying a thin coat of ice on after. This method at once proved eminently successful, and has remained unsurpassed for rapid running with heavy loads, despite numerous experiments made with other materials by various expeditions. It has, however, the disadvantage of being a lengthy and difficult process in its application.

The first requisite is to find the peat; or failing this,

lichen or moss. The mass should in any case be entirely free from sand or grit. It has then to be thawed, crumbled in the hands, mixed with tepid water and kneaded to a thick paste which is spread on the runners in the form of a ski, broadest in front just where the runners curve upward. Even in very severe cold it requires a day to freeze thoroughly on, and not until then can the coating of ice be applied. This is done by smearing it with water, using a brush or a piece of hide. The water must be lukewarm, as the sudden cooling gives a harder and more durable form of ice. With this shoeing, even a heavily laden sledge will take quite considerable obstacles, as long as the movements are kept fairly smooth, avoiding any sudden drop that might crack the coating of ice. Should this occur, it is a troublesome business to repair it. In the course of a long day's journey, the ice gets worn through, and has to be renewed once or twice; it is therefore necessary to carry water, in order to save the loss of time occasioned by first melting snow or ice.

With a good ice shoeing and reasonably level ground, even heavy loads will run as smoothly as in a slide, without fatiguing the teams.

It was hopeless, of course, to go out in the blizzard hunting for peat, so we had recourse to another means in this case. Mr. Cleveland had plenty of flour at the store; we purchased some of this, and worked it up with water into a dough which proved excellent for the purpose. And lest any should consider it a sinful waste of foodstuffs in a region ill provided with the same, I may reassure my readers

YOUTH AND BEAUTY

A girl from Repulse Bay, with the big fur hood falling down over one shoulder.

with the information that the flour thus used still fulfilled its proper mission in the end. As soon as the weather grew milder and ice shoeing was no longer needed, the dough was scraped off and given to the dogs, who regarded it as a delicacy of the highest order.

We were rather late in starting, and got no farther that day than a camp of snow huts on the western side of Repulse Bay. Here we were kindly received by an old couple who had settled down on the spot with their children and nearest of kin. On entering their hut, we found, to our astonishment, rosaries hung above the blubber lamps and crucifixes stuck into the snow walls. Our host, divining the question in our minds, explained at once that he had met a Roman Catholic missionary far to the south some time before, and had been converted with all his family. He had formerly been an angakoq himself; and it was plain to see that he was an honest man, earnestly believing in his powers and those he had invoked. But, he informed us, from the moment he first listened to the words of the stranger priest, his helping spirits seemed to have deserted him; doubt entered into his mind, he felt himself alone and forsaken, helpless in face of the tasks which had called forth his strength in earlier days. At last he was baptized, and since then, his mind had been at rest. All his nearer relatives had followed his example, and all now seemed anxious to make us understand that they were different from the ordinary heathen we had met. The others of their tribe had given them the name of Majulasut, which means, they who crawl upward, as indicating that they had already relinquished their foothold upon earth, and sought only to find release from the existence to which they were born.

We started early the next morning, there was a broad spit of land to cross at Beach Point, and we were eager to see how our ice shoeing took it. The pace was good enough; but we had hardly begun to congratulate ourselves on this before we discovered that what we had gained for the dogs we had lost for ourselves. Travelling overland in Greenland is quite good fun for the most part, and little obstacles need not be taken too seriously; the iron runners will take no harm from an occasional stone or point of rock. Here, however, we have to leap off at the first sight of any such hindrance ahead, and guide the sledge carefully to avoid damage to the fragile covering of ice. Save for this, however, the general result is admirable. The sledges glide as if their heavy loads were feather light, and we can keep at a sharp trot all day, despite the hilly going. It is a pleasure to see how little exertion is required on the part of the dogs; the sledges run almost by themselves, with just a momentary pull every now and again.

We halted that night on the edge of a lake, and built a snow hut for shelter.

It was a cheerless country we were driving through. Everything one saw was like everything else; today's journey was just yesterday's over again; no mountains, only small hills, lakes and level plain.

Next afternoon, to our great surprise, we met a

fellow traveller on the road. A sledge appeared in
the distance, coming straight towards us, and shortly
after we had the pleasure of a first encounter with
the famous Royal Canadian Mounted Police. Both
sledges halted as we came together, and a tall, fair
young man came forward and introduced himself
as Constable Packett, of the Mounted Police Headquarters at Chesterfield Inlet, on his way out to
inspect our station.

It was strange to us to meet with police in these
regions; and we were at once impressed by the energy
with which Canada seeks to maintain law and order
in the northern lands. The mounted police, a service
popular throughout the country, has here to relin-
quish its splendid horses and travel by dog sledge,
making regular visits of inspection over a wide extent
of territory. Originally, the headquarters here was
at Cape Fullerton, a couple of days' journey north-
east of Chesterfield; the whaling vessels used to winter
there, and the somewhat mixed society of the whaler's
camp required a good deal of looking after. The
whaling has now ceased, but the Mounted Police
remains as a permanent institution in the Canadian
Arctic, representing the Government of the country
and its laws, in regard to white men and Eskimos
alike.

I explained to Constable Packett that he would
find Bosun's wife and some of our Eskimos at the
station; and recognizing that I could not go back
with him myself without giving up the journey I
had planned, he very kindly agreed to make do with
a report, which I promised to hand in at Chesterfield,

instead of requiring my personal attendance. He himself, however, would have to go on to our headquarters, in accordance with his instructions.

I confess to being somewhat impressed by the Canadian Mounted Police as undaunted travellers. Our friend here, for instance, was out for a little run of some two thousand kilometres. He reckoned to be two and a half months on the way, and during the whole of that time, he would have no shelter but a snow hut, save for the few days at Captain Cleveland's and our station. We bade him a hearty farewell, and were soon out of sight.

At noon on the 3rd of April we came up with the icebound vessel *Fort Chesterfield* at Berthie Harbor, a little to the north of Wager Bay. Despite all good resolutions as to not breaking the journey while it was light enough to see, we found it impossible to pass by these cheery seamen's door without a halt. Captain Berthie himself was away, investigating the possibilities of some new harbor works. I had met him before, and spent some days with him on the road. Berthie had all the good qualities of the French Canadian, and in addition, was thoroughly familiar with all forms of travel in the Arctic, and speaks Eskimo fluently. His crew, consisting exclusively of young men from Newfoundland, were full of praise for their captain; and entertained us in his absence with cheerful hospitality.

A little village of immigrant Netsilik natives had sprung up about the vessel, and I took the opportunity of paying them a visit. The oldest inhabitant was an aged veteran from the region of the North

Pole, named Manilaq. He had been a great fighter in his day, but was now reduced to resting on his laurels. He lived in a big snow hut with his children and grandchildren, who still regarded him with great respect, treating him indeed, as if he were their chief. He was an excellent story-teller, and always sure of a large audience. Unfortunately, I had not time myself to draw upon his stock of folk lore and personal recollections. It was essential to my plans that we should get as far on into the Barren Grounds as possible while the winter lasted. I hoped, however, to have an opportunity of meeting the old fellow later. As it turned out, this was not to be. A little while after we had left, he committed suicide, in the presence of his family, preferring to move to the eternal hunting grounds rather than live on growing feebler under the burden of days.

The time passed rapidly now, and our sole object was to get on as far as possible. We took short cuts wherever we could, though travelling overland was always an anxious business, unaccustomed as we were at first to the use of this delicate ice-shoeing. Thus we cut across the flat country from Berthie Harbor due west down to Wager Inlet; the mouth of the great fjord here is never frozen over, owing to the strength of the current. From here we came up on land again, and at last, on the 10th of April, reached Roe's Welcome, at a bay called Iterdlak. We could now follow the coast right down to Chesterfield, and though the country itself was very monotonous, there was plenty to interest us here. Every

time we rounded a headland we came upon the ruins
of some old settlement, which were eagerly investigated. They were not the work of the present population, but of some earlier inhabitants, evidently of
a high degree of culture and well up in stone architecture. The ruins consisted of fallen house walls,
store-chambers, and tent rings—all of stone—with
frameworks for kayaks and umiaks, such as one
finds in Greenland, where the boats are set up to
keep the skins from being eaten by the dogs. There
was evidence of abundant hunting by sea, in the form
of numerous bones scattered about wherever the
ground lay free from snow. Meat cellars were also
frequently found, and to judge from their size, there
should have been no lack of food. Every little
headland was fenced in by stone cairns placed so
close together that they looked from a distance like
human beings assembled to bid us welcome. They
were set out along definite lines across the ground,
and had once been decked with fluttering rags of
skin on top, serving to scare the caribou when driven
down to the coast, where the hunters lay in wait in
their kayaks, ready to spear them as soon as they took
to the water.

All these ruins were the work of the "Tunit";
and from all that we could see, this highly developed
coastal race with their kayaks and umiaks, must
have been identical with the Eskimos that came into
Greenland from these regions a thousand years ago.
Both Miteq and Arnaruluk felt thoroughly at home
in these surroundings. Much of what they had met
with among the living natives of the present day was

strange to them, but these relics of the dead from a bygone age were such as they knew from their own everyday life at home.

We followed the coast southward, keeping close in to shore, as the ice here was good and level. On the 16th of April we passed Cape Fullerton, where some empty buildings still remain from the great days of the whaling camps. It was late in the afternoon, and the sun shone warmly over the spit of land, as if in welcome. It was tempting; here we could find shelter in a real house if we wished; but we had heard that there were natives at Depot Island, and our eagerness to meet them outweighed considerations of mere creature comfort. We drove on, therefore, until the twilight forced us to camp on the site of a famous ruin, known as Inugssivik. It had evidently been a big village at one time, and the huge stones that had been placed in position showed that the folk who lived there were not afraid of hard work. Our guide, Inujaq, informed us that in the olden days, there was always war between these people here and the tribes from Repulse Bay; hostilities had continued throughout a number of years, until the villagers here had been entirely exterminated.

Next morning, as soon as it was fully light, we perceived a small hillock far to the south amid the ice. This was Depot Island, which juts up out of the great white expanse like the head of a seal come up to breathe. It was some distance away, but we hoped to reach it before dark. We have given the dogs an easy time lately, and it would do them no harm to let them know we were in a hurry. A good driver should have the power of communicating his feelings to his team, so that the animals feel his own eagerness to get forward in case of need. And it was not long before our dogs realized that the old steady jogtrot would not do today; something more was needed. And accordingly, they were soon at full gallop; the sledges, lightened of all the dog-feed we had used up since leaving Repulse Bay, flew over the ice at such a pace that the occasional jerks at the traces threw them sideways on, and us nearly off. A little after noon we reached the island, having covered the distance at an average speed of ten kilometres an hour.

It was not long before we came upon fresh sledge tracks, and following them down to the coast, drove across a little headland without sighting any human being. Then suddenly we almost fell down a steep incline, and dashed full into a cluster of snow huts half buried in loose snow. Wooden frames stood up here and there, with skins and inner garments hung out to dry or bleach; two fat dogs came out and started barking—here evidently was the place we had been seeking. Miteq ran up to the window and shouted down to those within: "Here we are; here we are at last," a piece of mischievous fun that brought out the inmates at once. There was a confusion of cries and shouting, as of women in a flutter, a sound of rapid steps along the passage way, and out among us tumbled—a black girl. A little negro lady as black as one could wish to see.

This was perhaps the most surprising encounter we

have experienced up to date. I noticed also, that the sight was almost too much for Miteq, who started back and stood with wide eyes fixed in wonder on the unexpected figure. Here we were come all the way from Greenland to seek out other peoples of the farthest northern lands; and all of a sudden we found ourselves face to face with a child of the tropic South; a creature of the sun leaping up out of the snow!

The girl herself was no less astonished at our appearance. She retreated hastily into the hut, and we stood there waiting in eager anticipation until steps once more were heard within, and the girl reappeared, this time in company with three older women of normal Eskimo type.

It is often almost a pity to have mysteries explained; the whole thing seems so natural once you know how it came about, that there is nothing marvellous or thrilling about it afterward. The oldest of the women came up to us at once and asked who we were. When we had introduced ourselves as lucidly as possible, she explained that her husband and those of the other two women were out hunting, but should be back in the course of the day. She named her companions one by one, and when it came to the dark young lady's turn, informed us that this was her daughter by a stranger, a man who had come to them from a land where it was always summer. A remarkable man, she explained, one who never went out hunting himself, but devoted his life to the task of preparing rare feasts and luscious dishes for his fellows. He had come to their country on a great ship, and had spent the winter in their huts.

It was all simple enough after this. The girl's father had been a negro cook on one of the American whalers.

The dwelling place consisted of three large roomy huts, built together. The party here had spent the summer and autumn inland, caribou hunting, and had moved out in the course of the winter for the walrus hunting on the edge of the ice. They had done very well, it appeared, at any rate, there was an abundance of food of all kinds. A series of store-chambers had been built side by side with the living rooms, so that by shifting a block of snow, one gained access to the larder, the different kinds of meat being stored in separate compartments; seal meat, caribou meat and salmon, with piles of walrus meat in a shed at one side of the passage. We were at once invited to take as much meat as we liked for our dogs, and while we were feeding them, three pots were set on to boil, that we might have our choice of meats when it came to our turn.

In the course of the afternoon, the master of the house returned. His name was Inugpasugssuk, and he belonged to the Netsilik, as did the rest of the party. It was not long before we became firm friends. This ready frankness and lack of all reserve on the part of the natives was a great asset to me in my work. Where else in the world could one come tumbling into people's houses without ceremony, merely saying that one comes from a country they do not know, and forthwith begin to question them on matters which are generally held sacred—all without the least offence?

We were now but one day's journey from Chesterfield Inlet, and as there seemed to be excellent walrus hunting in the neighborhood, I decided to stay here for a while. Inugpasugssuk was too valuable a find to be dropped all at once. I stayed eight days, in the course of which time we went all through the folk-lore and legends of the people, without the slightest sign of impatience on his part. After we had done a hundred of the stories, we agreed that he should go with us to Chesterfield, where it would be more convenient to write them down.

We had arrived at Depot Island nearly out of provisions, as our arrangements had been made to include re-stocking at Chesterfield, and we had not reckoned on making any stay here. As it was, however, these good folk, whom we had never seen before, provided us with food for the whole party— five men and twenty-four dogs—throughout our stay, and seemed to regard it quite as a matter of course.

We were all busily occupied meantime. Arnaruluk was making new spring jackets for us, as the hard and heavy winter furs would soon be too hot. Miteq was out walrus hunting all day with the men of the place. At last, when he had got two walrus on his own account, I decided to set out for Chesterfield. Two sledges belonging to the party here helped us to carry our loads of meat, and on the 22nd of April, a calm, warm sunny day, we started for the white men's settlement of which we had heard so much.

A couple of hours' journey away, however, we were overtaken by a blizzard which came down on us so suddenly that we lost sight of the others. It was hopeless to go searching about in the dark and the driving snow; we camped, therefore, in three separate parties, none knowing where the others were, and waited for the morning.

Waking up in fine weather after camping hurriedly in a blizzard the night before is always full of surprises. One sees now, from the tangled tracks, how the sledges had been driven this way and that in the darkness and the gale, seeming to pick out the very worst spots. The last part of our journey on the previous night had led us in among a host of little reefs and islets, pressure ridges and fissures, till we brought up finally on a low point of land where a snowdrift offered the site and material for a hut.

Now, all was bathed in the morning sunlight, and the fresh April weather gave a brightness to every hummock and hill; beyond the farthest flat point to the south lay the settlement we had failed to reach. Without waiting for the other sledges, we started off, making our way slowly across the bay, which was deep under snow. Just as we were coming up on to the land again, we found ourselves driving in our own tracks of yesterday, and realized to our surprise that we had been almost in to Chesterfield the night before, but with the wind lashing our faces had turned off a little from the straight and come round in a wide curve.

The ascent from the bay was thick with sledge

tracks, and before long the dogs got scent of human dwellings. We raced at full speed over some low hills, and at last, reaching the main ridge of the peninsula, came in sight of the little group of houses that form the colony. We opened our eyes at the sight; for after our long sojourn among little snow hut encampments, this was a city by comparison. On the extreme east lay some neat white-painted houses belonging to the Hudson's Bay Company, forming a kind of suburb in themselves. Then a roughly built warehouse—a perfect skyscraper it seemed to us—and then a yellow wooden edifice entirely surrounded by snow huts, the open entrances to which gave the whole the appearance of a rabbit warren. Now too we perceived the barracks of the Canadian Mounted Police, in lordly isolation on the farther side of a creek which divided the town into two parts.

But the one thing which most of all impressed us as civilized and city-like was a wooden church on the shore of a tiny lake. It had a slender tower rising above the rest of the buildings, and just as we came out on to the lake, the deep, full tones of a bell rang out, as if to greet us. The sound of a church bell made a deep impression on our minds; it was as if we had passed a thousand years in heathen wilds, and now returned to Christendom and peace.

The bell was ringing for service; and there was something affecting in the mere sight of so many people moving, in the old accustomed way of a congregation, slowly, all towards the open doors.

We drove up to the Hudson's Bay Company's

offices and were hospitably received by the Station manager, Mr. Phillips. He very kindly invited me to stay with him, but this I declined, as it was essential that I should live as much as possible among the natives in their own free and easy fashion. He then at once placed an empty house at our disposal; we moved in at once, and revelled in the unaccustomed luxury of ample room, coal fires and comfort generally. Anarulunguaq kept house for us, and we decided to live Eskimo fashion on the stores of walrus meat we had brought down with us.

At the Mounted Police barracks I found only a Corporal at home; Sergeant Douglas, who was in charge of the station was away up country investigating a dual murder committed by an Eskimo. The last reports from his patrol stated that travelling was most difficult; deep snow, shortage of food for the dogs, and starving Eskimos all round. This was poor encouragement to us, who were to follow the same route, and farther up country.

The little church whose bell had greeted us so prettily on our arrival belonged to a Roman Catholic Mission, under Father Turquetil and two younger priests, all Jesuits, highly cultured and most interesting to talk to. They opened their house to us with the greatest hospitality, and I spent many an instructive evening in their company. Father Turquetil, a learned man who spoke Eskimo and Latin with equal fluency, had lived in these parts for a generation, and was greatly looked up to by the natives. Converts were not numerous, but the church was full every Sunday.

CHESTERFIELD: THE WHITE MEN'S PLACE

Premises of the Hudson's Bay company in the foreground. Chesterfield was first founded in 1912, and now is the centre of all trade with the Eskimos between Igdlulik and the Barren Grounds.

MOVING DAY

In March we began to feel the heat of the sun and moved into a tent for the spring.

On the 3rd of May we said goodbye and drove our separate ways.

The mild weather brought with it all the advantages we had been waiting for so long. The snow was moist underfoot, and the stout iron runners made as easy going as the troublesome ice shoeing. We had already decided to follow the narrow gut of Chesterfield Inlet right up to Baker Lake, instead of trying short cuts over hilly and unknown country.

On the morning of the 4th of May we halted to camp; the weather fine and calm, temperature a little over 1 degree. For the first time during the whole trip we could pitch a tent and call it summer.

All about we found puddles of clean fresh water from the newly melted snow; it was pleasant to kneel and drink from these. Along the slopes, the snow had vanished already, and we could lie down on a luxurious carpet of heather and herbage, eating crowberries and whortleberries by the handful, while chattering ptarmigan tumbled about our ears like snowballs.

But we had now to make the most of the little snow that remained for travelling, and pushed on therefore with all speed, and on the 12th of May we arrived at the little island in Baker Lake where Birket-Smith had been waiting impatiently for our coming. This is the most westerly outpost of the Hudson's Bay Company, and the centre of trade for all the Barren Grounds Eskimos right out to Hikoligjuaq, the Kazan River and the region of the Back or Great Fish River.

We were at once greeted with the good news that

there was excellent going on the overland route as long as one travelled by night. And, another point of equal importance to our progress; the caribou were moving up from the south. This was as encouraging as could be wished.

The principal difficulty we had to face was that of getting into touch with our fellow men at all. The only definite information we could gather on this head was, that if we followed the course of the Great Kazan River far enough up, we should meet with two inland tribes. The nearer of the two was called the Harvaqtormiut, or the people of the eddies; farther inland, near Lake Yathkied, or Hikoligjuaq, were the Padlermiut, or Willow-folk. Where the various families were now to be found, no one could say; they followed the moving caribou up in the interior.

We saw no reason to spend any time among the people in the neighborhood of Baker Lake, as these, the Qaernermiut, had for a long time past had dealings with the whalers, and much of their original character had been lost. We therefore transferred our attention without delay to the unknown interior.

CHAPTER V

OUR way lay through a flat, wild, desolate country, with little to guide the stranger. Although it was the latter part of May, the snow still covered such landmarks as there were, even the rivers were indistinguishable from the plains. All was white save the southern slopes of the hills where the sun had thawed a few bare patches of earth. Hour after hour we travelled on, never seeming to get any farther, and with an uncomfortable feeling all the time that we might be going wrong; as if the sense of direction were at fault. But as a matter of fact, it mattered little which direction we took, for from the day we left the coast we had realized that no information could be gleaned even from one settlement as to the position of another, since the various parties were always on the move, taking up their quarters here or there according to the movements of the game.

On the 18th of May we camped on the top of a ridge of hills, looking out over a wide landscape which, while still under snow, resembles in many ways the inland ice of Greenland, save that moraine takes the place of ice. Isolated masses of rock rising up here and there amid the innumerable lakes and streams, remind one of the Greenland nunataks:

mountain tops thrust up above the submerging flood
of ice.   There are ridges and ranges of hills here,
too, as in Greenland, at intervals on the way, until
one reaches farther into the interior, when all is
merged into one vast level plain.

Standing outside the tent one feels the country
like a desert.   There is not a sign of life; all game
seems to be extinct at this season of the year.   No
white man ever comes here; unless some crime or
other calls for the presence of the ubiquitous Mounted
Police.   Only a few days back we had heard about
Sergeant Douglas' last excursion in quest of a local
murderer.   He had been up in the coldest season,
when the prevalent north-west winds give a degree
of cold that few places in the world can surpass.
Everywhere he had met with starving natives, moving vainly from place to place in search of food.
The caribou had disappeared, the salmon had left
the rivers and lakes, and all their hunting failed to
yield the barest means of livelihood.   The police
patrol itself had found the greatest difficulty in
getting through to the coast, the dogs being ready
to drop with weakness and fatigue; and Douglas
himself was known as a clever and experienced
traveller.

Toward evening the desolate landscape was tinged
with beauty.   Light and shade stood out sharply
contrasted; but as the sun went down, and all melted
and merged into white billows of snow, one was again
reminded of the inland ice.   Following Chesterfield
Inlet, and afterwards Baker Lake, we had not this
impression of a vast expanse, but here, with nothing

but land to see on every side, we began to realize that these are indeed the Barren Grounds.

Geologically speaking, these are the ruins of what was once a mountainous country, the mountains having been gradually worn away in the course of millions of years. The disintegrating force of alternating heat and cold, action of water, and the rest, have done their work. In the glacial period, a great ice-cap, the Keewatin Glacier, covered all the land. The ice has rounded off all projecting summits, worn away all softer parts, and strewn boulders, great and small, over the whole, until we have now a tract of primitive rock, buried beneath a thick layer of moraine deposit; clay sand and gravel, with only a solitary peak, or its worn remains, jutting up here and there.

On the 19th of May, we passed the first settlement of the Harvaqtormiut, the People of the Eddies. We have decided, however, to use the general term, Caribou Eskimos, for all these inland tribes, the caribou being the principal factor in their life.

We had made excellent going up to now, the snow firm as a dancing floor under the night's frost. Being, however, four men to one sledge, and that with a heavy load, I preferred to go ahead on ski. We had just topped a rise when to our surprise we discovered a village down by the shore of a tiny lake, with people running in and out of their snow huts in confusion; alarmed, it would seem at our appearance on the scene. When we reached the huts, all the women and children had disappeared, and only two men remained outside, seated on a block of snow, back to back, ready to receive us. Evidently, they were not sure we came as friends. Our whole equipment, with the Greenland sledges and dogs, would be strange to them; they might take us perhaps for a party of the Kitdlinermiut from the shores of the Arctic, or Indians from somewhere up country. Both these they regarded as enemies, the Indians especially, as we learned later on, being looked upon with dread. For centuries past, the Eskimos and the Indians had been at feud, and the atrocities on both sides were not yet forgotten.

While at Baker Lake, I had met a man from the shores of the Arctic, who informed me that there was a special form of greeting used when encountering any of the inland Eskimo. The natives from the coast often went all the way down from the region of the North-west Passage to the timber belt, in quest of wood. And it was their custom on meeting the inland folk, to say at once: *Ilorrainik tikitunga*, which means: "I come from the right side" *i.e.*, from the proper, friendly, quarter.

I shouted the conventional greeting accordingly, at the top of my voice; and hardly were the words out of my mouth when the two men sprang up with loud cries and came running towards us, while the remainder of the party came tumbling out from their huts.

We now learned that the place was called Tugdliu-vartaliik, the Lake of Many Loons. They had had a very severe winter, and numbers of men and dogs alike had died of hunger in various parts. They

PUKERDLUK, CHIEF OF THE PEOPLE OF THE EDDIES

had camped throughout the winter on the eastern side of the Kazan River, and had now moved west to meet the caribou coming from the south. Two sledges had been sent out to a neighboring settlement on the Kazan River, at Nahigtartorvik, or The Outlook; from here the caribou could be seen as soon as their advance guard appeared. This being duly reported to the camp, the whole party would move off and shift their quarters to fresh hunting grounds.

Despite the fact that we were but a few days journey from the trading station at Baker Lake, we found that some of the women and children here had never seen white men before. Our cameras were regarded with the greatest astonishment, and a peep through the finder seemed a marvel beyond words. The people here were anxious to trade, and brought along their stores of fox skins, asking in return, however, our most indispensable pots and pans. When we declined to barter these, and explained that we did not care for fox skins, but would rather have old clothes, hunting implements and other curios of ethnographical interest, it was plain to see that we had fallen in their estimation.

We halted for a few hours, made some tea and some pancakes, and on this simple menu stood treat to the whole village. While the impromptu banquet was in progress, in came the two sledges which had been sent out reconnoitring. Long before they reached us we could hear the men shouting: "The caribou are coming; the caribou are coming"; and in a moment the entire assembly was in a tur-

moil of extravagant rejoicing.   Here was the end of
winter; the caribou were come, and with them summer and its abundance.   And one can imagine what
this means to people who have struggled through a
whole long winter in the merciless cold of their snow
huts, with barely food enough to keep them alive.

On leaving Baker Lake, we had laid our course
over land in a curve to the south-east of the Kazan
River, having learned that it was inadvisable to
follow the lower reaches of the river itself.   Now,
however, we had to move down to the river in order
to get into touch with the natives.   One of the young
men who had just come in offered to go with us to
the next village as a guide, and with his aid, we soon
reached the river, which was fairly broad at this
point.   We crossed over to the spot where the village
had been, but found the place deserted; the party
had gone off after the caribou.   We then sent our
guide back at once, and went farther up country,
in the hope that we might again manage unaided
to get into touch with people here.

The Barren Grounds were now so thick with game
that it was hard to make any progress by sledge
with dogs used to hunting.   Herds of caribou came
trotting by, great and small, one after another,
numbering from fifteen or twenty-five to fifty, sometimes over two hundred head.

Although it was late in June, we again had winter for a spell.   The snow had frozen hard again,
caking over everything, and we could make better
going now.   We followed the winding river through
the low-lying country, where the stream itself re-

peatedly spread out to great width. Here and there the water had begun to eat its way up through the ice, and we had to be very careful in| the neighborhood of these eddies. Towards evening we came upon a deserted snow hut, a sure sign that there were people not very far away. But where? There was a confusion of sledge tracks to choose from, but most of them pointed in a direction opposite to that we were inclined to take.

We had left the river now and had reached a lake of such extent that it could hardly be any but Hikoligjuaq itself where the Padlermiut were supposed to have their summer camp. We had followed the eastern bank of the river, as advised, and now at last a man appeared on the summit of a hill, watching us intently. We stopped and waved to him; he answered by stretching out both arms, a sign which said he is a friend. We drove forward accordingly, and soon arrived at his camp.

Here at last we found we had reached our goal. We were among the Padlermiut, the Willow-Folk— the head tribe of the Caribou Eskimos.

It was a tiny camp, consisting for the moment of but three tents. Igjugarjuk, the head of the party, unlike the majority of his fellows, greeted us with fearless cordiality, and his jovial smile won our hearts at the outset. I knew a good deal about him, already, from his neighbors on the Kazan River, and had heard the story of how he procured his first wife. It was, to say the least, somewhat drastic, even by Eskimo standards. He had been refused permission to marry her, and therefore went out one day with his brother and lay in wait at the entrance to the lady's hut, and from there shot down her father, mother, brothers and sisters—seven or eight persons in all, until only his chosen herself was left.

I was somewhat surprised then, to find a man of his temper and antecedents introducing himself immediately on our arrival as the accredited representative of law and order. He handed me a document with the seal of the Canadian Government, dated from his camp in April, 1921, when the police had visited there in search of a criminal. Briefly, it set forth that the bearer, one Ed-joa-juk (Igjugarjuk) of She-ko-lig-jou-ak, was by the undersigned, Albert E. Reames, His Majesty's Justice of the Peace in and for the North-west Territory, hereby appointed Special Constable in and for the said territory for the purpose of bringing to justice one Quaugvak, of the Padlermiut, the said Quaugvak being accused of two murders . . .

I read through the document with due solemnity, and handed him in return a bit of old newspaper from a parcel. He took it with great dignity, and studied it with the same attention I had given to his. And from that moment we were friends, with perfect confidence in each other.

As a matter of fact, Igjujarjuk was no humbug; and when I run over in my mind the many different characters I met with on that long journey from Greenland to Siberia, he takes a prominent place. He was clever, independent, intelligent, and a man of great authority among his fellows.

He invited us at once into one of his tents; and we

found that as befitted his position, he had two wives. The elder of the two, Kivkarjuk, the cause of the massacre above mentioned, was now dethroned by a younger beauty named Atqaralaq, and it was to her tent we were now invited.

To my great relief, the famine we had expected to encounter was already a thing of the past. In front of the tents lay a pile of dead caribou, so many indeed that it was difficult to count them. A month before, the people here had been on the verge of starvation, but now all was changed. Igjugarjuk at once gave orders for an extravagant banquet in our honor, and two large caribou were put on to boil in huge zinc cauldrons.

I had expected to find these people living in quite a primitive state, and in this respect, was disappointed beyond measure. What we did find was the worst kind of tinpot store and canned provision culture; a product of trading expeditions to the distant Hudson's Bay Company's Stations. And when a powerful gramophone struck up, and Caruso's mighty voice rang out from Igjugarjuk's tent, I felt that we had missed our market, as far as the study of these people was concerned. We were about a hundred years too late. Save for their appearance, which was of pronounced Eskimo type, they were more like Indians than Eskimos. Their tents were of the pointed Indian pattern, made of caribou skins with a smoke hole at the top, and in each, on the left hand side, burned the Uvkak, or tent fire. All the women wore colored shawls over their skin dresses, just as the Indian women do; and to my astonishment

I found that they wore watches, hung round their necks. These ornaments, however, were divided up among the party, some wearing the case, others going shares in the works.

The only unadulterated Eskimo element we had to work on was the language; and to the satisfaction of both parties, we found that our Greenland tongue was understood immediately, though there was naturally some difference in pronunciation and idiom. Igjugarjuk, who was not beyond flattering a guest, declared that I was the first white man he had ever seen who was also an Eskimo.

The banquet took some time to prepare, and while it was being got ready, we went out to feed our dogs. This gave rise to astonishment not unmixed with horror among our hosts. We had still some of the walrus meat we had brought up from the coast, and this we now brought out. But no such meat had ever been seen on Lake Yathkied, and strange meat was strictly tabu. Here was a difficulty. Igjugarjuk, however, whose travels had made him somewhat a man of the world, met the situation with tact. The young men of his party, he declared, must on no account touch the strange meat, but there would be no harm in our cutting it up ourselves, and feeding our own team with it, as long as we used our own knives.

This little episode showed that our friends were not so hopelessly civilized after all. And when one of the young men, named Pingoaq, came up and asked me whether seal had horns like the caribou, I forgot my disappointment altogether. True, tango

IGJUGARJUK, CHIEF OF THE WILLOW FOLK AND A NOTABLE WIZARD

He fell in love with our Greenland dress at first sight, and we had to present him with a costume. He would never consent to be photographed in his own caribou-skin dress.

SIMIGAQ AND HER TWO HUSBANDS, NILAK AND INORAJUK

melodies were now welling forth from the gramophone, and the meat for our dinner was seething in genuine imported ironmongery; yet these people were plainly different in manners and habit of mind from the ordinary type of Eskimo to whom seal and walrus are the main factor in everyday life. And though I was aware that white men had visited these regions before, I knew also that no one had yet made a thorough study of the people here.

My meditations were interrupted by a shout informing the whole camp that dinner was ready. I have sat down to many a barbaric feast among Eskimos in my time, but I have never seen anything to equal this. Only the elders used knives, the younger members of the party simply tore the meat from the bones in the same voracious fashion which we may imagine to have been the custom of our earliest ancestors. Besides the two caribou, a number of heads had been cooked, and one was served out to each member of our party. The heads were an extra, and we were allowed to keep them till after, to eat in our own tent, on condition that none of the leavings should under any circumstances be touched by women or dogs. The muzzle especially was regarded as sacred meat, which must not be defiled.

Then came dessert; but this was literally more than we could swallow. It consisted of the larvæ of the caribou fly, great fat maggoty things served up raw just as they had been picked out from the skin of the beasts when shot. They lay squirming on a platter like a tin of huge gentles, and gave a nasty little crunch under the teeth, like crushing a black-beetle.

Igjugarjuk, ever watchful, noted my embarrassment and observed kindly: "No one will be offended if you do not understand our food; we all have our different customs." But he added a trifle maliciously: "After all, you have just been eating caribou meat; and what are these but a sort of little eggs nourished on the juices of that meat?"

That same afternoon a whole party of sledges came in from an island out in the lake. It was a remarkable procession to any accustomed to the Eskimos of the coast and their swift teams. Here were six heavily laden sledges, fastened three and three, each section drawn by two dogs only, men and women aiding. The only person allowed to travel as a passenger was an old woman, a mummy-like figure, very aged, and generally looked up to among the Padlermiut on account of her knowledge of tabu and wisdom generally. The fact that she was Igjugarjuk's mother-in-law doubtless counted for something as well.

By the time we had been there one day we began to feel ourselves at our ease among these strange folk. They treated us, apparently, with entire confidence, and endeavored in every way to satisfy our curiosity. In the evening, I ventured to touch on my special subject, and explained to Igjugarjuk, who was famous as an angakoq throughout the whole of the Barren Grounds, that I was most anxious to learn something of their ideas about life, their religion and their folk-lore. But here I was brought up short. He answered abruptly that he was an ignorant man, knowing nothing of his people and its past; if any had said he was an angakoq, they lied.

I realized that I was going too fast, and had not yet gained the confidence of my host in full.

It was well on in the forenoon before we turned out on the following morning, and Igjugarjuk at once volunteered to show me the country round.

Just behind the camp was a high range of hills, and from here one had an excellent view of the surroundings. The lake, I found, was enormous, the low-lying coasts vanishing away into the horizon; it looked more like the sea than an inland water. The Indians call it Lake Yathkied, but the Eskimo name is Hikoligjuaq, which means the great water with ice that never melts. The name is justified by the fact that the ice in the middle of the lake rarely if ever thaws away completely.

Igjugarjuk drew for me with surprising readiness a chart of the lake and its shores, noting the names of all the different settlements. A generation or so earlier, there had been some 600 people here; now there were hardly 100. The introduction of firearms has affected the movements of the caribou, and the animals have begun to avoid their old routes and crossings; and when the caribou hunting fails, it means famine to the Eskimo.

The weather was wonderful; the brutal change on change with snow, storm and rain was gone, and everything was at peace. The ice of the lake had melted close to the mouth of the river, and the heavy tumbled winter ice made way in its midst for a smooth sheet of water with a veil of warm mist above. Hosts of swimming birds had found a playground here, and laughed and chattered as new flocks alighted.

On land, one heard all around the little singing sound of melting snow; and the daylight beat so fiercely on the whiteness of the lake that one had to shade one's eyes. Spring had come to the Barren Grounds, and soon earth and flowers would rearise out of the snow.

Small herds of caribou on the move approached within easy distance; but today we were friendly observers only, and felt nothing of the hunter's quickened pulse on seeing them at close range. We had meat enough for the present.

Here again we found the stone barriers, shelters and clumsy figures built to represent a human form, with a lump of peat for a head—relics of the days when caribou hunting was carried on systematically by driving the animals down to the water, where the kayak men were ready to fall upon them with the spear.

With the introduction of firearms, this method of hunting has gone out of fashion, and there will soon be hardly a kayak left in the Barren Grounds. But not many years ago, these inland people were as bold and skilful in the management of a kayak as any of the natives on the coast.

Igjugarjuk and I walked down towards the camp. Far out on the horizon one could see the extreme fringe of the forest, but the sunlight was deceptive, and I could hardly make out for certain whether it were trees or hill. I asked Igjugarjuk, and he answered at once: "Napartut" (the ones that stand up). "Not the true forest where we fetch wood for our long sledges; that is farther still. It is our belief that the trees in a forest are living beings, only that they cannot speak; and for that reason we are loth to spend the night among them. And those who have at some time had to do so, say that at night, one can hear a whispering and groaning among the trees, in a language beyond our understanding."

All the wild creatures were greeting the spring in their mute, humble fashion. We could see hares and lemmings, ermine and marmot snuggling up in the tall grass, with never a thought of feeding, but only enjoying the light and warmth. They were dreaming of an eternal summer, and gave themselves up to the delight of the moment, forgetting all their mortal enemies. Even the wolves, forever lying in wait at other seasons, now resorted to their old den and gave themselves up to domestic bliss. In a fortnight there would be a litter of cubs to look after, and the parents then must take turns to go abroad, for the foxes are quick to scent out anything in the shape of young, even when the sun is at its hottest.

But by the open waters of the lake there was an incessant chattering among the gulls and terns and duck who cannot make out why the loon should always utter such a mournful cry in its happiest moments. There was a blessedness of life and growth here in the spring, when the long-frozen earth at last breathed warm and soft and moist, and plants could stretch their roots in the soil and their branches above. The sand by the river bank gleamed white; showing clearly the footprints of the cranes as they moved. All the birds were talking at once, heedless of what was going on around them, until a flock of wild geese came swooping down, raising a mighty commotion in the water as they alighted. And in face of these, the smaller fry were silent and abashed. But who can paint the sounds of spring? The nature lover will not attempt it, but will be content to breathe its fragrance with rejoicing.

The sun was low on the horizon, the sky and the land all around aglow with flaming color.

"A youth is dead and gone up into the sky," said Igjugarjuk. "And the Great Spirit colors earth and sky with a joyful red to receive his soul."

CHAPTER VI

NOMAD'S LIFE IN THE BARREN GROUNDS

AFTER our first introduction here, I allowed a few days to pass without pressing my actual errand, spending the time in hunting and bartering a little for ethnographical material. I realized that it would take some time to gain the complete confidence of the natives here.

We lived in our own tent. Among the natives of the coast we had always preferred as far as possible to live in the houses of the natives as we found them, which gave us a better chance of making friends and being regarded as members of the family. In the present instance, however, we kept to our own quarters, not only because we had more time, but also because our hosts here were—to put it mildly— so uncleanly in their habits that it would have been difficult to accommodate ourselves to such conditions.

The men were leading a life of idleness just at present, but the women were busy; we were indeed astonished at the amount of work which fell to their share. It was the women who went out gathering fuel, often from a considerable distance, which meant heavy toiling through the swampy soil; they had also to skin and cut up all the caribou brought in, and

attend to the fires and the cooking. Their hard
life had set its mark upon them; it was not always
age, but often simply toil, that had wrinkled their
faces; their eyes were often red and rheumy from
the smoke of the fires, their hands coarse and filthy,
with long, coarse nails. Their womanly charm had
been sacrificed on the altar of domestic utility; none
the less, they were always happy and contented, with
a ready laugh in return for any jest or kindly word.

It suited our purpose well enough that the men
were idle, as we had thus more opportunities of
gathering the information we sought. In regard to
all matters of everyday life they were willing enough
to tell us all they knew. The thing which most of
all impressed us was their entire independence of the
sea. True, they had had some dealings with the
natives of the coast districts, a few having made
journeys for purposes of trade, but many of the men
here had never even seen the sea. And this also
accounted for the fact that all sea meat was strictly
tabu. Old men were of opinion that their forefathers
had always lived inland, their sole means of livelihood
being based on caribou, salmon, and birds. Nor
was there anything in their material culture to suggest any previous acquaintance with the sea. During
the past generation, however, intercourse with neighboring tribes had been somewhat more general, and
there had lately been some emigration from the
southern end of Hikoligjuag down over the great
lakes to the coast at Eskimo Point. The country
here was now inhabited by natives from the inland
districts. Nevertheless, the natives with whom we

were living at present seemed for the most part to regard it as inconceivable that anyone could prefer the blubbery, evil-smelling beasts of the sea to the splendid game that was to be had on land.

Each hunter had a modern rifle, and there was no difficulty in catching foxes enough to pay for the ammunition required. But they did not seem to realize that the use of firearms was in itself largely responsible for the frequent periods of famine. In the olden days, it is true, hunting was more confined to certain definite seasons; but the ingenious methods and implements of capture gave so rich a yield as to cover also the dead seasons when no game was to be had, as long as the hunting had been fairly good and sufficient meat stored for the winter.

The first essential was to find a site for the village directly on the route followed by the caribou in their migrations, and as these routes differed for spring and autumn, the natives led a somewhat nomadic existence. They always returned, however, to the same spots, as extensive preparations were needed. Hundreds of stone cairns had to be erected covering a range of several kilometres, and the ground had to be chosen so that the caribou could be driven in exactly the direction required. Hunting in the open with bow and arrow gave but a poor return; it was necessary to work up within close range of the animals, which might be a matter of days. And one could never reckon on bringing down more than a couple of head, even where the herds were numerous.

The caribou were shy, and the bow was only

effective at short range. This difficulty was met by the following arrangement:

Oblong boulders were set up, or stone cairns built, in two lines, forming an avenue. On top of each stone, or heap of stones, was set a lump of peat or tuft of grass, to look like a head. The avenue was very broad at one end, and so placed that the caribou in flight, coming over a hill, would find themselves between the two lines of figures. Behind were women and children acting as beaters, waving garments and shouting like wolves. The animals seeing themselves, as it appeared, pursued by their enemies from the rear and hemmed in by a line on either side, had no choice but to go straight ahead. As they did so, the space between the lines narrowed in, like an old-fashioned duck decoy, and at the farther end, shelters were built where the hunters lay in wait. The caribou had now to pass within close range of the shelters, and the hunters were able to take toll of them on the way.

The same system of stone figures was employed on the lakes and rivers, at spots where the caribou were accustomed to take to the water. In this case, however, the hunters would lie in wait on the shore, ready to put out in their kayaks. Caribou do not swim very fast, and it was then an easy matter to overtake them and kill them with the spears which were specially fashioned for this form of hunting. Given a broad crossing place and numerous herds, great numbers could be slain in this manner, till the water was choked with the bodies. Some were also taken in winter, in regions where they

AKJARTOQ, THE OLDEST WOMAN IN THE TRIBE

She is boiling down caribou bones to extract the fat.

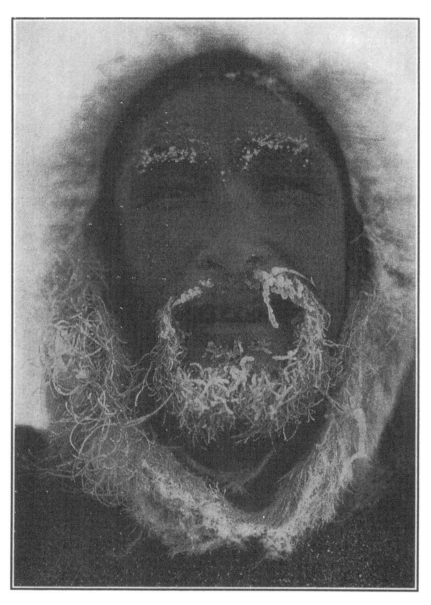

TATILGAQ, WHO DESCRIBED THE NATIVE METHODS OF HUNTING

were to be found at that season, by a system of pit-falls.

Compared with the caribou, all other forms of game were but of minor importance. Fish were caught by spearing or with hook and line; birds, hares, lemmings and marmot taken in snares. The feathered game was mostly hunted in the autumn, when the birds are moulting and cannot rise easily. They are then pursued on the water in kayaks, and killed with small harpoons.

Unfortunately, the kayak is now being superseded altogether by the gun, and it will not be long before kayaks are a thing of the past. The gun has immediate advantages, but it is doubtful whether it pays better in the long run. Naturally, it is tempting to employ a weapon which does away with the need for elaborate preparation of dummies and shelters, and there is little difficulty on thinning out the herds with a long-range rifle. But it should be borne in mind that arrow and spear did their work silently, and without scaring the rest, so that the caribou continued for centuries to follow the same routes from the forests to the Barren Grounds and back again. Now, since the introduction of fire-arms, a change seems to have taken place in this respect; the animals tend more and more to avoid the native villages, and famine has frequently resulted. In some districts, during the last few years, the inhabitants have been completely exterminated by starvation.

Another difficulty which the Caribou Eskimos have to reckon with is the fact that the moving of the caribou in summer and autumn comes just at those seasons when travelling is most difficult. The great stretches of tundra are a pathless waste, and the rivers are available only as their course lies, often tending in the wrong direction for pursuit of the caribou. It is not until late in the autumn, when the rivers and lakes are frozen over, and the country is covered with snow, that they are able to cover any distance; but under these conditions, they are splendid travellers, skilful and untiring. In the days before the trading stations were established at Baker Lake and Eskimo Point, they would go south as far as Fort Churchill, and west to the region of Schultz Lake and Aberdeen Lake. Here they had their meeting place at the famous Akilineq, a ridge of hills south of the great lakes in the neighborhood of the Thelon River. Here they procured timber for sledges, kayaks and tent poles, from Lake Tivsalik, where great tree trunks, brought down by the river from far up country, were washed ashore. One can imagine the patience required in those old days for any kind of wood work, when the only tools available were odd scraps of iron. Now, of course, the saw is generally in use; and sawn timber cut to standard sizes can be obtained at the trading stations.

Akilineq was the meeting place for the natives from Baker Lake and Kazan River, who encountered here the tribes from regions so far distant as the North-west Passage, likewise coming up in search of timber. There was naturally a good deal of trading between the different tribes thus brought into contact. The inland folk traded white men's goods brought from Churchill, mostly knives, in exchange for seal skin thongs which were in great demand.

There were also forests by the shores of these lakes, but as the trees were regarded as living beings, they were rarely visited. There was a widely current tradition, of ancient date, that the tree-folk would not suffer any human being among them for more than ten nights.

It says much for the skill and endurance of the Eskimos as travellers that these long journeys were made with very small teams, rarely more than two, and never more than five dogs, owing to the difficulty of procuring food for the animals. Both men and women, however, were hardy walkers, and would cheerfully harness themselves to the sledge and haul as well as any dog. Despite their small teams, these natives here use, curiously enough the longest sledges known to exist anywhere; ten metres in length by only 43 centimetres across are by no means unusual measurements. Thanks to the ice shoeing, however, they were easy to haul, and their length made for steadiness and buoyancy in soft loose snow.

We were anxious to ascertain whether any stone houses existed up inland, such as we had found all along the coast; our informants here, however, were positive that none such had ever been seen. Houses of this type would also be inconsistent with their mode of life, which involved a constant moving from place to place at certain seasons of the year.

The only form of winter dwelling known to the inland Eskimo is the snow hut; but having no oil or blubber, they are unable to heat them, though the thermometer in the cold season may often fall below minus 50°. During the long, dark evenings, their only light is a sort of primitive tallow dip, made of moss and caribou fat. So hardy, however, are these people that they declare they never feel cold indoors, however severe the weather may be; and their houses are also protected against the blizzards by being simply smothered in snow, till they are hardly distinguishable from the drift in which they are built.

Just outside the living room proper, and connected with it by a passage is the so-called iga, or kitchen, built straight up with steep walls, to prevent the snow from melting. Here the food is cooked, when any fuel is available; this, however, is by no means an everyday occurrence when the whole country lies deep in snow. For days in succession they may have to make do with frozen meat, and not even a mouthful of hot soup to help it down.

Water supply is ensured by building the snow hut close to the shore of a lake, and a hole is kept open in the ice all through the winter, a small snow hut being built above the opening to keep it from freezing. Like all other Eskimos living exclusively on meat, these inland folk drink enormous quantities of water.

The only serious difficulty they have to contend with is that they have no means of getting their footwear dried after a long day's hunting. If they have skins enough, the wet things are thrown away and replaced by new ones; failing this, the old wet things have to be dried at night by laying them next to the body.

In May, the snow huts begin to melt, and tents are then called into requisition, often of great size and magnificence, made on the Indian pattern, with smoke hole at the top, and of caribou skin throughout. In front of the house-wife's seat is the fireplace, and all meals are cooked here, inside the tent, the weather as a rule being very windy. One might imagine that the moving into tents meant a period of comfort and ease; this, however, is by no means the case. The cooking indoors precludes the use of a curtain at the entrance, and one has thus either to sit in a roaring draught, or in a smother of smoke from the fireplace. Often we had to jump up half stifled and hurry outside to breathe, though the rest of the inmates appeared to find no discomfort from the atmosphere.

This, roughly, is the ordinary everyday life of the inland Eskimos, probably the hardiest people in the world. Their country is such as to offer but a bare existence under the hardest possible conditions, and yet they think it the best that could be found. What most impressed us was the constant change from one to another extreme; either they are on the verge of starvation, or wallowing in a luxury of abundance which renders them oblivious of hard times past, and heedless of those that await them in the next winter's dark.

Igjugarjuk, who had so vehemently asserted that he was no magician, and knew nothing of the past history of his people, soon changed over when he found that he could trust me, and realized that I was earnestly interested in such matters. And in the end, I learned from him a great deal about aspects of Eskimo culture which were quite new to me.

I found it impossible to get a clear and coherent account of their religious beliefs; as soon as one began to ask about matters outside the sphere of tangible reality, the views expressed were so contradictory that one could make nothing of them together. Nothing definite was known, nor did it seem to matter that the wise men of the tribe held different views one from another; the one thing certain was, that all study of such matters was attended with the greatest difficulty, and much remained beyond our knowledge. The general view of life after death is best shown in the following story, which was told to me by Kivkarjuk:

"Heaven is a great country with many holes in. These holes we call the stars. Many people live there, and whenever they upset anything, it falls down through the stars in the form of rain or snow. Up in the land of heaven live the souls of dead men and beasts, under the Lord of Heaven, Tapasum Inua.

"The souls of men and beasts are brought down to earth by the moon. This is done when the moon is not to be seen in the sky; it is then on its way to earth, bringing souls. After death, we do not always remain as we were during life; the souls of men, for instance, may turn into all kinds of animals. Pinga looks after the souls of animals, and does not like to see too many of them killed. Nothing is lost; and blood and entrails must be covered up after a caribou has been killed.

"So we see that life is endless; only we do not know in what form we shall reappear after death."

The easiest way to learn, of course, was to inquire of an angakoq, and in the course of my long conversations with Igjugarjuk I learned many interesting things. His theories, however, were so simple and straightforward that they sound strikingly modern; his whole view of life may be summed up in his own words as follows: "All true wisdom is only to be learned far from the dwellings of men, out in the great solitudes; and is only to be attained through suffering. Privation and suffering are the only things that can open the mind of man to those things which are hidden from others."

A man does not become an angakoq because he wishes it himself, but because certain mysterious powers in the universe convey to him the impression that he has been chosen, and this takes place as a revelation in a dream.

This mysterious force which plays so great a part in men's fate, is called Sila, and is very difficult to define, or even to translate. The word has three meanings: the universe; the weather, and finally, a mixture of common sense, intelligence and wisdom. In the religious sense, Sila is used to denote a power which can be invoked and applied by mankind; a power personified in Silap Inua, the Lord of Power, or literally, the one possessing power. Often also, the term Pinga is used, this being a spirit in the form of a woman, which is understood to dwell somewhere in space, and only manifests itself when specially needed. There is no definite idea as to her being the creator of mankind, or the origin of animals used for food; all fear her, however, as a stern mistress of the household, keeping watch on all the doings of men, especially as regards their dealings with the animals killed.

She is omnipresent, interfering as occasion may require. One of her principal commandments appears to be that daily food should be treated with respect, care being taken that nothing is wasted. There are certain ceremonies, for instance, to be observed on the killing of a caribou, as mentioned in the story just quoted.

All the rules of tabu are connected with Sila, and designed to maintain a balance of amicable relations with this power. The obligations imposed by Sila are not particularly burdensome, and perhaps for that very reason trespass is severely punished; as for instance by bad weather, dearth of game, sickness, and the like; in a word, all that is most to be feared.

The angakoq serves as interpreter between Sila and mankind. Sila's leading qualities are those of healing in sickness or guarding against the illwill of others. When a sick person desires to be cured, he must give away all his possessions, and is then carried out and laid on the earth far from any dwelling; for whoever would invoke the Great Spirit must have no possessions save his breath.

Igjugarjuk himself, when a young man, was constantly visited by dreams which he could not understand. Strange unknown beings came and spoke to him, and when he awoke, he saw all the visions of his dream so distinctly that he could tell his fellows all about them. Soon it became evident to

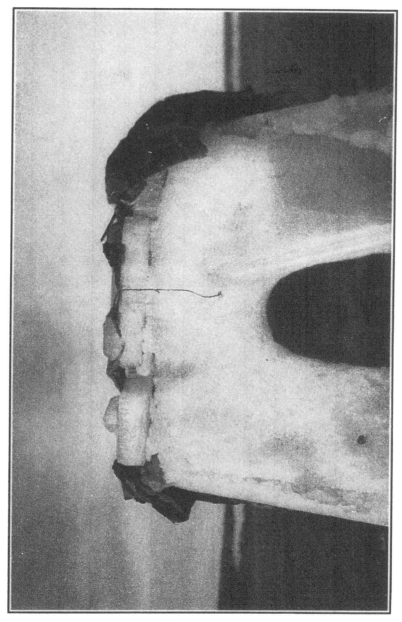

A HUT OF ICE BLOCKS

The lakes generally freeze before the snow comes. The natives then cut out blocks of ice and with great skill build houses of these, using wet snow as mortar, which soon freezes hard. These huts are cosy and comfortable, and there are no tabu restrictions as to needlework, etc., so the women can get to work on the skins for new clothes, which at this time of year may be sorely needed.

all that he was destined to become an angakoq and an old man named Perqanaoq was appointed his instructor. In the depth of winter, when the cold was most severe, Igjugarjuk was placed on a small sledge just large enough for him to sit on, and carried far away from his home to the other side of Hikoligjuaq. On reaching the appointed spot, he remained seated on the sledge while his instructor built a tiny snow hut, with barely room for him to sit cross-legged. He was not allowed to set foot on the snow, but was lifted from the sledge and carried into the hut, where a piece of skin just large enough for him to sit on served as a carpet. No food or drink was given him; he was exhorted to think only of the Great Spirit and of the helping spirit that should presently appear—and so he was left to himself and his meditations.

After five days had elapsed, the instructor brought him a drink of lukewarm water, and with similar exhortations, left him as before. He fasted now for fifteen days, when he was given another drink of water and a very small piece of meat, which had to last him a further ten days. At the end of this period, his instructor came for him and fetched him home. Igjugarjuk declared that the strain of those thirty days of cold and fasting was so severe that he "sometimes died a little." During all that time he thought only of the Great Spirit, and endeavored to keep his mind free from all memory of human beings and everyday things. Towards the end of the thirty days there came to him a helping spirit in the shape of a woman. She came while he was asleep, and seemed to hover in the air above him. After that he dreamed no more of her, but she became his helping spirit. For five months following this period of trial, he was kept on the strictest diet, and required to abstain from all intercourse with women. The fasting was then repeated; for such fasts at frequent intervals are the best means of attaining to knowledge of hidden things. As a matter of fact, there is no limit to the period of study; it depends on how much one is willing to suffer and anxious to learn.

Every wizard has a belt, which often plays a great part in his invocations of the spirits. I was fortunate enough to acquire one of these belts from a woman who was herself a witch doctor, named Kinalik. It consisted of an ordinary strap of hide on which were hung or strung the following items: a splinter from the stock of a gun worn in recognition of the fact that her initiation had taken place by means of visions of death; a piece of sinew thread, which had formerly been used to fasten tent poles with, and had on some occasion or other been used for a magic demonstration; a piece of ribbon from a packet of tobacco; a piece of an old cap formerly belonging to her brother—the brother was now dead, and was one of her helping spirits—a piece of white caribou skin, some plaited withies, a model of a canoe, a caribou's tooth, a mitten and a scrap of sealskin. All these things possessed magnetic power, by virtue of their having been given to her by persons who wished her well. Any gift conveys strength. It need not be great or costly in itself; the intrinsic value of the object is nothing, it is the thought which goes with it that gives strength.

Kinalik was still quite a young woman, very intelligent, kind-hearted, clean and good-looking, and spoke frankly, without reserve. Igjugarjuk was her brother-in-law, and had himself been her instructor in magic. Her own initiation had been severe; she was hung up to some tent poles planted in the snow and left there for five days. It was midwinter, with intense cold and frequent blizzards, but she did not feel the cold, for the spirit protected her. When the five days were at an end, she was taken down and carried into the house, and Igjugarjuk was invited to shoot her, in order that she might attain to intimacy with the supernatural by visions of death. The gun was to be loaded with real powder, but a stone was to be used instead of the leaden bullet, in order that she might still retain connection with earth. Igjugarjuk, in the presence of the assembled villagers, fired the shot, and Kinalik fell to the ground unconscious. On the following morning, just as Igjugarjuk was about to bring her to life again, she awakened from the swoon unaided. Igjugarjuk asserted that he had shot her through the heart, and that the stone had afterwards been removed and was in the possession of her old mother.

Another of the villagers, a young man named Aggjartoq, had also been initiated into the mysteries of the occult with Igjugarjuk as his teacher; and in his case, a third form of ordeal had been employed; to wit, that of drowning. He was lashed to a long pole and carried out on to a lake, a hole was cut in the ice, and the pole with its living burden thrust down through the hole, in such a fashion that Agg-jartoq actually stood on the bottom of the lake with his head under water. He was left in this position for five days and when at last they hauled him up again, his clothes showed no sign of having been in the water at all and he himself had become a great wizard, having overcome death.

These inland Eskimos are very little concerned about the idea of death; they believe that all men are born again, the soul passing on continually from one form of life to another. Good men return to earth as men, but evildoers are re-born as beasts, and in this way the earth is replenished, for no life once given can ever be lost or destroyed.

CHAPTER VII

W E very soon realized that the culture of these Caribou Eskimos was of inland origin. It was the most primitive we had encountered during the whole of the expedition, and all the facts tended to show that we were here well on the way to a solution of one of our most important problems.

Their religion, for instance, was of a pronounced inland type, differing essentially from that of the coast peoples, and in respect of tabu especially unlike that of the sea and shore. The ceremonies attending birth and death in particular were far simpler than those in use among the coast Eskimos. Plainly, the people who first found their way to the sea had seen in it, and in the mode of life which it involved, new and mysterious elements which had given rise to their complicated mythology and ceremonial.

The fact that the sea was new to them was further confirmed by the entire absence of any implements, whether among those in use or others now obsolete, such as would be used by dwellers on the coast.

Nevertheless, we soon found that they had many traditions in common with the Greenland Eskimos; indeed, a number of their folk-tales and legends are altogether identical with Greenland stories.

Out of fifty-two stories which I wrote down among

the Padlermiut at Hikoligjuaq, no fewer than thirty were identical with ones I had already heard in Greenland, and this despite the fact that for thousands of years past, no intercourse had taken place between the two groups of people.

An unquestionable connection exists between the Greenlanders and their Canadian kinsfolk in the matter of story and legend. These stories moreover show that the poor Eskimo can at times find room for thought of things beyond the mere material needs of the day; many of them show a forceful simplicity, a touch of epic strength, and a poetic sense, which command our admiration.

Here are several of the shorter ones:

The Owl that Wooed a Snow Bunting

There was once a little snow bunting; it sat on a tuft and wept because its husband was dead. Then came a big fat Owl and sang:

> Foolish one, weeping
> For a miserable husband
> With a spear
> Made of grass.
> I—I will be
> Your husband.

The little bird answered:

> Who would ever
> Have you for a husband?
> With your lumpy, clumsy feathers
> And that ugly-fashioned beak,
> Podgy legs, and fat round face
> And a head without a neck!

But the owl was so angry at this, that it swooped down on the little snow bunting, and struck it in the breast and then, when it cried in pain, the owl jeered at it, saying: "Ho, what a woman, that can feel pain in the breast and yet have such a sharp tongue!"

Told by KIVKARJUK, of Hikoligjuaq.

(Known throughout the whole of Greenland.)

HOW THE WHITE MEN AND THE INDIANS CAME

There was once a maiden who refused all men who wished to marry her. At last her father was so annoyed at this that he rowed off with her and his dog to an island out in the lake of Haningajoq, not far from Hikoligjuaq, and left her there with the dog. Then the dog took her to wife, and she gave birth to many whelps. And her father brought meat to the island, that they might not die of hunger. One day when they were grown up, their mother said to them: "Next time your grandfather comes out to the island, swim out to meet him, and upset his kayak."

The dogs did so and the girl's father was drowned. Thus she took vengeance upon her father for having married her to a dog. But now that he was dead, there was no one to bring the dogs meat, so the girl cut the soles out of her kamiks, and placed them in the water, and worked magic over them. Then she set some of the dogs on one sole, and said: "Go out into the world and become skilful in all manner of work!"

And the dogs drifted out away from the island and when they had gone a little way, the sole turned into a ship, and they sailed away to the white men's country and became white men. And from them, it is said, all white men are descended.

But the rest of the dogs were set on the other sole, and as it floated away, the girl said: "Take vengeance for all the wrong your grandfather did to me, and show yourselves henceforward thirsty for blood as often as you meet one of the Inuit."

And the dogs sailed away to a strange land, and went ashore there and became the Itqigdlit. From these are descended all those Indians whom our forefathers dreaded, for they slew the Inuit wherever they could find them. And this they continued to do until their brothers, the white men from the island of Anarnigtoq, took land in their country and taught them gentler ways.

Told by I<small>GJUGARJUK</small>.

(This story is known in Greenland.)

T<small>HE</small> R<small>AVEN</small> <small>AND THE</small> L<small>OON</small>

In the olden days, all birds were white. And then one day the raven and the loon fell to drawing patterns on each others feathers. The raven began, and when it had finished, the loon was so displeased with the pattern that it spat all over the raven and made it black all over. And since that day all ravens have been black. But the raven was so angry that it fell upon the loon and beat it so about the legs that it could hardly walk. And that is why the loon is such an awkward creature on land.

(There is a Greenland version of this.)

T<small>HUNDER</small> <small>AND</small> L<small>IGHTNING</small>

In the olden days, nobody ever stole anything. But then one day when a great song festival was being held, two children were left alone in a house. Here they found a caribou skin with the hair off, and a firestone, and desired to have these things for their own. But hardly had they taken them when a great fear came upon them.

"What shall we do," cried one, "to get away from people?"

"Let us turn ourselves into caribou," answered the other."

"No; for then they will catch us; let us turn into wolves."

"No; for then they will kill us. Let us turn into foxes."

And so they went on, naming all the animals there were, but always fearing that men should kill them. Then at last one said: Let us be thunder and lightning. For then men could not reach them. And so it came about; they went up into the sky and became thunder and lightning. And now when we hear the thunder it is one of them rattling the dry skin, and when we see the lightning it is the other one striking sparks from the stone.

Told by Arnarqik, of Nahigtartorvik, Kazan River.

(Also known in Greenland.)

THE OWL AND THE MARMOT

There was once an owl who went out hunting, and seeing a marmot outside its house, it flew towards it and sitting down in front of the entrance, sang:

"I have barred the way of a land beast to its home. Come and fetch it, and bring two sledges."

But the marmot answered: "O mighty owl, spread your legs a little wider apart, and show me that powerful chest."

And the owl hearing this was proud of its broad chest, and spread its legs wider apart.

Then the marmot cried: "Wider, wider still."

And the owl feeling even prouder than before spread its legs a little wider still, and stretched its chest as far as it could.

But then the marmot slipped between its legs and and ran off into its hole.

Told by Kivkarjuk.

I was told that there should be a larger settlement on the southern shore of Hikoligjuaq, and I determined to cross and pay a visit to the natives there. On the day before our departure, a grand song festival was arranged, to be held in Igjugarjuk's tent. In the afternoon the guests arrived, as many as the tent would hold. The singer stood in the middle with closed eyes, accompanying his song with a swaying movement of the hips, while the women, seated in a group on the bench, joined in the chorus every now and then, their voices contrasting pleasantly with the deeper tones of the men.

Here are the words of some of the songs:

IGJUGARJUK'S SONG

Yai—yai—yai
Ya—ayai—ya
I ran with all speed
And met them on the plain,
The great Musk Ox with brilliant black hair—
Hayai—ya—haya.

It was the first time I had seen them,
Grazing on the flowers of the plain,
Far from the hill where I stood,
And ignorantly I thought
They were but small and slight . . .

But they grew up out of the earth
As I came within shot,
Great black giant beasts
Far from our dwellings
In the regions of happy summer hunting.

AVANE'S SONG

Lo, alas, I look and seek
All impatient, eagerly,
For the caribou in the hills;
Am I old and worthless now,
Since I hunt in vain?
I who once could stand and shoot
Swiftly without aiming
Striking down with sudden arrow
Bulls with spreading horn;
Saw the great beast fall and lie
With muzzle deep in mire.

Women do not as a rule sing their own songs. No woman is expected to sing unless expressly invited by an angakoq. As a rule, they sing songs made by the men. Should it happen, however, that a woman feels a spirit impelling her to sing, she may step forth from the chorus and follow her own inspiration. Among the women here, only two were thus favored by the spirits; one was Igjugarjuk's first wife, Kivkarjuk, now dethroned, and the other Akjartoq, the mother of Kinalik.

KIVKARJUK'S SONG

I am but a little woman
Very willing to toil,

Very willing and happy
To work and slave . . .
And in my eagerness
To be of use,
I pluck the furry buds of willow
Buds like beard of wolf.

I love to go walking far and far away,
And my soles are worn through
As I pluck the buds of willow,
That are furry like the great wolf's beard. . . .

AKJARTOQ'S SONG

I draw a deep breath,
But my breath comes heavily
As I call forth the song . . .

There are ill rumors abroad,
Of some who starve in the far places,
And can find no meat.

I call forth the song
From above,
Hayaya—haya.

And now I forget
How hard it was to breathe,
Remembering old times,
When I had strength
To cut and flay great beasts.
Three great beasts could I cut up
While the sun slowly went his way
Across the sky.

In addition to ordinary hunting songs and lyrics there are songs of derision, satires with a mercilessly personal address; two men will stand up in turn and accuse each other before the assembled neighbors. These accusations, even when well founded, are received with surprising calmness, whereas "evil or angry words" may have far more serious effects.

I give here Utahania's impeachment of one Kanaijuaq who had quarrelled with his wife and attempted to desert her, leaving her to her fate out in the wilds; the woman, however, had proved not only able to stand up for herself in a rough-and-tumble, but left her husband of her own accord and went to shift for herself, taking her son with her.

> Something was whispered
> Of man and wife
> Who could not agree.
> And what was it all about?
> A wife who in rightful anger
> Tore her husband's furs across,
> Took their canoe
> And rowed away with her son.
> Ay—ay, all who listen,
> What do you think of him,
> Poor sort of man?
> Is he to be envied,
> Who is great in his anger
> But faint in strength,
> Blubbering helplessly
> Properly chastised?
> Though it was he who foolishly proud
> Started the quarrel with stupid words.

Kanaijuaq retorted with a song accusing Utahania of improper behavior at home; his hard words however, seemed to make no difference to their friendship. Far more serious was the effect of malicious words in the case of Utahania's foster-son who was once upbraided by his foster-father as follows:

"I wish you were dead! You are not worth the food you eat." And the young man took the words so deeply to heart that he declared he would never eat again. To make his sufferings as brief as possible, he lay down the same night stark naked on the bare snow, and was frozen to death.

Halfway through the festival it was announced that Kinalik, the woman angakoq, would invoke her helping spirits and clear the way of all dangers ahead. Sila was to be called in to aid one who could not help himself. All the singing now ceased, and Kinalik stood forth alone with her eyes tightly closed. She uttered no incantation, but stood trembling all over, and her face twitched from time to time as if in pain. This was her way of "looking inward," and penetrating the veil of the future; the great thing was to concentrate all one's force intently on the one idea, of calling forth good for those about to set out on their journey.

Igjugarjuk, who never let slip an opportunity of exalting his own tribe at the expense of the "salt water Eskimo," informed me at this juncture that their angakoqs never danced about doing tricks, nor did they have recourse to particular forms of speech; the one essential was truth and earnestness—all the rest was mere trickwork designed to impress the vulgar.

QINGARUVDLIAQ, THE WOMAN WHO KNEW ALL THE MEN'S SONGS AND PROMPTED
THEM WHEN THEY FORGOT THE WORDS

YOUNG WOMEN

They were always happy and smiling, and handsome as well.

When Kinalik had reached the utmost limit of her concentration, I was requested to go outside the tent and stand on a spot where there were no footmarks, remaining there until I was called in. Here, on the untrodden snow, I was to present myself before Sila, standing silent and humble, and desiring sky and air and all the forces of nature to look upon me and show me goodwill.

It was a peculiar form of worship or devotion, which I now encountered for the first time; it was the first time, also, that I had seen Sila represented as a benign power.

After I had stood thus for a time, I was called in again. Kinalik had now resumed her natural expression, and was beaming all over. She assured me that the Great Spirit had heard her prayer, and that all dangers should be removed from our path; also, that we should have success in our hunting whenever we needed meat.

This prophecy was greeted with applause and general satisfaction; it was plain to see that these good folk, in their simple, innocent fashion, gave us their blessing and had done all they could to render it effective. There was no doubting the sincerity of their goodwill.

On the following night we were racing at full speed over the wintry surface of Lake Hikoligjuaq. The firm ice was spread with a thin layer of soft, moist snow, acting as a soft carpet to the dogs' paws, and the long rest in complete idleness with plenty of fresh caribou meat had given them a degree of vitality that made it a pleasure to be out once more.

We had two lads with us as guides, who had borrowed Igjugarjuk's dogs, but it was not long before they were hopelessly out-distanced, and we had to content ourselves with a guess at our direction.

Early in the morning, before the sun was fairly warm, we reached the southern shore of the lake and camped in a pleasant little valley, fastening the dogs in a thicket of young willow that stood bursting in bud to greet the spring.

In the course of the day we went out to reconnoitre. And it was not long before we came upon a solitary caribou hunter observing us from a little hill. He was just taking to flight when the two lads from the last village, who had now come up, recognized him and called him by name, when he walked up smiling to meet them. He informed us that there was a village of five tents a couple of hours' journey farther inland, and that we could reach the place without difficulty, although the ground was bare. We tried to persuade him to come back with us to the camp, but he preferred to go on ahead and tell his comrades of the strange meeting. And before we had gone far, the whole party came down and overtook us, they had been too impatient to wait for our arrival. It was hard work for the dogs to get the sledge over the numerous hills, and even the level ground was difficult going, sodden as it was with water and broken by tussocks and pools. There were plenty of willing hands, however, and we made our way, albeit slowly, with a great deal of merriment. Miteq and I had to face an endless rain of questions. These inland folk look upon the sea as something wonderful and mysterious, far beyond their ken; and when we explained that we had had to cross many seas in coming from our own land to theirs, they regarded our coming in itself as something of a marvel. And we agreed with them in their surprise at our being able to understand one another's speech.

Suddenly speech and laughter died away; the dogs pricked up their ears, and a strange silence fell upon all. There, full in our way, lay the body of a woman prone on the ground. We stood for a moment at a loss. Then the men went forward, while we held back our dogs. The figure still lay motionless. A loud wailing came from the party ahead, and Miteq and I stood vaguely horrified, not knowing what it meant. Then one of the men came back and explained that we had found the corpse of a woman who had been lost in a blizzard the winter before—and he pointed to one of those bending over her; that was her husband.

It had been a hard winter, and just when the cold was most severe, six of those in the village had died of hunger. A man named Atangagjuaq then determined to set out for a neighboring village in search of aid, and his wife, fearing lest, weak as he was, he might be unable to complete the journey, had followed after him. She herself, however, had been lost in the snow before coming up with him. They had searched for her that winter, and in the following spring, but without result; and now here she lay, discovered by the merest accident right athwart our course.

I walked forward to view the body of this woman

who had lost her life in a vain attempt to help her husband.   There was nothing repulsive in the sight; she just lay there, with limbs extended, and an expression of unspeakable weariness on her face.   It was plain to see that she had walked on and on, struggling against the blizzard till she could go no farther, and sank exhausted, while the snow swiftly covered her, leaving no trace.

The body was left lying as it was; no one touched it. We drove on, and in an hour's time reached the Eskimo camp.

These people are quick to change from one extreme of feeling to another.   We had not gone far on our way before the dead woman, to all seeming, was forgotten, and the merriment that had met with so sudden a check broke out afresh.   As soon as we had put up our tent, the men got hold of our ski, and went off to try them in a good deep snowdrift that still lay in a gap.   They had never seen ski before, and great shouts of laughter greeted the first attempts of those venturesome enough to try them.   One of the gayest of the party was Atangagjuaq, who but a few minutes earlier had stood weeping beside the body of his wife.

By the 21st of June, we were once more on the ice of Lake Hikoligjuaq, and on the morning of the 22nd, just at sunrise, we reached the spot where the others of our party were encamped.   That sunrise was, I think, the most remarkable I have ever seen.   To the north, on the horizon, was a dense white mass of cloud, like a reflection from the lake itself, but with a narrow belt of delicate green below.   The country round was outlined in masses of black. Then suddenly there was a glow of fire, a tongue of flame broke through the pale green below the cloud, lighting up all the sky; light, fragile veils of rosy cloud-stuff floated by overhead, and the ice below was tinged with the palest mauve. The contours of shore and hill stood out now darker than before, while flowers of fire appeared on the horizon like fairy-lamps lit one after another, gradually merging into one great conflagration. Then up came the sun itself, and all the varied colors were lost in one stark red glow reflected in our faces as we looked.

It was like driving into a burning city; and we remained spellbound until the barking of dogs and shouts of welcome from our companions brought us back to reality and busy freshness of a new day. . . .

CHAPTER VIII

BETWEEN TWO WINTERS

IGJUGARJUK had for some time past been talking
of making a trip down to Baker Lake, and was
now getting ready for the journey. Then one day a
canoe came up from the south, in charge of a young
man, Equmeq, by name. It was decided that Birket-
Smith and Bangsted, with the greater part of our
ethnographical collections, should start with this
party for Baker Lake, Igjugarjuk taking the rest,
and Miteq and I going by sledge—a plan which
caused much head-shaking among the natives, who
regarded sledging as dangerous or impossible at this
season.

Certainly, our journey turned out worse than we
had expected. The ground was soft and wet, and
very uneven, at the best, added to which we came
every now and then to swollen streams, often so deep
that we had to follow them some distance up to find
a practicable crossing among the ice of the lakes.
The constant detours, again, took up so much time
that we had little left for hunting, and had to reduce
our rations and those of the dogs accordingly.
Igjugarjuk and the lake party had simply to follow
the river and we were supposed to come up with them
every evening. Actually we often failed to make
their camp in time, but Igjugarjuk always waited

faithfully till we did come up, and gave us directions for the next day's route. On one occasion we came within a hair's breadth of losing the canoe with its precious load. We had just got in to camp, on the bank of a stream flowing into the main river, and found that our companions had laid out some newly slain carcases on the other side. Crossing in the canoe, we suddenly perceived the dogs making straight for the meat, and in hurrying to save it, we omitted to pull the canoe far enough up shore; when we turned, it was floating rapidly away down to the main channel. Guns, ammunition, cameras, diaries, and everything of value was on board; in addition to which, the canoe itself was our only practicable means of transport.

The feverish chase that followed was beyond description. Igjugarjuk,—who, by the way, could not swim—joined me in a mad obstacle race in and out of water, each of us with one end of a line fastened round the body. There were masses of loose ice in the fairway, and I managed to swim from floe to floe, hauling up Igjugarjuk to each before making for the next. So we went on, clambering and struggling desperately in pursuit. Fortunately, the canoe itself was checked in its progress by these same masses of ice; nevertheless, we dared not relax our efforts. Our hands were torn and bleeding from the sharp ice crystals; and when at last we reached the canoe itself and dragged it into safety, we were so exhausted that we sank down helplessly beside it. Another few yards and it would have been carried into the main river, to certain destruction—and ourselves with it.

I noted a curious thing in connection with this little adventure, as showing the effect of intense effort and strain on the sense of time. Both Igjugarjuk and I agreed that the struggle could only have lasted some few minutes. But when our friends came up and got us back to camp and boiling hot tea, we found that the actual chase, from the time the canoe broke loose to its recapture had taken us two and a half hours.

On the 3rd of July we reached the settlement of Nahigtartorvik. I was anxious to push on, and made a detour to avoid the settlement. Unfortunately, however, our way was barred by a stream so deep and wide that there was no crossing it without the canoe, and we had therefore to camp and wait for the others. When they came up, Igjugarjuk reported that the country ahead of us was destitute of game, and there was famine lower down the Kazan River, where several families had died of starvation already. Moreover, the river was now in a dangerous state owing to masses of ice coming down from above. Birket-Smith and Bangsted with their party had gone by a few days before, and had difficulty in getting through; it would be worse for Igjugarjuk with only a couple of lads, his wife and two small children. It was therefore agreed that he should go on with me for two days more, after which I could manage by myself. First of all, however, we must call at the settlement and obtain food for myself and the dogs.

Pukerdluk, the headman of this particular village received us most hospitably. The caribou hunting had been very successful, and they were well off for meat. They gave us an excellent meal, and we had no difficulty in making arrangements for further progress. Pukerdluk himself was to go on with Igjugarjuk the next day, and a young man named Kijoqut—a remarkably handsome young fellow by the way—was to accompany us down to Baker Lake.

Next day, after a hearty farewell to Igjugarjuk, and not least, to his wife, who had looked after us like a mother, we set off overland to the spot where we were to meet the canoe. The same evening we drove up into the native camp on the Kazan River at the point where we were to cross. Contrary to the usual procedure, no one came out to meet us, and there was no answer to the vociferous barking of our dogs.

On entering the tent, we found the explanation and a sorry one indeed it was. Half a score of human figures lay about in various attitudes, all in such a stage of exhaustion that they could not walk. We at once made some tea, and when they had had as much as they could drink, they livened up a little. It was an extraordinary instance of Eskimo limitations thus to find men at the point of death in a starvation camp within a few miles of plenty.

Hilitoq, the head of the party, whom we had met before, and his two young sons, were not quite so far gone as the rest, and we persuaded them to come out hunting with us the same night. After some hours search, we came upon a herd of fourteen caribou; we shot three, and sent one back to Hilitoq's people at the camp.

It is difficult for a Greenlander to understand how these natives here can give up and lie down to die in a country so rich in game. But it is not laziness. I fancy the wretched footwear they use in summer has a great deal to do with it. They have not the thick stout sealskin or walrus hide, but only light caribou skin, pleasant enough in winter on the cold dry snow, but miserably inadequate in the swampy tundra during summer, and with no sort of wear in it over rocky ground; a couple of days will wear through perfectly new soles.

Late that night we reached the river Kunuag. After a difficult crossing, we took leave of our companions, who with their kayaks on their heads hurried back to their own people. We built a great fire, and roasted steaks of freshly killed meat on flat stones. All was clear ahead now, down to Baker Lake; the weather was fine, and as sleep is not so essential in summer, we were soon on our way once more.

It was slow going over the swampy tundra, that squelched underfoot at every step. By six the next morning we reached a group of three tents, and were surprised to find the inmates here also on the verge of starvation. We had the better part of two caribou carcases with us, and seeing no reason to carry a heavier load than needed, we invited the village to a feast. The fine fresh meat was disposed of with remarkable celerity, and I had once more an opportunity of witnessing the feats of which an Eskimo is capable in this direction. Hunger however, had by no means impaired the spirits of these good folk; they smiled as they showed us their cooking pots, scraped clean and empty for the past week. And they broke up their tobacco pipes to get a taste of tobacco after the heavy meal.

We were past astonishment when a gramophone was produced, and kept going for the rest of the afternoon. The natives declared, in sober earnest, that jazz tunes were no less comforting to an empty stomach than soothing to a full one.

We had hoped to push on from here without further delay, but many obstacles lay between us and our return to Chesterfield,—too many to recount. The partial break-up of winter ice meant for us that progress by boat and progress by dog sledge were alternately barred. Once, native kayaks which we hired were crushed in the rocky narrows of a swollen river. Again, we had to cross a lake on a block of ice, with our dogs drawing the whole mass across by swimming in harness. And when, after days of soggy going, we finally' reached Baker Lake, we could not rouse the people of the trading post out on the island, though we burned signal fires for eight hours continuously. So we finally ferried across on an ice floe, using our skis as paddles.

We found Birket-Smith and Helge Bangsted at the island, but they wished to continue their botanical studies, so we pushed on to Chesterfield without them. We met with more delays on the way down to the Inlet,—chiefly from ice jams,—and not until July 31 did we reach our destination.

We had first visited Chesterfield in winter, and passed it in a blizzard, when everything was as arctic as could be; when one's nostrils froze in the icy blast and the blood fairly hardened in one's cheeks. Our own experience had taught us to appreciate the natives' power of adapting themselves to their surroundings. Their extraordinary clothing, of soft caribou skin from head to foot, inside and out, enabled not only the men, but also women and children, to move abroad in all manner of weather; as long as they could manage to procure food enough, the cold of winter seemed hardly to affect them at all.

Coming back now, in the summer, we found all changed to a surprising degree. The handsome dresses of caribou skin, so admirably suited to the racial type of the wearers, and to their surroundings, had given place to the cheap and vulgar products of the trading station. The men went about in jerseys and readymade slacks, their flowing locks surmounted by a cheap cloth cap, while the women had exchanged their quaint swallow-tailed furs, long boots and baggy breeches, for shapeless European dresses of machine-made stuff, in which grace and character alike were utterly obliterated.

So also with their dwellings; the wonderful snow huts, fashioned, as it were, of the cold itself as a protection from the cold, were now replaced by big white canvas tents, which made the place look more like a holiday camp than an Eskimo settlement. And one could not go near them without finding one's ears assailed by the noise of some modern mechanical contrivance, either a gramophone or a sewing machine.

I noted now for the first time how oddly these

quondam inland folk—they were mainly from the neighborhood of Baker Lake—felt lost and out of their element here on the shore of the open sea. Just outside Chesterfield Inlet was a veritable highroad for the seal; and all round the adjacent Marble Island the walrus might be seen blowing and steaming at the surface of the water; yet never a man in all the settlement went out hunting either. The natives here, despite their astonishing agility and skill with kayak and spears among the turbulent waters of the rivers, were content now to let all this meat go by, while they themselves lived on tea and pancakes. The most they ever attempted in the way of hunting was to lay out a net in the bay just outside their tents and catch a few fish.

This indifference to the abundance offered them by the sea was not due to laziness however, but rather a peculiarity of their inland culture itself. They could not dispense with their caribou; and it was a principle handed down through generations that one could not mingle sea hunting with that of the land without losing the latter altogether.

After a pleasant two-weeks stay at Chesterfield, during which Birket-Smith and Bangsted rejoined us, and during which we received and sent off letters by the Hudson's Bay steamer, *Nascopie*, we set off on the long journey back to headquarters at Danish Island. It was already later in the summer than I wished, and plans which we had hopefully made for spending the summer in useful work together began to grow impracticable. I was anxious to see what the rest had been doing,—Mathiassen and Freuchen in their investigation of ancient culture, particularly.

We were fortunate in getting passage by motor-schooner as far as Repulse Bay, which we made in three days. Here we should, by agreement, have found Peter Freuchen encamped waiting for us with the motor boat we had built especially for summer work. The migratory ice, however, had kept him from getting out with it.

We accordingly hired a whaleboat belonging to an Eskimo from Southampton Island, who was known to the traders as "John Ell." As it turned out, we needed him for various errands during most of the winter following, so we grew to know and admire John Ell.

He was a man in many ways unlike the average type of native, having been educated to begin with on board a whaler, thus learning not only to speak English fluently, but also to manage a boat with remarkable skill, especially among the ice. He was looked up to as a leader by his fellows, and was also a man of property, having a fine team of dogs and a range of sledges designed for work at different seasons, a well-equipped whaleboat, and furthermore, a motor boat of his own. This last is uncommon among the Eskimos; John Ell had bought it for 75 fox skins. He carried on an extensive correspondence with people in the neighborhood, using the sign language invented by a missionary named Peck, which is here generally employĕd. And he kept a regular account of his income and expenditure throughout the year. It was the more remarkable, seeing how much he had lived and learned among

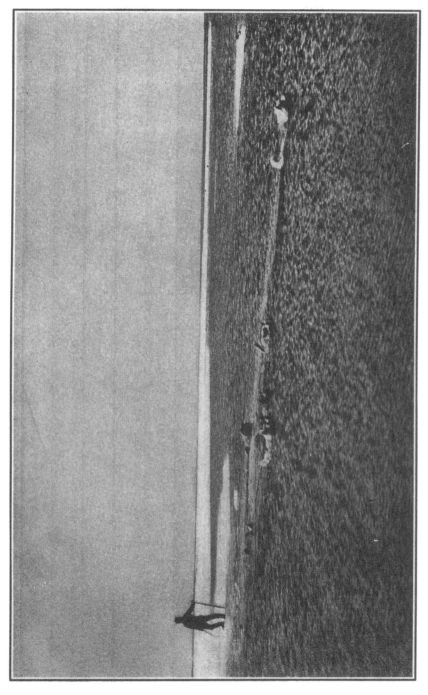

ICE ON THE LAKES

Generally a belt of open water close to the shore was left, and we had then either to paddle across, using our skis as paddles, or harness the dogs to an ice-floe and let them swim to land with us and our gear as here shown.

REMAINS OF ESKIMO DWELLINGS

Ruins of this type, where peat and stone often eked out with bones of the whale were used as building material, were found by the Expedition in many places throughout regions where only snow huts are now in use. All the finds from these winter dwellings point towards a gradual development from an inland form of culture, based on hunting of land game, to that of a coast people living on seal and walrus. The transition appears to have taken place in Alaska.

white men, to find that he was a distinguished anga-koq, with a faith in native magic equal to his reputation.

Winter weather on land and ice in the channel held us at Repulse Bay till September 1, and then we crossed in a day as far as Hurd Channel. Here again we were held up for twelve days. We used the interval in hunting meat for our dogs, and other employments. Then we crossed at a favorable moment to Vansittart Island, and three days later got through to headquarters.

We found an empty house. Whereas we had expected a rousing welcome after our long absence, there wasn't even a letter to tell us where our other comrades were.

However, Freuchen and the Eskimos were only out at the hunting grounds, and they hadn't believed that we could get through the broken ice. We went out and found them, and our reunion was as joyous as any meeting in the Arctic is likely to be between companions long separated.

Mathiassen, with Jacob Olsen, was still at South-ampton Island studying the traces of former Eskimo culture. It was not until February 18, and only after causing us anxiety for his safety, that he finally returned, and completed the final reunion of our party.

Meantime, the rest of us were held at Danish Island, or nearby, for most of the winter. Freuchen, who started out in January for Baffinland, to begin studies later to be carried out in cooperation with Mathiassen, was quickly brought back with a bad case of frostbite which made him temporarily an invalid. Birket-Smith and Bangsted were held at headquarters looking after him.

I was occupied during the winter with two main tasks,—completing my study and comparison of the various ethnographical collections, and rounding them out with materials secured on another visit to the natives around Lyon Inlet.

With regard to one item of our study, I felt that we had already secured satisfactory data; namely, the investigation of the culture of the Tunit. Therkel Mathiassen's work[1] here proved to be of greatest importance to our study of the people and their history as a whole.

There are no written sources for the early history of the Eskimo people; it is to the spade that we must turn if we would learn something of their life in ages past. We have to dig and delve among the ruins of their dwellings, in the kitchen middens of their settlements, for proof of how they lived and hunted, how they were housed and clad. It is often a laborious task, but not less interesting on that account. And it was one of the principal tasks of the Fifth Thule Expedition to investigate, by means of archæological excavations, the history and development of the Eskimo people, and their migrations into Greenland. Our work in this field has brought to light some six or seven thousand items which afford a good

[1] Space forbids the inclusion here of my companions' reports in full, and I can give but the briefest indication of their main features. Both Freuchen's and Therkel Mathiassen's reports are published—or shortly to be published—in English elsewhere. The pages here following are taken from Therkel Mathiassen's own text.

idea as to the mode of life prevailing among the Central Eskimos here in those distant ages.

Naujan lies on the northern shore of Repulse Bay, a little to the east of the trading station. The name, which means "the place of the young seamews," is taken from a steep bird cliff on the banks of a small lake. From the lake, a valley runs down towards the shore, where it opens out into a bay, and it is in this valley, just south of the lake, that the great settlement of Naujan existed in ancient times.

The Eskimos of the present day in these regions use only snow huts in winter; it was the more surprising therefore to come upon remains of quite a different type of house. We found at Naujan a whole little township of these houses, constructed of stone, turf, and the bones of whales. They were built so as to be partly underground and must have been far more substantial and warm, though less hygienic perhaps, than the light, cool, healthy snow huts of today. Various features placed it beyond question that at the time when these houses were built, the land must have lain some ten metres lower than it does now; and this, too, explains why the settlement was found at some distance from what is now the beach, instead of practically on it as is customary. Similarly, in confirmation of our theory, we found, on a little island near by, a pair of kayak stands—pillars of stone on which the skin kayaks are laid to be out of reach of the dogs—some 15 metres up from sea; actually, of course, they would have been built at the water's edge, to save hauling up and down.

The houses themselves had fallen to pieces long since, and the remains were scattered, weatherworn and overgrown with grass and moss to such an extent that our excavations gave but a poor idea of their original appearance. The implements and objects found among the ruins, however, gave an excellent view of the culture of the period from which they were derived. The materials comprised bone, walrus tusk and caribou antler, flint, slate and soapstone, whalebone, some wood, and occasionally metal, this last in the form of cold hammered copper (probably obtained by barter from the Eskimos of the west), with a single fragment of meteoric iron forming the point of a harpoon.

It is of course impossible to mention more than a very few of the finds here; often, too, the most insignificant objects to all outward seeming prove most important from the scientific point of view. Among our most valuable finds, for instance, were three odd broken fragments of rough earthenware vessels. These are only known to exist among the Alaskan Eskimos, and the finding of them here was of importance; few, however, would have attached any value to those three dirty scraps of pottery.

And now as to the age of this Naujan material. We may at once assert that nothing was found which could suggest any intercourse with Europeans. There were no glass beads—which are ordinarily the first thing the Eskimos procure, and always found in their villages—and the only fragment of iron found was of meteoric origin. This at once carries us back 300 years. Beyond this, we have only the alter-ation in the level of the land to fall back upon. It takes a considerable period, of course, for the land to rise ten metres, but there is no definite standard by which to measure the lapse of time involved. In the north of Sweden, for instance, the land rises 1 metre in a hundred years; allowing the same rate of progress here, this would give us an age of 1000 years—but this is, of course, mere guesswork.

As to the people who lived here in those days, they were beyond doubt genuine Eskimos; they lived on the shore in regular winter dwellings, drove dog sledges, and hunted whale, seal and walrus, besides bear and caribou; they trapped foxes, and caught salmon. They had at any rate no lack of meat, to judge from the enormous quantities of bones, which indeed, almost smothered the remains of the houses themselves. If we ask the present inhabitants of these regions, the Aivilik, as to the folk who dwelt in these now ruined houses, they will say, it was the Tunit. These Tunit were a race of big, strong men who lived in permanent dwellings and hunted whale and walrus; the men wore bearskin breeches and the women long sealskin boots just like the Polar Eskimos of today. When the Aivilik settled on the coast, the Tunit moved away to the northward; only on the inaccessible Southampton Island did a party remain, and the Sadlermiut, who died out here in 1903, were the last descendants of the Tunit in the country. Thus the Aivilik tradition, and it agrees in all essentials with the results of our investigations.

For on comparing these Tunit of ancient Naujan with the present inhabitants, we find a great difference between them. The Naujan Eskimos lived on the shore, hunted the whale, and built their houses from the skeletons. The Aivilik live in snow huts, and spend most of the year hunting caribou up in the interior. Many of the implements and utensils in use among the Naujan folk, such as the bola, the bird dart, and earthenware vessels, are unknown among the Aivilik; the latter, on the other hand, have others unknown to the ancients, such as combs, big ladles made of musk ox horn, and toggles for dog harness. And on examining the types of implement in use among the two peoples, many distinct points of difference are found.

Where did the Naujan Eskimos come from, and what became of them?

It soon becomes apparent that they link up in two directions across the Eskimo region; with Alaska on the one hand and Greenland on the other. At Thule, in northern Greenland, a find has been made, the oldest of any extent from the whole of Greenland, which points to precisely the same type of culture as that which we found at Naujan; and we have therefore called it the Thule type. Similar finds have been made both in west and north Greenland, and the Polar Eskimos of the present day are very much like these Thule folk in many respects. The Greenland Eskimos, then, must have passed through these central regions at a time when they were still inhabited by the Thule folk.

Looking now to the westward, we find in Alaska a race of big men, who hunt the whale, live in permanent dwellings on the coast, use the bola, make earthenware, and have almost the same types of implements generally as those we found at Naujan; old finds from Alaska also exhibit even more marked resemblance to the Naujan type. The Thule folk then, must have come from Alaska, this is beyond question. They spread in a mighty wave from west to east, reaching right across to Greenland. At some time now far distant there was a more or less uniform type of culture prevailing throughout the whole of the Eskimo region; that which we now call the Thule type; then, in the central districts, an advance took place of people from the interior represented by the present-day Central Eskimo: the Aivilik, Netsilik, Copper Eskimos and Baffinlanders. These people, with their culture based on snow huts and caribou hunting, made their way down to the coast, where their mode of life was gradually adapted to some extent, so as to include the hunting of marine animals, while the ancient Thule culture disappeared from the central regions where now only the numerous ruins of stone and bone houses remain as evidence of the culture of earlier times. Thus too we have an explanation of many otherwise inexplicable similarities between the two topographical extremities of Eskimo culture; Alaska and Greenland; features found in the extreme east and in the extreme west, but lacking in the central region.

CHAPTER IX

FAITH OUT OF FEAR

BY the middle of January, I had the ethnographical collections in shape so that I could leave Danish Island for good. But we still needed a few items. I wanted a few more skin dresses to round out the collection, and I wished to make a final study of the spiritual beliefs of the Eskimos of the region. Accordingly, I set off for the hunting camp at the mouth of Lyon Inlet, to visit my old friend Aua.

Aua's hunting camp lay midway out in Lyon Inlet; I reached it late one afternoon, just as the setting sun was gilding the domes of the snow huts.

It was known that I was on the way, and above each hut waved a little white flag—a sign that the inmates had relinquished their old heathen faith and become Christians. As I drove up, men, women and children trooped out and formed up in line outside Aua's hut, and as soon as I had reined in my team, the whole party began singing a hymn. The tune was so unlike what they were accustomed to in their own pagan chants that they bungled it a little, but there was no mistaking the earnestness and pious feeling which inspired it. There was something very touching in such a greeting; these poor folk had plainly found in the new faith a refuge that meant a great deal in their lives.

When it was over, they stepped forward one by one and shook hands. And here I could not but recall my first meeting with these same people a year ago, at Cape Elizabeth. Then, they had come leaping and capering round me in an outburst of unrestrained natural feeling; now, all was ceremonial and solemn to an almost painful degree. It was not long, however, before this wore off, and the old easy merriment showed forth again. The carcase of a seal was brought out and thrown to the dogs, and while they were busy with it, I was regaled with the latest news. Then my sledge was hoisted up onto a stand built of blocks of snow, and I myself invited indoors to thaw. Aua's wife, Orulo, good friendly soul, had a fine big bowl of steaming hot tea for me, and when this had driven out some of the cold I could settle down at ease among my old friends.

It was the most difficult time of the year just now; the stores of meat accumulated during summer had been used up, and it was a question of procuring fresh supplies for men and dogs, from day to day. Seal were hunted now either at the breathing holes or in the open water beyond the edge of the ice. The weather was rough and stormy, snow falling every day, and the thermometer rarely above minus 50°C. The days were short, and in order to make the most of them, the hunters set off before daylight and returned after dark. All meat brought in was cut up and distributed at once throughout the camp, and as there was generally no more than would suffice for one day, the arrival of the next instalment was looked forward to with anxiety literally equal to that with which hungry folk look forward to a meal.

The men had little rest these days. It is a weary business to be out for ten hours at a stretch, first searching about to find the blowhole of a seal, and having found it, to stand motionless in the driving snow waiting for the seal to come up to breathe. A seal has always a number of blowholes open at once, and it might often be hours before it appeared at the one actually under observation. No wonder then, that the hunters were stiff and sore by the time they returned. Throwing off all but their innermost clothing, they threw themselves down on the bench in the warmth of the hut, while the women busied themselves cutting up the carcases into juicy red fillets edged with rich yellowish blubber. Then, when the pots began to boil, came the reward of the day's toil, in the shape of a steaming cup of thick blood-soup. The next course was meat, speared up from the cauldron on long bone skewers, and dumped down upon a wooden tray enriched with the juices of many a former meal. A sense of warmth and comfort spread and grew, the little triumphs or disappointments of the day were recounted with good humor; material wants were satisfied for the time being, and peace and plenty reigned.

These evenings, when we lay stretched at ease after a hearty meal, and the most taciturn had thawed into some degree of geniality, were the times I most looked forward to for converse with my hosts.

In the collecting of folk lore, one is altogether

dependent upon the character and temper of one's sources; it is essential to have native authorities not only qualified in regard to knowledge of their subject but also gifted with the right appreciation of it themselves. They must be reliable, so that one can listen without criticising all the time, and one should if possible be on friendly terms with them throughout. Aua and his wife Orulo eminently fulfilled these conditions; we were excellent friends, and the two old folk, pooling the experience and learning of their respective lives, combined to furnish a mine of information. What one did not know the other did. The reader will recollect Aua from a previous chapter. and the account of his snow palace at Cape Elizabeth; it was he who then gave me the accounts of native belief as to the life after death, and the methods of native wizards in their spirit flights and the like.

In addition to Aua himself, there were three other wizards in the camp, differing considerably in type and character. I endeavored throughout as far as possible to get them to take part in the conversation, in order to obtain as varied a general view as possible. One of them was a young man named Anarqaoq. He was not particularly skilful as a hunter, and had been more or less of a vagabond all his life. He had come originally from one of the Netsilik tribes in the neighborhood of King William's Land, where his first introduction to the practice of magic had taken place. He was a man of a very nervous temperament, easily influenced, and his speciality, as one might say, consisted mainly in the remarkable visions which came to him as soon as he was out alone caribou hunting in the interior. His imagination peopled the whole of nature with fantastic spirit creatures that came to him either while he slept, or even when fully awake and engaged on his normal occupations. In some way he could not explain, these spirits gave him an enhanced power of penetrating into the realms of mystery; and though his own accounts of such experiences often appeared naïve to say the least, they sufficed to impress his fellows with a sense of his importance as one familiar with the unknown powers. I gave him a pencil and paper one day and asked him to draw some of these "visions." After some hesitation he complied. And I could not but feel that he was himself convinced of their reality; he did not simply sit down and draw the things at once, but would remain for some time manifestly under the influence of strong emotion, trembling often to such a degree that he could hardly draw at all.

It is difficult indeed for the ordinary civilized mentality to appreciate the complexity of the native mind in its relations with the supernatural; a "wizard" may resort to the most transparent trickwork and yet be thoroughly in earnest. Anarqaoq himself, afforded an instance of this. One evening a child came in crying, but unable to say what was the matter—a not uncommon happening with children as everyone knows. Our wizard, however, grasped and utilized the opportunity. He dashed out into the darkness and returned some time later covered with blood and with great rents in his clothing, having fought and defeated the "evil Spirits" that

MITEQ CUTTING UP A NEWLY CAPTURED SEAL

SNOW HUTS

These are built with the first snows of autumn.   Skins of newly killed caribou are hung out to dry.

were seeking to harm the child. No one suspected that he had snatched up a lump of half frozen seal's blood from the kitchen, and with this, and a few self-inflicted wounds upon his garments, supplied the needful evidence to impress his fellow villagers with the truth of his story.

Another wizard was Unaleq, also a Netsilik. I chose out these two in particular for occasional interrogation because the Igdlulik, to which tribe Aua himself belonged, regarded the Netsilik as their inferiors, and Aua was thus impelled to be more communicative himself.

Unaleq was, I think, the most trustful and optimistic soul I have ever met. Actually one of the poorest and most unskilful hunters for some distance round, he was nevertheless convinced that his "helping spirits" had endowed him with supernatural powers enabling him to assist his fellows. I got him to draw these spirits for me, as Anarqaoq had done, though again, not without considerable difficulty, despite the tempting nature of the prize offered—a knife bigger and brighter and sharper than he had ever owned in his life. When he had finished, I assured him that he would be successful in his hunting on the following day, as I had dreamt I saw him catching a seal. Whether due to laziness or lack of skill, he had caught not a single seal all that winter. But on the following day he did. The confidence with which my dream inspired him had, perhaps, encouraged him to effort beyond his usual capacity; at any rate, he brought home a seal.

And finally, there was Aua's brother, Ivaluartjuk,

whose contribution to our stock of legends and myths was of the greatest value. We met him for the first time at Repulse Bay. He was a duly qualified wizard, but rarely practised his art, his speciality being folk tales, of which over fifty were written down from his dictation. Space forbids the inclusion of further stories at length, but there is one important point in this connection which must be noted, to wit, the similarity, or indeed, identity of many of the Canadian Eskimo folk tales with those already known from the Eskimos of Greenland. A few instances have been noted in the foregoing; and the further evidence afforded by this later material places the question of kinship beyond all doubt. The following are a few of the themes in the stories told by Ivaluartjuk having counterparts or very close variants in different parts of Greenland:

The coming of men: at the very beginning of the world, women went out and found children sprawling among the bushes. Later, they grew to be many throughout the world.

Day and night. In earliest times, all was dark; the fox wished it to be dark that it might steal from the dwellings of men. But the raven could not see to find food in the dark, and wished for light. And there was light.

The raven that married a goose, and was drowned when the birds flew over the sea.

The fatherless boy who was ill-used by his fellows, till a spirit (the moon) took pity on him and made him a strong man, when he returned and took vengeance.

Igimarajugjuk, who ate his wives.

The soul that lived in the bodies of all beasts.

Sun and moon—brother and sister who loved each other, till the sister, ashamed, fled away by night, the brother in pursuit. Both carried torches, but the one went out, hence the faint glow of the moon compared with the sun.

The man disturbed in his hunting by children at play; he shuts them up in a mountain where they starve to death.[1]

There are, of course, numerous themes common to the folklore of many different countries and races, so that the subject itself does not always count for much. But in the case of these stories we often find, not only close resemblance in points of detail, but precisely identical words in the dialogue.

Aua of course, as a wizard himself, was an authority not only on folklore and customs generally, but more especially on all matters connected with the supernatural, as well as the complicated rites and observances coming under the head of tabu. His account of the origin of his own profession is worth noting. Briefly, it was as follows:

In very early times there were no wizards, and people generally were ignorant of many things pertaining to their welfare. Then it came about that there was great famine at Igdlulik, and many died of starvation. One day, many being assembled in one house, a man there present declared that he would go down to the Mother of the Sea. None of those present knew what he meant by that. But he

---

[1] A representative collection of these Greenland stories is given in *Eskimo Folk Tales*, by Knud Rasmussen and W. Worster, London, Gyldendal.

insisted, and begged to be allowed to hide behind the skins, as he was about to undertake something for the good of all.   They allowed him to do so, and presently, pulling the skins aside, they saw that he was already almost gone, only the soles of his feet remaining above ground. It is not known what inspired him to do this thing, but some say he was visited by spirits that came to him out in the great solitude.   And he went down to the Mother of the Sea, and brought back her good will and the grant of game for the hunters, so that thenceforward there was no longer dearth, but great abundance of food, and all were happy once more.   Since then, the angakoqs, have learned much more about hidden things, and aided their fellows in many ways.   They have too their own sacred speech, which is not to be used for common things.

A young man wishing to become an angakoq must first hand over some of his possessions to his instructor. At Igdlulik it was customary to give a tent pole, wood being scarce in these regions.   A gull's wing was attached to the pole, as a sign that the novice wished to learn to fly.   He had further to confess any breach of tabu which he might have committed, and then, retiring behind a curtain with his instructor submitted to the extraction of the "soul" from his eyes, heart and vitals, which would then be brought by magic means into contact with those beings destined to become his helping spirits, to the end that he might later meet them without fear.   The ultimate initiation always took place far from all human dwelling; only in the great solitude was it possible to approach the spirits. Furthermore, it was essential that the novice should start young; some, indeed, were entered to the profession before they were born. Aua himself was one of these, his mother declaring that her coming child was one that should be different from his fellows. His birth was attended by various remarkable features, special rites were observed, and strict discipline imposed on him during childhood and early youth; "nevertheless, though all was thus prepared for me, I tried in vain to become an angakoq by the ordinary methods of instruction." Famous wizards were approached and propitiated with gifts, but all in vain. At last, without knowing how, he perceived that a change had come over him, a great glow as of intense light pervaded all his being (this is a recurrent feature in the process) and a feeling of inexpressible joy came over him, and he burst into song.

"But now," he went on, "I am a Christian, and so I have sent away all my helping spirits; sent them up to my sister in Baffin Land."

Occasionally, the spirits themselves lay hold of a man and of their own accord invest him with supernatural powers; this is generally reckoned as a painful process, attended by terrifying phenomena.

It is the business of an angakoq to heal the sick, to protect the souls of his fellows against the machinations of hostile wizards, to intercede with the Mother of the Sea when seal are scarce, and to see that traditional customs are properly observed. Infantile diseases, for instance, are generally reckoned as due to some breach of tabu on the part of the mother; famine may likewise be sent as a punishment for similar neglect, and the angakoq has then to find and persuade the culprit to confession.

Such manifestations as I had an opportunity of witnessing myself were, I must confess, disappointing to the critical observer. Acquainted as he would be with his neighbors' life and doings, it was not difficult for the angakoq to hit upon something done or left undone by one or another. The trance-like state into which he cast himself was not impressive in itself, and as for the spirits supposed to be present, one can only say they did not make their presence felt. The wizard stood in the middle of the hut with his eyes closed, talking in a strained, unnatural voice; the rushing of mighty wings, which in the old stories accompanies such spiritual visitations, was conspicuous by its absence.

I had frequently brought the conversation round to the subject of tabu with a view to ascertaining the purpose of these highly complicated and apparently meaningless observances; this thing insisted on, and that strictly forbidden. But here lay the difficulty. Everyone knew, and all were unanimously agreed, as to what must be done or avoided in any given situation, but as to the why and the wherefore, none could advance any explanation whatever. They seemed, indeed, to regard it as unreasonable on my part to demand, not only a statement, but a justification, of their religious rites and ceremonies. Aua was as usual the one I mainly questioned, and one evening, when I had been endeavoring to extract some more positive information on this head, he suddenly rose to his feet and invited me to step outside.

It was twilight, the brief day was almost at an end,

but the moon was up, and one could see the storm-riven clouds racing over the sky; every now and then a gust of snow came whirling down. Aua pointed out over the ice, where the snow swept this way and that in whirling clouds. "Look," he said impressively, "snow and storm; ill weather for hunting. And yet we must hunt for our daily food; *why?* Why must there be storms to hinder us when we are seeking meat for ourselves and those we love?"

Why?

Two of the hunters were just coming in after a hard day's watching on the ice; they walked wearily, stopping or stooping every now and then in the wind and the snow. Neither had made any catch that day; their watching had been in vain.

Why?

I could only shake my head. Aua led me again, this time to the house of Kuvdlo, next to our own. The lamp burned with the tiniest glow, giving out no heat at all; a couple of children cowered shivering in a corner, huddled together under a skin rug. And Aua renewed his merciless interrogation: "Why should all be chill and comfortless in this little home? Kuvdlo has been out hunting since early morning; if he had caught a seal, as he surely deserved, for his pains, the lamp would be burning bright and warm, his wife would be sitting smiling beside it, without fear of scarcity for the morrow; the children would be playing merrily in the warmth and light, glad to be alive. Why should it not be so?"

Why?

Again I could make no answer. And Aua took me

to a little hut apart, where his aged sister, Natseq, who was ill, lay all alone. She looked thin and worn, and too weak even to brighten up at our coming. For days past she had suffered from a painful cough that seemed to come from deep down in the lungs; it was evident she had not long to live.

And for the third time Aua looked me in the face and said: "Why should it be so? Why should we human beings suffer pain and sickness? All fear it, all would avoid it if they could. Here is this old sister of mine, she has done no wrong that we can see, but lived her many years and given birth to good strong children, yet now she must suffer pain at the ending of her days?"

Why? Why?

After this striking object lesson, we returned to the hut, and renewed our interrupted conversation with the others.

"You see," observed Aua, "even you cannot answer when we ask you why life is as it is. And so it must be. Our customs all come from life and are directed towards life; we cannot explain, we do not believe in this or that; but the answer lies in what I have just shown you.

"*We fear!*

"We fear the elements with which we have to fight in their fury to wrest out food from land and sea.

"We fear cold and famine in our snow huts.

"We fear the sickness that is daily to be seen amongst us. Not death, but the suffering.

"We fear the souls of the dead, of human and animal alike.

"We fear the spirits of earth and air.

"And therefore our fathers, taught by their fathers before them, guarded themselves about with all these old rules and customs, which are built upon the experience and knowledge of generations. We know not how nor why, but we obey them that we may be suffered to live in peace. And for all our angakoqs and their knowledge of hidden things, we yet know so little that we fear everything else. We fear the things we see about us, and the things we know from the stories and myths of our forefathers. Therefore we hold by our customs and observe all the rules of tabu."

Aua's explanation was reasonable enough from his point of view. There was no more to be said.

But I will endeavor now to give a brief summary of the leading principles in the system of tabu, with its ordinances and prohibitions.

It is to begin with very largely a matter of propitiatory rites and ceremonies attending the treatment of the animals killed; preparing food, skins, etc. Here, there is a fundamental distinction between land game and the products of the sea. The fauna of each has its own distinct origin, and it is believed that any contact between the two is offensive to both, involving punishment of the person responsible. The caribou of the land have their "mother," as the seal and walrus together have theirs, and the two must never be confused.

Then it is a matter of faith that all living creatures have souls; and the souls of animals slain for food or other useful purpose by man are affected by the manner in which their bodies are treated after death; even, indeed, by the manner of their killing. There are a host of little apparently trivial things that must be done or must on no account be done, in connection with hunting, cooking, making clothes and the like; and they are regarded so much as a matter of course that it is difficult,when living among the natives and observing them, to pick out this or that little matter and get at the purpose underlying it. The whole system is further complicated by "name" principle running through daily life and observances in a similar way. A person's name is always derived from that of someone deceased, and carries with it the namesake's qualities; one becomes, indeed, a member of the great community of all who have borne the same name back to the ultimate distant past. Each living human being is thus attended by a host of namesake-spirits, who aid and protect him as long as he is faithful to rule and rite, but become inimical on any transgression.

The soul of the caribou detests everything pertaining to the creatures of the sea; in caribou hunting, therefore, all implements and material associated, with hunting at sea must be left behind. On the other hand, footwear which has been used for caribou hunting must on no account be used when hunting seal or walrus. Caribou are moreover, peculiarly sensitive in regard to "contamination" by women; when slain, they must be skinned in such a fashion that certain parts of the carcase are protected against direct contact with a woman's hands. Women at certain periods, and in certain conditions, are for-

bidden to touch either the meat or the skin.   Dogs
must not gnaw the bones of caribou during the
hunting season.   A piece of the meat and a piece of
the tallow must be placed under a stone near the spot
where the animal was killed; this is an offering to the
soul in the hope that it may attract other caribou to
the hunter.

Walrus hunting has its own special rules, which
again are to some extent distinct from those which
apply to seal.   Salmon, curiously enough, are reckoned as "land meat" and may not be eaten on the
same day as seal or walrus meat.

Tabu at Igdlulik was particularly strict, as it was
here, according to tradition, that the Mother of the
Sea met with her fate, and she is thus nearer and
more easily offended than elsewhere.   It was said
that she hated the caribou because they were not of
her own creation; hence the rule that whale, seal and
walrus meat must never be eaten on the same day as
caribou; must not even be found in the same hut at
the same time.

Some of the sea-beasts are of the "dangerous"
order, and have to be propitiated after death; thus
whale, ribbon seal and bear.   No work may be done
in the huts for so many hours after the killing; parts
of the carcase must be hung up together with certain
implements.   Ordinary seal are easier to manage, but
here again there are complicated rules as to refraining
from this and that until it has been skinned.   Certain
articles must not be touched, women must not comb
their hair.   Sinews of the seal must never be used for
sewing, on pain of premature death.

Birth and death have their own peculiar rites and observances. Various means are employed to facilitate birth, mainly of the magic order, such as the wearing of certain amulets, or dressing the hair in a certain way. No assistance may on any account be rendered to the woman at the actual birth; she is placed beforehand in a separate tent or hut, and there left until the child is born. She is then moved to another house where she lives by herself for two months; others may visit her, but she must not enter any other house. For a whole year after she is not allowed to eat raw meat, or the meat of any animal save those killed in certain ways. There are endless observances designed to secure good luck or useful accomplishments for the child when it grows up.

Death involves first of all the attendance of the nearest relatives for a period of three days if the deceased be a man, four days if a woman; during this time the soul is supposed to remain in the body, which must not be left alone. No work must be done, nor any hunting save in extreme need, during these first days of mourning. No one is allowed to wash, comb hair or cut nails. Curious methods are employed for purification of the hut or tent, and certain magic formulæ are used. The body is never buried or enclosed in a cairn, but simply laid out on the earth at the chosen spot, with a few loose stones placed at head, shoulders and feet. In winter, a small snow shelter may be built above the corpse. Models in miniature of implements used by the dead, suitable for man or woman as the case may be,

A PROMISING YOUNG HUNTER ON THE LOOK-OUT FOR GAME

TERTAQ, THE "AMULET BOY"

This poor little fellow has to drag about with him no fewer than eighty amulets, wherever he goes, as a protection against mishap.

are fashioned and placed beside the corpse for use "on the other side."

Persons tired of life and wishing to hang themselves—a recognized form of suicide—are required to do so while alone in the house, and by certain methods; it is also a rule that the suicide shall leave the lamp burning in order that his body may be at once observed as soon as anyone enters the hut.

A woman who has lost a near relative is regarded as unclean for a year after; she may not work on caribou skin, or speak of any animal used for food except in the peculiar terms employed for magic incantations. A man who has lost his wife may not drive or strike his own dogs for a year after.

When any breach of these irksome regulations has been committed, the only means of making reparation and warding off the evil consequences that would otherwise ensue, is for the delinquent to confess at once to his fellows. There is, however, a natural unwillingness to do so; and furthermore, the complexity of the whole code renders it very easy for one to offend unwittingly. Even where every reasonable care is taken, there is constant danger of incurring the enmity of spirits and supernatural powers; and it becomes the task of the angakoq, then to intervene.

All these observances however, are mainly negative; designed to avoid actual disaster; they do not make for any positive advantage beyond the ordinary level of security. He who would achieve anything further must have recourse to amulets and charms, or spells.

Amulets consists mainly of certain portions of the body of certain animals, which are sewn into the clothing. The Igdlulik natives, unlike those of Netsilik, use very few amulets, but their idea as to the purpose and effect is the same. The virtue lies in the soul of the creature represented, though it is only certain parts of its body which can convey the power. A woman with a newly born infant for instance, will use a raven's claw as a fastening for the strap of her *amaut* (the bag in which the child is slung on her back); this is supposed to give strength and success in hunting to the child later on.

The mystic power of an amulet is not invariably at the service of the person wearing it; the actual object for instance, may be given away to another, but its inherent activity will not operate on his behalf unless he has given something in return. It is a regular thing for a young hunter to obtain a harpoon head from some aged veteran no longer able to hunt for himself; the "luck" of the former owner then passes with the chattel to its new possessor. Clothes may be lucky in themselves. One lad at Igdlulik whose father was always unlucky at caribou hunting, was given the sleeve linings of a particularly successful hunter, and these were fitted successively to every tunic he wore, and brought him luck. There are amulets for various qualities, such as making the wearer a good walker, preserving him from danger on thin ice, keeping him warm in the coldest weather, giving extra stability to his kayak, and so on.

Then there are "magic words" for use in various emergencies. The efficacy of these is impaired as soon as they are made known to others, and it is therefore difficult as a rule to get hold of them. They consist mainly of fragments from old songs, handed down from earlier generations. They can be bought, at a high price, or bequeathed by the "owner" on his deathbed to another. But they must never be heard by any save the one who is to use them, or their power will be gone.

Aua himself had, as a young man, learnt certain charms of this sort from an old woman named Qeqertuanaq, in whose family they had been handed down from generation to generation dating back to "the very first people on earth." And by way of payment Aua had undertaken to feed and clothe her for the rest of her life. They had always to be uttered in her name, or they would be of no avail.

Here is one of them, designed to lighten heavy loads. The speaker stands by the fore end of his sledge, looking ahead and says:

I speak with the mouth of Qeqertuanaq, and say:
I will walk with leg muscles strong as the sinews on the shin of a little caribou calf.
I will walk with leg muscles strong as the sinews on the shin of a little hare.
I will take care not to walk toward the dark.
I will walk toward the day.

(This may be said also when setting out on a journey on foot.)

A charm for curing sickness among neighbors may be uttered by one who is well. The speaker gets up early in the morning before anyone else is astir, takes the inner upper garment of a child, and drawing down his own hood over his head, thrusts his arms into the sleeves of the child's garment as if to put it on.   Then these words are uttered:

I arise from my couch with the grey gull's morning song.
I arise from my couch with the grey gull's morning song.
I will take care not to look toward the dark,
I turn my glance toward the day.

Words to a sick child:

Little child! Your mother's breasts are full of milk. Go to her and suck, go to her and drink. Go up into the mountain. From the mountain's top shalt thou find health; from the mountain's top shalt thou win life.

A charm to stop bleeding:

This is blood from the little sparrow's mother. Dry it up! This is blood that flowed from a piece of wood. Dry it up.

A charm for calling game to the hunter:

Beast of the sea! Come and place yourself before me in the dear early morning!
Beast of the plain! Come and place yourself before me in the dear early morning!

These charms, quaint or meaningless as they may seem, are used by the Eskimos in all sincerity and pious faith, as prayers humbly addressed to the mighty powers of Nature.

CHAPTER X

AUA'S wife Orulo was one of those women who give themselves up entirely to their housewifely duties. She was never idle for a moment from morning to night and could get through a wonderful amount of work. Her favorite occupation was sewing, and of this there was plenty, as the men's clothes were constantly in need of repair after the wear and tear of hunting. But she had many other things to attend to besides. It was her business to fetch in snow for water, and keep the hut supplied, to have a stock of meat thawing near the lamp for immediate use, and a supply of food for the dogs ready cut up when the men came home. There was blubber to be pressed and beaten that the oil might run out, the lamp itself to be tended carefully and kept from smoking. If the temperature inside the hut rose beyond a certain point, the roof would begin to drip, and had to be plastered with fresh snow from within. Occasionally, when a part of the roof or wall thawed through, she had to go out and cut away the weakened portion, fitting fresh blocks of snow into the hole. There was blubber to be scraped from the raw skins of newly killed seal, the skins themselves stretched out to dry on the frame above the lamp, and pieces of hide intended for boot soles had to be chewed from their original state, which was almost as hard as wood, until they were soft enough for working. All these manifold duties however, she took cheerfully as part of the day's work, and went about humming a scrap of some old song, as happily as could be. And there was sure to be a cheerily bubbling pot on the boil—more welcome music still—by the time her menfolk came in from their hunting.

With it all she found time to look in and see that all was well with her neighbors, lending a helpful hand where needed, and finding a bit of meat, or a lump of blubber, from her own store for those who were badly off.

I had often asked her to tell me something of her life, and such of her experiences as she reckoned the most important, but she always turned it off as a joke, declaring that there was nothing of the least importance to tell about. At last one day when we had the hut to ourselves, she returned to the subject of her own accord. I was busy with my own work, and hardly conscious of her presence, when she began without preamble. And there, sitting cross-legged on the skins, working the while at a pair of waterproof boots, she told me the story of her life.

"I was born at a place near the mouth of Admiralty Inlet, but while I was still quite small, my parents left Baffin Land and came to Idglulik. The first thing I can remember was that my mother lived

alone in a little snow hut. I could not understand
why my father lived in another, but then I was told
that it was because my mother had just had a child,
and must not be near the hunters. But I was allowed
to visit her myself; only when I went there first, I
could not find the entrance. I was so little at that
time that I could not see over the big block of snow
that the others stepped over when they went in, and
there I stood crying out 'Mother, Mother, I want to
come in, I want to come in.' At last someone came
out and lifted me over and into the hut. Then when
I got inside it seemed that the couch of snow she
was lying on was ever so high, that I could not get up
there by myself, and again someone had to lift me.
Yes, I was as little as that at the time when I first
can remember.

"The next thing I remember is from the time we
were at Piling, up in Baffin Land. I remember having the leg of a bird to eat, ever so big it was, but
that was because I was only used to having ptarmigan, and this was the leg of a goose. I remember
thinking what a huge big bird it must be.

"Then I cannot remember any more until one day
it seems to wake up again, and we were living at a
place called the Mountain. My father was ill, and
all the others had gone away hunting caribou and we
were left alone. My father had pains in his chest
and lungs, and grew worse and worse. And there we
were all alone, my mother and two little brothers and
myself, and mother was very unhappy.

"One day I came running into the tent crying out:
'Here are white men coming!' For I had seen some

figures that I thought must be white men.   But when
my father heard me, he sighed deeply and said,
'Alas, I had thought I might yet be suffered to draw
the breath of life a little while; but now I know that I
shall never go out hunting any more.'

"For the figures I had seen were evil trolls; no white
men ever came to our country in those days.   And
my father took it as a warning that he was about to
die.

"I made no secret of what I had seen, but told it to
the others without thinking either way about the
matter.   But my little brother Sequsu kept it secret;
and he died of it shortly afterwards.   When one
sees evil spirits, it is a great mistake to keep it secret.

"Father grew worse and worse, and when at last
we saw he could not live much longer, we put him on
a sledge and carried him off to a neighboring village,
where he died.   I remember they wrapped him up in
a skin and carried him away; the body was laid out on
the bare ground, with its face toward the west.   My
mother told me that this was because he was an old
man; when old men die, they are always placed so as
to look toward the quarter whence the dark of evening comes; children must look towards the morning,
and young people towards the point where the sun
is at noon.   This was the first I ever learned about
the dead, and how we have to fear them and follow
certain rules.   But I was not afraid of my father,
who had always been kind to me.   And I thought it
was unkind to let him lie there out in the open, all
in the cold with no covering; but then my mother
explained that I must no longer think of him as in

TYPICAL WOMEN OF THE TRIBE

that body, for his soul was already in the land of the dead, and there he had no longer any pain.

"After this we went to live with an old man who took my mother to be another wife to him, and we lived in his hut. It was soon after this that my brother Sequsu fell ill; he had pain in his stomach, and his liver swelled, and then he died. I was told that it was because he had seen those evil trolls with me before our father died, and because he had kept it secret, it had been his death, for it is always so.

"In the autumn, when the first snow had fallen, the others went off hunting up inland, and my other brother went with them. I remember my mother was very anxious about this, for she did not think the old man could get any game, having only a bow and arrows. But she could not get food for herself, and so had to let my brother go with them.

"A strange thing happened a little after this. My mother had cooked some walrus ribs and was sitting eating, when the bone she had in her hand began to utter sounds. She was so frightened she stopped eating at once and threw down the bone. I remember her face went quite white, and she cried out: 'Something has happened to my son!' And so it was; for in a little while they came back and instead of walking straight into the hut, the man went to the window and called to my mother and said: 'Dear Little Thing, it is through my fault that you have no longer a son.' Dear Little Thing was a name he had for my mother. And then he came in and told us how it had come about. They had been for several days without food and were seeking the spot where he had cached a caribou some time before, but could not find the spot. So they separated, his wife going one way and he with the two boys the other. But still they could not find it. It was autumn, the first snow had fallen, and a cold wind sent it whirling about them every now and then; and their clothes were poor for such hard weather. So at last they lay down behind a stone shelter, worn out and almost perishing with cold. The days were short now and the night seemed very long, but they must wait for daylight before they could begin their search again. Meantime, the woman had found the meat, but now she had no means of knowing where to find the others. Being anxious about them she ate but little herself, and gave the child she was carrying a tiny piece of meat to suck. She had made a shelter of stones, as the others had done, and lay there half dozing, when suddenly she awoke, having dreamed of my brother. The dream was that she saw him quite plainly before her, very pale and shivering with cold. And he spoke to her and said: 'Now you will never see me again. This has come upon us because the earth-lice are angry at our having touched their sinews before a year had passed after my father's death.'

"I remember this so distinctly myself, because it was the first time I ever heard about not doing certain things for a year after someone had died. When he said earth-lice, he meant caribou; that is a word the wizards use.

"Now the woman could sleep no more that night because of her dream. My brother was very dear to her, and she used to say magic words over him to make him strong.

"Next morning, when it was light and the others were ready to start again, my brother was so weak that he could not stand, and the two others were too exhausted to carry him. So they covered him up with a thin caribou pelt and left him. Afterwards they found the meat, but they did not return to my brother. He was left to freeze to death.

"My stepfather had his old mother still living; she was blind, and I remember I was terribly afraid of her because I had heard that once, in a time of famine, she had eaten human flesh. A wise woman had said charms over her to cure her blindness, and she had just begun to see a very little, but then she ate some blubber, and that is a thing one must never do when being cured of anything by magic; after that she became quite blind again and nothing could make her see.

"The following spring we left that place and came to Admiralty Inlet. We got there just at the time when everyone was getting ready to go up country hunting caribou. One of the women had just given birth to a child before her time, and could not go with the rest, so my mother went instead, and took me with her. We stayed up country all that summer. The hunting was good, and we helped the men to pile up the meat in store places or cut it up into thin slices and laid it out on stones to dry. It was a merry life, we had all kinds of nice things to eat, and the day's work was like so much play. Then I remember one day we were terrified by a woman from one of the tents crying out: 'Come and look, Oh come and look.' And we all ran up and there was a spider letting itself down to the ground. We could not make out where it came from, it looked as if it were lowering itself on a thread from the sky. We all saw it quite plainly, and then there was silence among the tents. For when a spider is seen to lower itself down from nowhere in that way, it always means death. And so it was. Some people came up from the coast shortly after, and we learned that four men had been out in their kayaks and were drowned; one of them was my step-father—and now we were homeless and all alone in the world once more.

"But it was not long before my mother was married again; this time to a young man, much younger than herself. They lived together until he took another wife of his own age; then my mother was cast off and we were alone again. Then my mother was married once more, to a man named Aupila, and now we had some one to look after us. Aupila wanted to go down to Pond's Inlet, to look for some white men. He had heard that the whalers generally came to that place in the summer. So he went off with my mother, and I was left behind with another man and his wife. But I did not stay with them long, for the man said he had too many mouths to feed already, and I was passed on to someone else. Then at last Aua came and found me; 'my new husband' that is my little name for Aua; and he took me away and that is the end. For nothing happens when you are happy, and indeed I have been happy, and had seven children."

Orulo was silent, evidently deep in thought. But I was eager to hear more, and broke in without ceremony:

"Tell me what is the worst thing that ever happened to you."

Without a moment's hesitation she answered:

"The worst that ever happened to me was a famine that came just after my eldest son was born. The hunting had failed us, and to make matters worse, the wolverines had plundered all our depots of caribou meat. During the two coldest months of winter, Aua hardly slept a single night in the hut, but was out hunting seal the whole time, taking such sleep as he could get at odd moments in little shelters built on the ice by the breathing holes. We nearly starved to death; for he only got two seal the whole of that time. To see him, suffering himself from cold and hunger, out day after day in the bitterest weather, and all in vain, to see him growing thinner and weaker all the time—oh, it was terrible!"

"And what was the nicest thing of all you remember?"

Orulo's kindly old face lit up with a merry smile; she put down her work and shifting a little nearer began her story:

"It was the first time I went back to Baffin Land after I was married. And I, who had always been poor, a child without a father, passed on from hand to hand—I found myself now a welcome guest, made much of by all those who had known me before. My husband had come up to challenge a man he knew to a song contest, and there were great feasts and gatherings, such as I had heard of perhaps but never seen myself."

"Tell me something about them."

"Well there was the Tivajuk, the Great Rejoicing, where they play the game of changing wives. A big snow hut is built all empty inside, just for the dancing, only with two blocks of snow in the middle of the floor. One is about half the height of a man and is called the jumping block, the other is a full man's height and is called the lamp block. Two men, they are the Servants of Joy, are dressed up, one like a man, the other like a woman, and both wear masks. Their clothes are made too small for them on purpose, tied in tightly just where they ought to be loose, and that makes them look funny, of course. It is part of their business to make everyone laugh.

"Then all the men and women in the place assemble in the dance hut, and wait for the two masked dancers. Suddenly the two of them come leaping in, the man with a dog whip and the one dressed as a woman with a stick; they jump over the jumping block and begin striking out at all the men in the hut, chasing them all out until only the women are left. The maskers are supposed to be dumb, they do not speak, but make signs to each other with great gestures only giving a sort of huge gasp now and again with all the force of their lungs. They have to leap nimbly about among the women, to make sure there are no men hidden; then out they go to the men waiting outside. One of the men waiting now goes up to the two, and smiles, and whispers the name of the woman he specially wants. At once the two maskers rush into the hut, and touch the woman named under the sole of the foot. Then all the other women are supposed to be ever so pleased to find that one of their number has been chosen. Then the three go out together; and every time the maskers go in and out they have to jump over the jumping block with long strides trying to look funny. They lead out the woman who has been chosen, and bring her back directly after with the man who asked for her; the women are never allowed to know who it is that wants them till they get outside. Both have to look very solemn when they come in, and pretend not to notice that the others are laughing. If they laugh themselves, it means a short life. All the others then call out 'Unu-nu-nu-nu-nu-nu' and keep on saying it all the time, in different voices, to make it sound funny. Then the man leads the women he has chosen twice round the lamp block, and all sing together:

> "Mask, mask, leaping, teasing mask,
> Twirl and writhe and dance with joy,
> Give him gifts now,
> Dry moss for lamp wicks;
> Mask, mask, leaping teasing mask!

"While this song is being sung, the two maskers have to keep on embracing each other, making it as funny as they can, so that the others have to laugh.

"So the game goes on until every man has chosen a woman, and then they go home.

"Another festival that is only held where there are a lot of people together is called Qulungertut. It begins with two men challenging each other to all kinds of contest out in the open, and ends up in the dance house.

"Each of them has a knife, and as soon as they meet, they embrace, and kiss each other. Then the women are divided into two parties. One side sings a song and they have to keep on with it all the time, a long, long song; the other side has to stand with arms up waving gull's wings all the time and see who can keep on longer. Here is a bit of the song:

"See here they come
Gaily dressed in fine new skins,
Women, women, all young women,
See, with mittens on their hands
They hold the gull's wings high aloft
See their skirt tails waving, waving,
All the time as they are moving.
Women, women, all young women,
You may know them by their motion
As they step towards the men who
Take them for their prize of contest.

"The side that first gives in has to step across to the others, who make a circle round them, and then the men come in and try to kiss them.

"After this game there was a shooting match with bow and arrows. A mark was set up on a long pole, and the ones who first hit it ten times were counted the best. Then came games of ball, and very exciting contests between men fighting with fists, until the end of the day, and then a song festival to end up with, and that lasted all night. Here are some of Aua's songs:

WALRUS HUNTING

I could not sleep
For the sea was so smooth
Near at hand.
So I rowed out
And up came a walrus
Close by my kayak.
It was too near to throw,
So I thrust my harpoon into its side
And the bladder-float danced across the waves.
But in a moment it was up again,
Setting its flippers angrily
Like elbows on the surface of the water
And trying to rip up the bladder.
All in vain it wasted strength,
For the skin of an unborn lemming
Was sewn inside as an amulet to guard.
Then snorting viciously it sought to gather strength,
But I rowed up
And ended the struggle.
Hear that, O men from strange creeks and fjords
That were always so ready to praise yourselves;
Now you can fill your lungs with song
Of another man's bold hunting.

BEAR HUNTING

I spied a bear
On the drifting floe
Like a harmless dog
It came running and wagging its tail towards me
But all so eager to eat me up
That it swung round snarling
When I leaped aside.

And now came a game of catch-me-who-can
That lasted from morning till late in the day,
But at last it was wearied
And could play no more,
So I thrust my spear into its side.

CARIBOU HUNTING

Creeping noiselessly I moved across the marsh
With bow and arrows in my mouth;
It was far, and the water icy cold,
And not a scrap of cover to be seen.
Slowly I dragged myself,
Dripping wet but still unseen,
Up within range.
The caribou were feeding,
Nibbling at ease the juicy moss
Till my arrow stood quivering deep in the breast
Of the biggest.
Then terror seized
Those heedless dwellers of the plains,
In a moment they scattered
And swiftly trotting hurried away
Beyond the refuge of the hills."

Orulo had spoken earnestly of her life, and I could
feel, as she went on, how the memories affected her
while she recalled them. When she had ended her
story, she burst into tears, as if in deep sorrow. I
asked her what was the matter, and she answered:
"Today I have been as it were a child again. In
telling you of my life, I seemed to live it all over
again. And I saw and felt it all just as when it was
really happening. There are so many things we

never think of until one day the memory awakens.
And now you have heard the story of an old woman's
life from its first beginning right up to this very day.
And I could not help weeping for joy to think I had
been so happy . . ."

CHAPTER XI

SEPARATE WAYS

THE prolonged absence of Therkel Mathiassen at Southampton caused us, at last, so much uneasiness that I began making preparations for a relief expedition, and even sent down to Repulse Bay for a guide, thoroughly acquainted with the region, to go with me.

February 21st was a perfect beast of a day, with a howling blizzard, and bitterly cold. Nobody stirred out of the house if he could help it. The Greenland Eskimos were indoors mending harness, the rest of us posting up our journals. Then, suddenly, the door burst open, and in tumbled Therkel Mathiassen, with Jacob Olsen at his heels, followed by John Ell, and a crowd of Southampton Islanders.

Mathiassen had been eight months absent. We gave him a rousing welcome, as may be imagined.

The expedition had done good work and met with not a few adventures by the way. Southampton Island is the most isolated piece of territory in the whole Hudson Bay district, and accessible by open boat for only a few days during the summer. They had planned to spend only a fortnight there, but unfavorable weather and other mishaps detained them. The local natives couldn't do anything for them, and when Mathiassen violated tabus by cracking caribou skulls with iron hammers, he

THE DANISH MEMBERS OF THE EXPEDITION
Photographed at West Greenland.

Kaj Birket-Smith   Therkel Mathiassen   Helge Bangsted
Peder Pedersen   Knud Rasmussen   Peter Freuchen   Jacob Olsen

aroused their fears. One night, Jacob Olsen over-
heard one of the locally employed Eskimos and his
wife plotting to kill Mathiassen and himself, and
frustrated the attack. The lack of personal malice,
however, was so evident, that the plotters were for-
given and allowed to continue with the party. The
difficulties arising from native prejudices, together
with an injury to Olsen's hand and a long sickness of
Mathiassen's, due at the beginning to his inability to
eat the rotten walrus meat, made the trip to Southampton Island, though fruitful of good expedition
material, a kind of nightmare. We were all glad to
forget it in the preparation for the next year's work.

For we had now come to the parting of the ways,
and the Fifth Thule Expedition was about to split
up into five separate projects each with its own field
of work, scattering over the greater part of the
Arctic Coast of Canada.

Mathiassen was to go by dog-sledge to Pond's
Inlet in Baffin Land, to supplement his ethnological
investigations with map-making and other studies
in that territory.

Birket-Smith with Jacob Olsen as interpreter,
was to continue with the Caribou Eskimos, and then
go on to the Chipywan Indians, near Churchill.

Peter Freuchen was to stay for a while to look
after the transportations of our collections, and then
survey the route to Chesterfield. The Greenlanders
would remain at headquarters, until they could be
taken back to Greenland by Freuchen.

And I, myself, was to start, about the 10th of
March, for my long sledge trip through the North-

west Passage, with only Miteq and Anarulunguaq to help me. Helge Bangsted would accompany me a little way, and then, after further excavations, would return to help Freuchen supervise the removal of our effects.

The rest of this account will have to do only with my own observations, but I carried with me for some time the regret of breaking off contact with companions with whom I had been so happily associated for eighteen months. And it is a pleasure to recall that our work together was never marred by the slightest discord among ourselves.

The Greenlanders, too, had done their part well. Like all other Arctic expeditions we had based our maintenance on the help afforded by these faithful hunters and workers. There was Arqioq, a steady sensible fellow of thirty odd, who had spent most of his life with one expedition or another, including two from America. Bosun, a few years younger, had been my foster son at Thule since he was ten years old. He was a dead shot, a good comrade, and cheerful under the most adverse circumstances. Their wives, too, had done all that was possible to make our headquarters homelike and comfortable.

Especial gratitude was due to Jacob Olsen, not only for his indispensable services to Mathiassen, but also for his abilities. In contrast with the others, who had lived always native fashion, and were only baptized just before we left Greenland, Olsen was a man of some education, having spent six years in a seminary and acquired a considerable knowledge of books, though he was no less adequate as a hunter on that account. He was valued as an interpreter, and was useful even in collecting ethnographical material.

I should like to close this part of the book with a recollection of one of our last evenings at home. I had just come in from a run over the ice, and was driving up in the twilight towards the house, where the light from the windows shed a glow on the space in front. Some of the dogs were sleeping, as if making the most of their time before fresh hard work set in; groups of men and women were at work by lantern light getting the new sledges ready for use. The daylight was not long enough for all there was to be done. Hammers rang, and the rhythmic back-and-forth of the plane spoke cheerily of work well in hand. A wild scene, maybe, yet not without a beauty of its own. Dark against the white plain rose the two peaks where we had raised memorial stones to those whom death had taken on the threshold; at the foot, stood the domed snow huts, with little ice windows twinkling like stars.

Into the midst of this I drove, my team scattering their sleeping companions to every side and bringing up against the wall where they were accustomed to lie themselves. And as we halted, I heard someone singing a little way off. The words seemed curiously appropriate to the occasion:

> Only the Air-spirits know
> What lies beyond the hills,
> Yet I urge my team farther on
> Drive on and on,
> On and on!

CHAPTER XII

STEPPING OUT

THE Arctic spring was full of promise on that March morning when we took leave of our companions and set out on our long sledge trip. Two continents lay between us and home.

Our party consisted of but three persons in all; Miteq, Anarulunguaq and myself. Miteq, a young man of twenty-two from Thule was a very old friend of mine; I had known him, indeed, from the time when he lay screaming lustily in his mother's amaut. He was a skilful and untiring hunter, and a good driver, besides being a cheery companion. Anarulunguaq, a woman of twenty-eight, was Miteq's cousin. Oddly enough, she had as a child been on the point of being killed off as a burden to the community, as is often done with fatherless children, but her little brother's intercession had saved her life. And here she was setting out upon a journey that was to make her the most famous woman traveller of her tribe. I could not have wished for better companions than these two.

Our equipment was the simplest possible. We had two long six-metre sledges of the Hudson Bay type, with ice shoeing, each drawn by twelve dogs, and with a load of 500 kilos. to each sledge. About

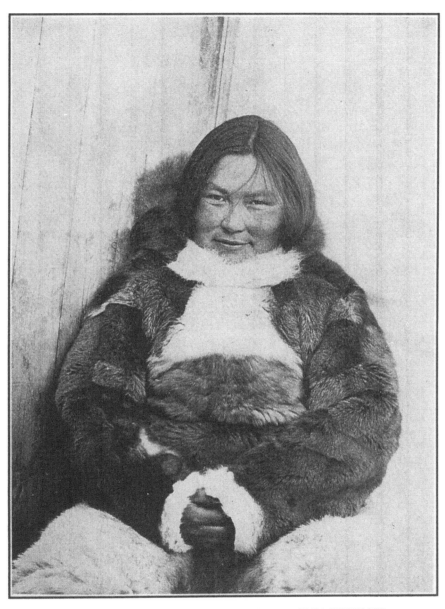

ANARULUNGUAQ, THE YOUNG ESKIMO WOMAN FROM GREENLAND

She accompanied the Expedition on the long sledge journey through the North-west Passage and round the north of Alaska, returning to Greenland via New York and Copenhagen.

A FAMILY PARTY SETTING OUT FOR REPULSE BAY

The journey out and home will take several months.

two-thirds of this load consisted of food for the dogs, the rest being made up of tea, coffee, sugar, flour, tobacco, trade goods for buying up ethnographical objects, clothes, guns, and ammunition for a year.

And now we were fairly off, our last link with civilization severed. There was no means of communication now until we reached a telegraph station somewhere in Alaska. All we had to look to for our lives was on our sledges, and they seemed none too heavy as we set off at a sharp trot along the North Pole River.

We crossed Rae Isthmus by short stages, and had then the lowlands of Simpson Peninsula between us and Pelly Bay. Before we could begin the crossing of this, however, we had to cover some distance along the ice foot on the shore of Committee Bay, the sea ice being too rough for our heavy loads. The incessant wind had carried away most of the snow from the plain, and clay and pebbles showed through everywhere; we had therefore to take the ice shoeing off the runners of one sledge in order to get the loads down to the ice foot.

On the 28th of March, in a tearing blizzard, we had our first meeting with the natives of these parts. We had built a snow hut, and were just deciding it was no use going on for the present, when Miteq, who had gone outside for snow to repair the wall, called in through the opening that there were men approaching.

And sure enough, two tall figures could be seen coming towards the hut. At about 300 metres distance they stopped, and I at once went forward to meet them and assure them we were friends. They carried long snow knives and sealing harpoons, but I thought it best to carry no weapon myself. They were greatly astonished to find a white man in these regions, and more so when I hailed them in their own tongue:

"You may lay aside your weapons; we are peaceable folk who have come from afar to visit your land."

On this the elder of the pair stepped forward and said:

"We are just quite ordinary people, and you need fear no harm from us. Our huts are near; our weapons are not meant to do you hurt, but it is well to have weapons here when meeting strangers."

We went back to our hut, and the two men, who had been somewhat shy at first, were soon at ease and friendly. They were particularly interested in the two Greenlanders, who came from so far a country and yet spoke the same tongue. They themselves, it appeared, were on their way down to Repulse Bay with fox skins, to buy new guns, their own having been lost in crossing a river some time before.

Despite the blizzard, we now decided to move over to our new friends' quarters. Orpingalik, the elder of the two, explained that they were but a short distance away. It cost us three hours fierce battling with the storm, however, before we reached the spot. There were two snow huts built together, cosy, well furnished and well supplied with food. The natives here were remarkably well built and handsome, differing in many ways from the ordinary

Eskimo type and rather like the Indians in feature, but their frank, open smile and character generally were those of the true Eskimo. We soon made friends with them.

Orpingalik was an angakoq, and well up in the legends and traditions of his people, and I was glad to avail myself of the time while my companions were busy getting our goods down, to have a talk with him about such matters. I was anxious in the first place to learn how many of the stories I had already written down among the Igdlulingmiut were known to him, and we went through at least a hundred of these together. Also, he gave me some rare magic songs, or spells, which I paid for in kind, giving him in return some of those I had obtained from Aua. The transaction was regarded as perfectly legitimate, as the magic would take no harm when it was a white man who acted as the medium of conveyance.

These magic songs and spells are difficult to translate, as the words themselves are often meaningless in the actual context; they have to be uttered in a peculiar way, with great distinctness and sometimes with pauses here and there; the virtue lies to a great extent in the way they are spoken.

One which Orpingalik regarded as of great value was the *Hunter's Invocation*, which is roughly as follows:

> I am ashamed,
> I feel humbled and afraid.
> My grandmother sent me out
> Sent me out to seek.

I am out on an errand
Seeking the precious game,
Seeking the wandering fox.
But alas, it may be I shall frighten away
That which I seek.

I am ashamed,
I feel humbled and afraid,
My grandmother and great-grandmother
Sent me out to seek.
I go on their errand after game,
After the precious caribou
But alas, it may be I shall frighten away
That which I seek.

When he had given me this, he declared that we were now almost like brothers. Another useful song is the *Poor Man's Prayer* to the spirits, which is spoken at dawn before setting out hunting, when the blubber is running low and fresh supplies are urgently wanted.

O father- and motherless,
O dear little one-all-alone
Give me
Boots of caribou.
Bring me a gift,
A beast of those beasts
That make luscious blood soup;
A beast of the beasts
From the depths of the sea
And not from the plains of earth.
Little father- and motherless one,
Bring me a gift.

This is used for seal; when hunting caribou, on the other hand, one must say:

> Caribou,
> Earthlouse,
> Longlegs
> One with Big Ears
> And stiff hair on the neck,
> Flee not from me.
> Here I bring skin for boot soles,
> Here I bring moss for lamp wicks,
> Come then gladly
> Hither to me
> Hither to me.

Orpingalik himself was a poet, with a fertile imagination and sensitive mind; he was always singing when not otherwise employed, and called his songs his "comrades in loneliness." Here is the beginning of one of them—written when he was slowly recovering from a severe illness. It is called *My Breath.*

> I will sing a song,
> A little song about myself
> I have lain sick since the autumn
> And now I am weak as a child,
> Unaya—unaya.

> Sad at heart I wish
> My woman away in the house of another
> In the house of a man
> Who may be her refuge,
> Firm and sure as the strong winter ice.

Sad at heart I wish her away
In the house of a stronger protector
Now that I myself lack strength
Even to rise from where I lie.
Unaya,—unaya.

Who knoweth his fate?
Here I lie, weak and unable to rise,
And only my memories are strong.

I asked Orpingalik how many songs he had made up, and he said "I cannot tell you, for I do not know how many there are of these songs of mine. Only I know that they are many, and that all in me is song. I sing as I draw breath."

Singing is indeed very prevalent among these people. They go about singing all day, or humming to themselves. The women sing not only their husbands' songs, but have songs of their own as well. Orpingalik taught me one that belonged to his wife. They had a son, Igsivalitaq, who had killed a man some years before, and was now living as an outlaw up in the hills near Pelly Bay, in fear of being brought to justice by the Mounted Police. His mother had made a song about him, as follows:

Eyaya—eya,
I find again
The fragment of a song
And take it to me as a human thing,
Eyaya—eya.
Should I then be ashamed
Of the child I once bore,
Once carried in my amaut,

Because there came news of his flight
From the dwellings of men?
Eyaya—eya.
Ashamed I may be,
But only because he had not
A mother flawless as the blue sky
Wise and without unwisdom.
Now the gossip of others shall teach him,
And ill repute follow that teaching.
I should indeed be ashamed,
I, who bore a child
That was not to be my refuge;
I envy instead all those
Who have a host of friends behind them
Beckoning on the ice
When they have taken leave at a merry feast before
    starting.
Alas, I remember a winter
When we set off from the island,
The air was warm
And the thawing snow sang under the runners.
I was as a tame beast among men.
But when the news came
Of the killing, and of the flight,
Then the earth became as a mountain peak,
Its summit needle-pointed,
And I stood trembling.

The song is interesting less for its form than for the evidence it affords as to the workings of the primitive mind.

On the 5th of April we took leave of Orpingalik and his people, the whole party shouting after us as we drove off:

"Tamavta tornaqarata ingerdlasa" ("May we all travel with no evil spirits in our train").

We had bought a store of meat from Orpingalik before leaving, and were to pick it up on the way from the spot where it was cached. Part was fish, the rest seal meat and caribou. The fish we found without much difficulty, and were delighted to find that we had purchased, for a pound of tea, a pound of sugar, twenty cakes of tobacco and a small pocket-knife, something like six hundred pounds of fine sea trout, besides the seal and caribou. To get at this last, however, we had first to hunt up Igsivalitaq the outlaw, who knew where it was. This was rather a delicate task, and Orpingalik had warned us to be careful how we approached him. We found his hut, but it was empty, and fresh tracks showed that he and his party had made off to the northward. Following up the tracks, we came up with him in the course of the day. I greeted him with the same words as his father had used at our first meeting:

"We are just quite ordinary people, and you need fear no harm from us."

The outlaw was evidently relieved to find that he was not being hunted down, but only receiving visitors with greetings from his family. He gave a shout of delight, and his wife came out from the snow hut and joined in the welcome.

Later, Igsivalitaq gave me an account of the circumstances which had led to his act of homicide—and certainly, he had acted under considerable provocation. I advised him in any case most earnestly to make no attempt at escape in the event

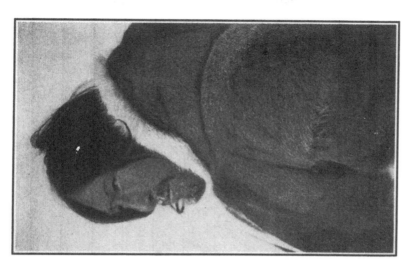

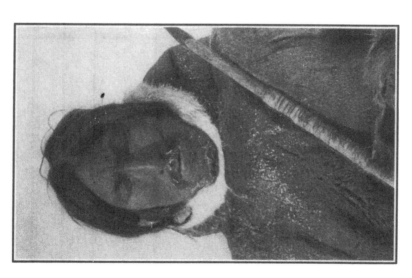

NATIVE FROM PELLY BAY

ESKIMO FROM THE MAGNETIC POLE, ARMED WITH BOW AND ARROW

of his being sought for by the Mounted Police, and above all not to resist capture by armed force; it was unlikely, I thought, that he could be punished very severely. At the same time I endeavored to instil into him some idea as to the sacredness of human life and the wickedness of killing a fellow-man; my exhortation here, however, was unfortunately impaired in its effect by what the poor outlaw himself had heard, through some traders from Repulse Bay, as to the doings of the white men in the Great War.

On the following day, under Igsivalitaq's guidance, we filled up our stores from the depot of seal and caribou meat, and drove on again to a camp of snow huts some distance out in the fjord.

Arviligjuaq, "The Land of the Great Whales," is a term used to denote the whole of the Pelly Bay district, and is derived not from any actual prevalence of whales in those waters—as far as I could learn, there are none—but from some hill formations on land, which viewed from a distance present the appearance of whales.

The people here were Arviligjuarmiut, a tribe related to the Netsilik group, but holding apart from them as regards their territorial limits, and keeping to the district between Lord Mayor's Bay and Committee Bay. This winter, they numbered in all but fifty-four souls, men, women and children, divided among three settlements, two on the ice in Pelly Bay and a third on the west coast of the Simpson Peninsula.

The whole region seemed to be one of plenty, and the Arviligjuarmiut informed me proudly that the scarcity and famine, such as the Netsilingmiut west of Boothia Isthmus often suffered, were altogether unknown among themselves. This was due to the variety of game at their disposal in sequence throughout the year; caribou, musk ox, seal and fish; should one form of hunting fail, there was always another to fall back on.

The Arviligjuarmiut, whose country lies right off the routes followed by white men through these regions, have from the first learned to rely on such material as their own territory afforded for the making of weapons and implements generally. Knives are made from a kind of yellowish flint, brought from a considerable distance, in the neighborhood of Back's River. Fire was obtained from "Ingnerit," i.e., firestone, iron pyrites, found near the sea west of Lord Mayor's Bay. Sparks were struck so as to fall on specially prepared tinder made from moss soaked in blubber. Soapstone for lamps and cooking pots was procured from the interior south of Pelly Bay.

The greatest difficulty was the scarcity of wood. Owing to the masses of drift ice always collecting out in Boothia Gulf, drift wood never came up into the fjord; the nearest place where it could be obtained was on the shores of Ugjulik, west of Adelaide Peninsula. Mostly, however, the natives here learned to manage without wood; they made long slender harpoon shafts of horn, the pieces being straightened out laboriously in warm water and joined length to length. Tent poles were fashioned in the same way, only one being used for each tent. Owing to the scarcity of iron and flint, harpoon heads were made from the hard shinbone of the bear.

When summer was at an end, and the tents no longer required, they were turned into sledge runners. This was done by laying out the skins in a pool to soak, and when thoroughly softened by this means, folding them over and over into long narrow strips of several thicknesses, and leaving the whole to freeze hard in the shape of a runner. Musk ox skins were used in the same way. These runners of frozen skins were further strengthened by a packing of raw fish or meat between the layers, the whole being frozen to a compact mass. Then in the spring, when warmer weather set in and the sledges thawed and fell to pieces, the tent skin runners did final service as food for the dogs, and the meat "stuffing" as food for their masters.

There were originally two trade routes offering means of communication with tribes from whom iron and wood could be procured in case of need. One was via Rae Isthmus down to Chesterfield, where, before the new trading station was established, knives could be procured from natives who had been down to Churchill. The other was across Back's River to Saningajoq, the country between Baker Lake and Lake Garry, and thence to Akilineq, the famous hill district on the Thelon River, where the Eskimos from the shores of the Arctic used to meet the Caribou Eskimos for purposes of trade. Wood, in particular, was brought from here.

And these hardy folk were not afraid of making long journeys by sledge, being away sometimes for a whole year, in order to procure some luxury which they could well do without; on the other hand the possession of a real knife, or a wooden sledge, conferred a certain distinction upon its owner, while the woman who could make and mend her husband's clothes with a needle of iron or steel was an object of envy among her less fortunate sisters.

It is generally believed that the wreckage of the Franklin Expedition was of great importance in the domestic economy of the North-west Passage Eskimos, and in particular, that their supplies of wood and iron were for years obtained from this source. I never found any confirmation of this; on the other hand, I did find that the Eskimos right from Committee Bay to Back's River, from King William's Land to the Kent Peninsula, possessed implements whose origin could be traced back to the John Ross Expedition, which appeared in Lord Mayor's Bay in the autumn of 1829 and wintered there. The natives round Pelly Bay had still many reminiscences of this expedition, and the sober fashion in which they spoke of these experiences, now nearly a hundred years old, goes far to show how trustworthy these Eskimos are when dealing with anyone who understands them.

They state that John Ross's ship was first observed early in the winter by a man named Avdlilugtoq, who was out hunting seal. On perceiving the great ship standing up like a rocky island in a little bay, he moved cautiously towards it, as something he had not seen before. The sight of its tall masts, however, convinced him that it must be a great spirit, and he turned and fled. That evening, and throughout the night, the men held council as to what should be done. Ultimately, it was decided that if they did not take active measures themselves, the great spirit would certainly destroy them; they therefore set off on the following day, armed with bows and harpoons, to attack it. They now discovered that there were human figures moving about beside it, and therefore hid behind blocks of ice in order to see what manner of beings these might be. The white men, however, had already sighted them, and came towards them. They stepped out then from their hiding places to show they were not afraid. The white men at once laid down their weapons on the ice, and the Eskimos did the same; the meeting was cordial, with embraces and assurances of friendship on both sides, though neither could understand the other's tongue. The Eskimos had heard of "white men" but this was the first time that any had visited their country. The white men afterwards gave them costly gifts—all manner of things which they could never have procured for themselves—and there was much intercourse between them, the natives going out with them on journeys and helping them in various ways from their knowledge of the country. The names of some who went out more often than the rest with the white men are still remembered: as Iggiararsuk, Agdlilugtoq, Niungitsoq and Ingnagsanajuk.

After the first winter, the ship was beset by the ice and ultimately sank in Itsuartorvik (Lord Mayor's Bay), but the "insides" of the ship were saved, being carried on shore in boats to Qilanartut; and when the strangers finally went away for good, they left behind them a great store of wood, iron, nails, chain, iron hoops and other costly things, which are still in use at the present day in the form of knives, arrow heads, harpoon heads, salmon spears, caribou spears and hooks.   Some time after, a mast came ashore, and from this sledges, kayaks and harpoons were made.   The mast was first cut up by saws made from barrel hoops; it took them all the summer and autumn to do it, but there was plenty of time.

There are interesting stories current also as to the Franklin Expedition.   One old man named Iggiararjuk relates as follows:

"My father, Mangak, was out with Terqatsaq and Qavdlut hunting seal on the west coast of King William's Land, when they heard shouts, and perceived three white men standing on the shore and beckoning to them.   This was in the spring, there was already open water along the shore, and they could not get in to where the others stood until low water. The white men were very thin, with sunken cheeks, and looked ill; they wore the clothes of white men, and had no dogs, but pulled their sledges themselves. They bought some seal meat and blubber, and gave a knife in payment.   There was much rejoicing on both sides over the trade; the white men at once boiled the meat with some of the blubber and ate it. Then they came home to my father's tent and stayed the night, returning next day to their own tent, which was small and not made of skins, but of something white as the snow.   There were already caribou about at that season, but the strangers seemed to hunt only birds. The eider duck and ptarmigan were plentiful, but the earth was not yet come to life, and the swans had not arrived. My father and those with him would gladly have helped the white men, but could not understand their speech; they tried to explain by signs, and in this way much was learned. It seemed that they had formerly been many, but were now only few, and their ship was left out on the ice. They pointed towards the south, and it was understood that they proposed to return to their own place overland. Afterwards, no more was seen of them, and it was not known what had become of them."

And lest any doubt should remain as to the veracity of his account, Iggiararjuk mentions the names of all those who were in the camp when the white men came: Mangak and his wife Qerneq, Terqatsaq and his wife Ukaliaq, Qavdlut and his wife Ihuana, Ukuararsuk and his wife Putulik, Panatoq and his wife Equvautsoq.

Among other visits from white men, they remember those of John Rae in 1847 and 1854.

I am quite ready to admit that there is nothing particularly exciting about these reminiscences in themselves, but this very fact: the lack of any special interest in the episodes, affords proof of the memory and reliability of these Eskimos. Their encounters with the white men were of the most casual order, and there was no time for them to become closely acquainted with the strangers; nevertheless, the accounts of such meetings are preserved, even after this long lapse of years, in a manner which speaks for itself as to their reliability. And if we look up the official reports of the respective expeditions concerned, we find that the native tradition is in excellent accord with the facts there stated.

The last day was given up to sports of various kinds, among which target shooting with bow and arrow was particularly effective. The targets were life size figures built of snow. And I noted here, that while the arrows might strike at a distance of 100 metres with force enough to kill, the shooting at this range was very uncertain. Accurate shooting was limited to a distance of 20 to 30 metres. Most of the men of course possessed firearms, which would naturally lead them gradually to neglect their practice with the bow and arrow. Nevertheless, the musk ox hunting of the previous autumn, in the neighborhood of Lake Simpson, had been carried out exclusively with bow and arrow, and twenty or thirty beasts would be brought down by this means.

The same evening, I had a visit from a man named Uvdloriasugsuk, who had come in from his camp a day's journey to the north-west. He was a big, broad-shouldered fellow with a long black beard; a steady and reliable man, greatly esteemed by all who knew him. Nevertheless, he had shot his own brother the winter before. And it was in connection with this killing that he wished to see me. The brother, it appeared, was a man of unruly temper, who went berserk at times, and had killed one man and wounded others in his fits. His fellow villagers therefore decided that he must be killed, and Uvdloriasugsuk, as head of his village, was deputed to act as executioner. Much against his will, for he was fond of his brother, Uvdloriasugsuk nevertheless consented, regarding it as a duty. He therefore went in to his brother and having explained the position, asked him to choose his own manner of death; by steel, thong or bullet. Without protest or sign of fear, he chose the last, and Uvdloriasugsuk shot him on the spot. He seemed anxious now to hear what I thought about it. I could only assure him that where the safety of all was threatened and all had agreed upon the measures to be taken in defence, he could hardly have acted otherwise.

On the following morning we took leave of our hosts and set off in different directions.

The dogs would wait no longer. I sprang to the sledge and waved a last goodbye as we drove off.

CHAPTER XIII

ONE day when we were lying out in Pelly Bay east of Boothia Isthmus, two men came running up out of the blizzard in front of the hut.

It was like a naked man suddenly knocking at the door. They had no sledge, no dogs, and carried no weapon save their long snow knives. And this was the more extraordinary since their dress showed that they came from a distance.

We got them in and thawed them up a little, and after a good meal they were able to give an account of themselves. They were two brothers from the neighborhood of the Magnetic Pole, out with a load of fox skins which they were going to trade for old guns with the natives at Pelly Bay. Qaqortingneq, the elder, was turning back now; and we decided to go back with him to visit his tribe.

The rest of his party were in camp some distance off; he brought them up and introduced them; two wives and a foster son. Quertilik, the prettier of the two women, had, he explained, cost him a whole wooden sledge; the other, Qungaq, had been purchased for the modest price of a bit of lead and an old file. He explained, however, that he had got her cheap, as her husband had just died of hunger. The boy had been bought in infancy, for a kayak and a cooking pot—men, of course, are worth more than women.

We did a little trading, ourselves, and I secured a blue fox skin for our collection at the price of a few beads. On the following morning we struck camp and set out together across Franklin Isthmus, making for an encampment of Netsilingmiut out on the ice between King William's Land and Boothia Isthmus.

On the 3rd of May we camped north of the Murchison River, in a great plain leading down to Shepherd Bay. An endless expanse of white spreads all around, broken only here and there by a few isolated hillocks jutting up like seals' heads from the waste. Qaqortingneq was an intelligent fellow, and thoroughly acquainted with the Netsilik district; also, he drew excellent maps. The camp, however, had been shifted since he left it, and it was not until the evening of the 5th that our dogs picked up the scent. Even then it was not the camp itself, but a curious indication. Ahead of us on the ice lay a long line of seal skulls, with the snouts pointing in a particular direction. This Qaqortingneq explained was the work of the hunters on shifting camp, it being generally believed that the seal would follow in the direction in which the snouts of the slain were set. In the present instance, it served as a guide to us, pointing the way the party had gone.

After some fruitless chasing about among confusing tracks, we came upon the village. Great blocks of snow were set up round it, not for shelter, but as frames on which to lay out the skins to dry. The

people of Kuggup Panga (The River Mouth) had
evidently no need of sheltering walls; they had, however, set up spears and harpoons in the snow outside
their huts, and long snow knives above the doorways,
to keep off evil spirits.

No white man had visited these people since the
coming of Amundsen twenty years before, and I was
a little anxious as to how they would receive us.
Coming upon them as we did in the middle of the
night there was no time for much in the way of
explanation.

I crept into a house, together with Qaqortingneq's
foster-son, Angutisugssuk, who was one of the party
that had accompanied us from Pelly Bay. It was
his mother's house we now entered.

"Here are white men come to visit us," he cried
excitedly. His mother jumped up at once from a
bundle of dirty skins, knelt down on the sleeping
bench and bared her breast, which the boy hurried
forward to kiss. This is a son's greeting to his mother
on returning from a long journey. In the midst of
these squalid surroundings, this recognition of the
bond between them, the son's homage to the mother's
breast, was to me doubly impressive.

We had hardly made ourselves known to them
when I observed that the women were gathering
in an odd sort of order about our sledges; and soon
they began marching round them in solemn procession. On enquiring the reason for this I was
informed that it was a ceremony designed to ward off
any possible danger from the "spirits" which had
accompanied us on our way unknown to ourselves.

QUERTILIK, NALINGIAQ'S PRETTY DAUGHTER, WIFE OF THE CHIEF QAQORTINGNEQ

THE ARRIVAL

When strangers arrive in a village, all the women who have borne children go out and step a circle round the sledges, in order to bind any evil spirits which may have accompanied the party without their knowledge. The track thus made forms a barrier which the spirits cannot pass. The illustration here shows mothers and children ready to receive us.

It is a custom on the coming of strangers, for all the women who have borne children, to step a circle round the sledge with its team; undesirable spirit entities are then "bound" within the magic circle and can do no harm.

By the time we had unloaded our goods and gear, friendly hands had built a hut for us, and we were hardly settled in our quarters when two huge seals were dragged up before the door as food for ourselves and our dogs.

Early the next morning we were awakened by the unceremonious entry of the village wizard, one Niaqunguaq. He was in a trance, and talked in a squeaky falsetto; the burden of his message being that his "helping spirits" had visited him during the night and declared that Qaqortingneq had eaten of forbidden food, videlicet, the entrails of salmon, while in our company. This is tabu during the seal hunting season. It was a safe guess anyhow, as the frozen fish were there among our stores when we unpacked the sledge, plain for all to see. Incensed authority was pacified, however, by the fragrance from our coffee pot, which I had quietly put on the oil stove while he was capering about. I took the opportunity to question him further as to these helping spirits of his, and learned that he counted about a score. One was a naked infant he had found sprawling on the bare earth far from human habitations; another was an Indian who had appeared to him with icicles in his hair and a flint knife stuck through his nose; a third was a lemming with a human face, which could also take the form of an eagle, a dog or a bear. This lemming was his special guardian angel. Despite the importance thus conferred, and his dignity as a wizard, he was not above enjoying a mug of coffee, and when he left, we were on the most friendly terms.

We spent the rest of that day going visiting from hut to hut. I soon discovered that we were in a hunting camp, where all were intent upon the most pressing of all our human occupations, the getting of their daily bread. It would be better therefore, for my purpose, to call on them some other time, later in the year, when they had settled in King William's Land. I decided accordingly to move on to the Magnetic Pole, where there was said to be a big camp.

I myself was anxious to make a collection of amulets from among the Netsilingmiut, where they were in use to an extent beyond what was customary with other tribes.

On the 11th of May I took leave of my comrades and set off to the northward through Rae Strait, taking with me one Alorneq, whose personality is best indicated by the fact that his gums were always dry from constant smiling.

We had no very precise idea as to where our people were to be found, as camps in the spring shift with the movements of the seal. We had first of all to get up to the north of Matty Island and into Wellington Strait, where we might hope to come upon sledge tracks leading in the right direction. It was difficult indeed to keep any sort of direction here. The compass itself was useless owing to the proximity of the magnetic pole, and the low south-eastern shore of King William's Land with Franklin Isthmus, is hardly to be distinguished from the sea ice, while the few mountain ranges are always wrapped in a veil of driving snow. We drove for two days without sight of a landmark anywhere; then we got a glimpse of the south-west coast of Boothia Isthmus, and on the third day went on up through Ross Strait, where we knew there had been a camp earlier in the winter. A fresh north-easter was blowing as we passed the north coast of Matty Island, and in Wellington Strait we began to look about on the chance of sighting bear, which not infrequently come in here hunting seal on their own account.

It was at Cape Adelaide, close to the Magnetic Pole, that we came upon the first snow huts; these were deserted, but the quaint little "offerings" of seal skulls pointed the way the hunters had gone; we followed up their tracks, and came upon more huts, first five, then three, then twelve, and then twelve again.

Alorneq is a magnificent tracker; he knows people by the way they build their huts, the way they lie down to sleep, as well as by their actual spoor, and long before we come up with the party he is able to tell who they are. When we did come upon them it was with a certain suddenness, our dogs disappearing headlong out of sight in what proved to be the entrance to a hut.

Alorneq went from one to another announcing our arrival, all turned out without the slightest hesitation and helped us to rights, and we were soon settled among them as comfortably as could be.

Amulet hunting is rather a delicate business, and I had to proceed with care. My business was to obtain, in the name of science, all that I could of these little odd trifles which are held by the wearers to possess magic power, and worn as a protection against ill. But it had to be done in such a manner that I should not be held accountable afterwards for any evil that might befall those who had parted with their treasures.

I spent the first day making myself known to all, and seeking as far as I could to win their confidence. This meant, incidentally, partaking of generous meals at the shortest intervals—for after all, humankind is much alike all over the globe, and one of the best ways of getting to know your neighbor is to dine with him.

Meantime, Alorneq had unpacked the trade goods and set them out for all to see. There were brand new glittering needles, taken out of their papers and laid in a heap, there were knives and thimbles, nails and matches and tobacco—little ordinary everyday trifles to us, but of inestimable value to those beyond the verge of civilization. I was pleased to note that there was a constant stream of visitors to our little exhibition.

That evening, on returning to the hut, I found it packed with eager men and women. All had something to offer in exchange, principally skins such as traders usually ask. There was a murmur of disappointment when I announced that I did not propose to trade on the usual lines. I explained that I had come from a distant land in order to learn the customs of other tribes, and had visited them in particular on account of their amulets, of which I had heard so much. I then gave them a lecture on the subject of amulets and their power, the gist of which was that as I was a foreigner from across the wide seas, the ordinary rules and regulations applying to amulets, tabu and the like did not apply to me. I had in the meantime made the acquaintance of their own medicine man, and quoted him in support of my arguments, together with other authorities—famous angakoqs of other tribes, whose names, it is true, they had never heard before, but whose words nevertheless carried weight. I pointed out that an owner of an amulet still enjoyed its protection even in the event of his losing the amulet itself—and this was agreed. How much more then, must he retain its protective power when, by giving away the article itself, he secured the material advantage of something valuable in exchange? Needless to say, I emphasized the fact that I was not trying to buy the power of the charm, which must remain with the original owner, but only the article itself, and its history.

Despite all arguments, it was plainly a matter that required thinking over. I left them to sleep on it, and decide next day whether they would trade or not.

It was late next morning before we awoke and removed the block with which the entrance to a hut is closed at night. This was a necessary preliminary to our receiving visitors, as it is not considered good manners to call on people until their hut had been opened.

Alorneq and I made some tea and had some breakfast, but nobody came along. I was beginning to fear the worst when a girl strolled casually down towards the hut and stood hesitating. I had noticed her the day before, admiring some of our beads. We invited her to come in, and she crawled through the passageway with all the amulets she was wearing on behalf of her son—when she should have one. Women rarely wear amulets on their own account. The Eskimo idea is that it is the man and not the woman who has to fight the battle of life, and consequently, one finds little girls of five or six years old wearing amulets for the protection of the sons they hope to bear—for the longer an amulet has been worn, the greater is its power.

This girl, whose name was Kuseq, now handed me a little skin bag containing all her amulets, newly removed from various parts of her clothing, where they were generally worn. I took them out and examined them, a pitiful little collection of odds and ends, half mouldy, evil-smelling, by no means calculated to impress the casual observer with any idea of magic power. There was a swan's beak—what was that for? Very sweetly and shyly the girl cast down her eyes and answered: "That I may have a man-child for my first-born."

Then there was the head of a ptarmigan, with a foot of the same bird tied on; this was to give the boy speed and endurance in hunting caribou. A bear's tooth gave powerful jaws and sound digestion; the pelt of an ermine, with skull attached, gave strength and agility; a little dried flounder was a protection against dangers from any encounter with strange tribes.

She had still a few amulets besides, but these she preferred to keep, so as to be on the safe side. Meantime, a number of others had found their way into the hut, young men and women, who stood round giggling and adding to our first customer's embarrassment. But their scornful smiles gave place to wonder when they saw what we gave her in return; beads enough for a whole little necklace, two beautiful bright needles and a sewing ring into the bargain. The girl herself could not conceal her satisfaction at the deal; and when she went out, I realized that this little daughter of Eve had set just the example that was needed.

In a couple of hours time there was such a run on the shop that I was really afraid the premises would be lifted bodily from their foundation, and before bedtime I was able to announce that we had "sold out." In return, I had a unique collection of amulets, comprising several hundred items.

Among those most frequently recurring and considered as most valuable, were portions of the body of some creature designed to convey its attributes; as the tern, for skill in fishing, foot of a loon, for skill in handling a kayak, head and claw of a raven, for a good share of meat in all hunting (the raven being always on the spot when any animal is killed), teeth of a caribou, worn in the clothing, for skill in caribou hunting. A bee with its brood sewn up in a scrap of skin gives "a strong head"; a fly makes the person invulnerable, as a fly is difficult to hit.

One of the few amulets worn by women on their own account is a strip from the skin of a salmon, with the scales along the lateral line; this is supposed to give fine strong stitches in all needlework.

We packed up our collection and stowed all away, ready to move off the next morning. Our departure was delayed however, at the last minute, by a visit from the local medicine man, whom I had, as already mentioned, appealed to as an authority in support of my theory as to the harmlessness of the transaction. He now demanded further payment in return. It was plain, he said, that I must be a man of remarkable power myself, and a lock of my hair, for instance, would be most valuable as an amulet in the event of trouble with spirits later on. He suggested that I should give a piece to each of those who had traded with me. I was rather taken aback at this; with every wish to give my friends a fair deal, I could not but remember that it was winter, in a chilly climate, and I was loth to set out on my further travels entirely bald. We compromised therefore with a few locks of hair for the most important customers, the rest being satisfied with bits of an old shirt and tunic divided amongst them.

The actual haircutting was the worst part of it, each lock being shorn, or rather sawn, off by the wizard himself with a skinning knife, and not over sharp at that. Scissors were unknown among these people. And by the time he had done with me, I am afraid my appearance was hardly what my hairdresser at home would consider that of a gentleman.

Finally, we got away about midday, instead of at

NIAQUNGUAQ, THE WIZARD

The white band across his forehead, made from the soft underskin of the caribou, marks
him as an angakoq, or witch-doctor.

daybreak as I had intended. But the whole village waved us a hearty farewell, and I had the satisfaction of feeling that we left them convinced of having obtained full value for what they had given, and something over.

CHAPTER XIV

AN INNOCENT PEOPLE

THE visit of Back, in 1833, was the first ever paid by white men to the Utkuhikhalingmiut—the name generally given to the natives inhabiting the delta and lower reaches of the Great Fish River. The word means "Dwellers in the Land of Soapstone" and refers to a deposit of the mineral south of Lake Franklin.

The white men were very kind, and gave the natives handsome and costly gifts. Nevertheless, so runs the tradition, there was a great fear of the strangers, and the angakoq had said that no good was to be looked for from that quarter. Therefore, when the white men took their departure, after only one night's stay, an elder of the tribe stood forth on a rock in the river and uttered a spell to prevent them from ever returning. "And that was in the olden days, when there was yet power in magic spells." Hence the fact that no white men have ever settled among the Utkuhikhalingmiut since that day.

Certainly, the story is in agreement with the facts insofar as the people of this region, near the mouth of the Great Fish River, as well as the kindred tribes farther up inland, are among the least known of all the Eskimos. No one has made any stay among them, and there is no description extant of their life and ways. The one occasion on which any Arctic expedition came into contact with them was the visit of Back above mentioned, in 1833, and this was a matter of a few hours only, the more unproductive from the fact that none of the white men understood the Eskimo tongue. The same was the case in 1855, when James Anderson, of the Hudson's Bay Company, following Back's route, encountered them on his way down to Montreal Island seeking news of the Franklin Expedition. And finally there was Schwatka, who in 1879 passed a settlement on the Hayes River on his way to King William's Land, likewise in search of news as to the fate of Franklin's men. None of these travellers could say more than that they had come upon a remarkable people in these regions; naturally therefore, I was eager myself to make their acquaintance.

Miteq and one of the Netsilik natives were to go on to the trading station of the Hudson's Bay Company, at Kent Peninsula, taking such collections as we had accumulated up to date and bringing back various supplies, notably of ammunition, some of that intended for our own use having been already disposed of in the way of exchange. We were to meet on the west coast of King William's Land, at the settlement of Malerualik, where most of the natives from that district would then be assembled for the fishing and caribou hunting.

I myself had with me Anarulunguaq and a Netsilik native called Inugtuk, with his wife Naulungiaq and two young sons. They were on their way to Lake Franklin to barter hide and blubber for powder and lead among the inland Eskimos there. Inugtuk was a skilful hunter, but like all the Netsilik, a very poor driver. And he proved an excellent comrade when I learned to know him a little better. At first I was inclined to regard him with some distrust, owing perhaps to what I had learned as to his antecedents. He had obtained his present wife by murdering her husband, Pujataq, at the same time adopting the two sons of the man he had killed. The whole family now lived together in the greatest harmony, and there seemed to be real affection between them all round—which was the more remarkable as the two lads would, on arriving at man's estate, be expected to take vengeance for the murder of their father. Inugtuk himself was a man of good family as such things go in these regions, and it was currently believed that his father had been carried up to heaven "as thunder and lightning" when he died.

According to the information I had received, the nearest settlement of the Utkuhikhalingmiut was at Itivnarjuk, near Lake Franklin, the same spot where they had been found in 1833 and 1855. The distance from there to the snow hut colony at south-west of Shepherd Bay was about 250 Km.

Early in the morning of the 31st of May, our dogs picked up the scent of something near at hand; and we were now just about the spot where we expected to find them. Sure enough, a few minutes later we drove full into a camp of nine tents.

The natives here received us with a certain dignity.

Despite the suddenness of our appearance, there was nothing of the shouting and confusion customary on such occasions. They could see at once from our clothes, our sledges and the manner in which our teams were harnessed, that we were strangers, and from a distance, but there was no rain of questions as to who we were and what we wanted, or the like. The men of the party came down towards us, not running inquisitively, but moving quietly and with some reserve. They were fine big men, well dressed, and with an earnest, almost solemn severity of countenance, more resembling Indians than Eskimos.

I explained who I was and what was my object in visiting them. The language occasioned no difficulty, and it was not long before they laid aside their first formal stiffness and began helping us to fasten the dogs, set up a tent and get our goods in order. This done, the spokesman of the party, whose name was Unaumitaoq, stepped up to me and looking me straight in the face, asked:

"Are you one of those white men who forbid the Eskimo to enter their tents?"

I explained that it was my earnest desire to learn as much as possible about my new friends in the short time I was able to stay there, and that anyone who cared to visit me would be welcome.

A murmur of approbation greeted this announcement. I added, that such trade goods and other property as I had with me would be left unguarded in the tent, since I took it for granted that they would be safe there. Upon which Ikinilik, one of the elders, answered proudly:

"Among our people, it is only dogs that steal."

I spent the rest of that day improving the acquaintance of my hosts. They had made a favorable impression on me from the first, and it was a relief indeed to find oneself among people positively *clean*, clean even to their hands and feet, after the indescribable dirtiness of the Netsilingmiut. They were, moreover, far more intelligent and quick of apprehension, and answered questions briskly and to the point. All were eager to give me information.

They were, I found, not altogether unacquainted with white men and white customs, though the nearest trading station was so far distant that it sometimes took half a year to get there and back. The journey was only made by the younger men, so that none of the older ones had ever seen a white man before.

Writing was a great source of wonder and amusement to them, and my journal, in which I was constantly making notes, occasioned much comment. All were delighted with the fineness of the paper leaves, which they took to be a specially delicate variety of skin. And when I wrote down what they said and afterwards read it aloud, they applauded; evidently, the "creature" had a good memory!

The Inland Eskimos, of the Great Fish River, or, as it is also called, from the name of its discoverer, Back's River, number only 164 souls in all, men, women and children. They divide themselves according to their villages into three groups, the Utkuhikhalingmiut in the Delta and lower reaches, especially the country south of Lake Franklin, the

Sangningajormiut farther up the river and in the district between Meadow Bank River and Baker Lake, and finally the Ualiardlet right up among the great inland waters, Lake McDougall, Lake Garry and Lake Pelly, which they call Imarjuaq, Qajarvik and Igdliviaq. This last group is now dying out, and numbers at present only 28 souls. All these people are entirely independent of the sea and never move down to the coast. This however, was not always the case; the Ualiardlet used to go down to Queen Maude Gulf, mostly about Ogden Bay, for the sealing, while the others went down to Elliot Bay and as far along as Cape Britannia.

Now, they use tallow in place of blubber for their lamps, that is, for lighting purposes; for cooking and heating they use lichen and moss and a kind of heather. As a matter of fact, there is very little cooking done, most of their food, both fish and meat, being eaten raw. Also, they dry their wet clothes on the body.

The temperature here is for several months of the year somewhere between minus 40° and minus 60° C. Nevertheless, these people declare that they do not feel the cold "much"; snow huts may be a little cold when newly built, but when covered with a good layer of fresh snow and filled with live human bodies, they soon get warm. The Utkuhikhalingmiut, indeed, regard themselves as much better off than the Netsilingmiut. Famine is not unknown, but is by no means of frequent occurrence, and only occurs when a long spell of extra bad weather prevents the men from hunting, or when the hunting itself proves fruitless both for caribou among the hills and fish in the lakes.

There is an old tradition to the effect that the Utkuhikhalingmiut were once a great people, so numerous that the hills around Lake Franklin were veiled in the smoke of their cooking fires. They were a warlike people, constantly fighting with their neighbors, and killing among themselves was of frequent occurrence.

As an illustration both of the spiritual culture and the manner in which it was revealed, I give the following account of an interview with Ikinilik, whom I have already mentioned as one of the elders of the tribe, and who was, also, a remarkable personality.

I tried to explain to him in the first instance, that I was interviewing him on behalf of a daily newspaper; that all that passed between us would be made known to many people through the medium of "talkmarks" such as he had seen me making in my note books, printed on sheets of the fine "skin" for men to learn what is happening each day.

But this in itself he regarded as a witticism, a humorous exaggeration; the world of the white men was big, no doubt, yet it could not after all be bigger than that a man might learn all the news there was by enquiring at the nearest tent.

In the following, I give question and answer word for word, according to my own notes written down on the spot. It will be observed that the parts dealing with religious beliefs are to some extent a repetition of what has already been given in my conversations with Aua; I have retained these however, on purpose,

NULIALIK, THE MOST SKILFUL CARIBOU HUNTER ON THE GREAT FISH RIVER

With his long hair about his ears, and circlet of white caribou skin, he looked more like
an Indian than an Eskimo—as did almost all of these inland folks.

TWO LITTLE GIRLS FROM LAKE FRANKLIN

as it seems worthy of note that two men from different parts, and of different types, should express almost identical views on the most important problems of life.

Ikinilik settled himself comfortably among the soft caribou skins, and lighting his pipe—the bowl of which was about the size of a small thimble—started off with a laughing allusion:

"From what you say, it would seem that folk in that far country of yours *eat* talk marks just as we eat caribou meat." And continuing the simile, he went on: "Well, now, begin with your questions and get your fire going; then I will cut up the meat and put it in the pot."

I began accordingly. "Tell me something about your religion. What do you believe?"

But at this all those present answered in chorus, so that I was barely able to distinguish Ikinilik's voice:

"We do not believe, we only fear. And most of all we fear Nuliajuk."

I tried again to explain to the party what an interview was. "Only one must answer," I said, and hoping they would take this as final, I went on:

"Who is this Nuliajuk?"

But every boy and girl in the place knew something of Nuliajuk from their nursery rhymes; it was too much to expect them to keep silence. All wanted to tell what they knew, and it was with difficulty that Ikinilik could make himself heard above the rest.

"Nuliajuk is the name we give to the Mother of Beasts. All the game we hunt comes from her; from her come all the caribou, all the foxes, the birds and fishes."

I asked him then: "What else do you fear?"

And this time the others refrained from joining in. Apparently they had at last understood that the interview was a matter between Ikinilik and myself. Ikinilik answered:

"We fear those things which are about us and of which we have no sure knowledge; as, the dead, and malevolent ghosts, and the secret misdoings of the heedless ones among ourselves."

"Do all human beings turn into evil spirits when they die?"

"No; only when those nearest to them have neglected to observe the customs laid down from the time of death until the soul has left the body."

"And when does the soul leave the body?"

Ikinilik shook his head and smiled, with an expression almost of pitying condescension in his fine, wise eyes: to think that a grown man should be so inquisitive! The onlookers, too, were smiling as he answered.

"If it is a woman, five days after death; if a man, four."

But I was not to be deterred from my questioning, and went on:

"Is there anything else you fear?"

"Yes, the spirits of earth and air. Some are small as bees and midges, others great and terrible as mountains."

"What happens to the soul when it leaves the body?"

Ikinilik shifted in his place, and the wrinkles round his eyes deepened a little; of all the ridiculous questions.

"When people die," he began, in his slow, rich

voice, "they are carried by the moon up to the land of heaven and live there in the eternal hunting grounds. We can see their windows from on earth, as the stars. But beyond this we know very little of the ways of the dead. Some few of the angakoqs in former times made journeys to the land of heaven, and told what they saw. They visited the moon, and in every case were there shown into a house with two rooms. Here they were invited to eat of most delicate food, the entrails of caribou; but at the moment the visitor reaches out his hand to take it, his helping spirit strikes it away. For if he should eat of anything in the land of the dead, he will never return. The dead live happily; those who have visited their land have seen them laughing and playing happily together.

"There was once a woman named Nananuaq; she died, and was carried off by the moon. But she did not stay long in the land of the dead; the moon changed her into a man and sent her back to her husband. The husband was very pleased to have his wife back again, but was sorely disappointed to find that she would not sleep with him. She told him what had happened, and when he had assured himself that it was the truth, he was so angry that he determined to kill her. He went out of the house to cut a hole in the ice: 'I must have water to drink,' he said, 'for that is the custom after one has died.' But the woman fled away to her grandchild, who lived near by, and when her husband came after her to fetch her back, she killed him as he entered the passage.

"This woman told her fellows on earth many things about life after death, and it is from her that we have our knowledge. Our angakoqs nowadays do not know very much, they only talk a lot, and that is all they can do; they have no special time of study and initiation, and all their power is obtained from dreams, visions or sickness. I once asked a man if he was an angakoq, and he answered: 'My sleep is dreamless, and I have never been ill in my life!' Now that we have moved up inland away from the sea we do not need to bother ourselves about what is tabu in connection with sea-beasts, and then also we have guns, which makes all hunting much easier than it was. Young hunters nowadays have too easy a time of it to trouble about consulting wizards. In the olden days when our food for the whole winter depended on the autumn hunting at the sacred fords, it was a very different matter; all the regular observances and many particular ones in addition were dictated daily by the angakoqs who knew all about such things. But now we have forgotten all the old spells and magic songs, and you will find no amulets sewn up in our inner garments. The people have food enough, and do not bother about their souls."

This opens the way for a question of importance.

"What do you understand by 'the soul?'" I asked.

Ikinilik was plainly surprised that I could ask such a thing; nevertheless he answered patiently:

"It is something beyond understanding, that which makes me a human being."

"Can you tell me any more about the life after death?"

"Only that we remain forever as we were when we died; old people do not become young, and the young do not grow old; children do not grow up at all."

Here the interview was brought to a close by the equivalent of the dinner gong, a summons which could not be ignored. It was moreover, my last public appearance among these friendly people, as I was leaving the same night. The river was breaking up and difficult to pass already.

Looking back upon my short stay among them, I cannot help noting that the esteem and admiration I felt for them at the time has been in no wise impaired by subsequent impressions elsewhere. I shall always look upon the Utkuhikhalingmiut as the handsomest and most hospitable, as well as the most cultured people of all those I met with throughout the whole length of my journey; and the cleanest and most contented to boot.

Oddly enough, the only information I had about them prior to my visit was from a letter written by Captain Joe Bernard, published in Diamond Jenness' book on the Copper Eskimos. Bernard, who went up to Victoria Land in 1918 and wintered there, based his opinion on the Netsilingmiut, and summarily disposed of the others in the following terse dictum:

"The Utkuhikhalingmiut are probably the most miserable people in the winter time I have ever seen or heard of."

Which shows how opinions may differ—and how careful one should be in forming an opinion as to one tribe from what one has heard through another.

It was a little after midnight when I started, and

the whole village, men and women, turned out to see us off, wishing us all that was good out of their own abundant content. The mountains were already bathed in cold white light, and we were anxious to get well out onto the sea ice before the heat of the sun made the work too fatiguing for our teams. Amid a chorus of farewells from our friends we struck off over the great water. One might almost say: through it; for a mush of sodden snow and water came threshing up over the sledges, and we ourselves were soaked through at once, having to go down on our knees in order to heave the sledges clear when they stuck fast.

Altogether about as wretched going as one could wish for the starting of a journey, but we took little heed of it, and laughed as we plunged into the icy mess through which we had to toil that day. The snow-broth seethed about the runners, and we drove through it singing.

"TAILS UP!"

Our dogs starting out on a long run.

NETSILINGMIUT CATCHES FISH AT AMTSOQ, KING WILLIAM'S LAND

At midnight, when the land was white with frost, they would leap out naked into the icy water, laughing and thoroughly enjoying the sport, though their limbs would be swollen and red with the cold when they emerged.

CHAPTER XV

O N the 13th of June we made King William's Land, at Malerualik, the spot where we had arranged to meet Miteq on his return from Kent Peninsula. Miteq was not there, but we found instead our old friend Qaqortingneq, together with a man named Itqilik (which means "The Indian") who had come all the way from Bellot Strait, having spent several years in North Somerset. These were just the people I wanted to meet, and learning at the same time that all the Netsilik folk from all villages between Adelaide Peninsula and Boothia Isthmus would be gathering in King William's Land, I decided that I could not do better than spend the summer here. I had always wanted to learn the ways of some primitive tribe more thoroughly than I had been able to do as yet, and the region in which I now found myself was one of the most isolated and inaccessible throughout the whole Eskimo territory. True, it was not altogether unexplored, since Schwatka, Roald Amundsen and Godfred Hansen had been here already, but their objects were not the same as mine, and without in the least detracting from the excellent work of these, my predecessors, I might fairly say I had struck a new field as far as my own branch of study was concerned. It was pleasant, also, to be able to look forward to a longer stay than hitherto, and make plans that allowed for good long spells of work, instead of hurrying from place to place.

On the 20th of June I made my first reconnaissance of the immediate surroundings. The country rises as one moves inland, in terraces marking the site of earlier beaches, with long narrow lakes in the hollows between, fed by small streams from the melting snow. There are a few ranges of hills, but as soon as one gets away from the sea, the country at this time of year presents the appearance of a great grassy plain. Spring was at its height, and the earth on every side was bursting into life. Geese, duck and waders were gathered in thousands on the lakes and marshy ground; red patches of saxifrage glowed among the rocks, the first of flowers to greet the light and warmth of the sun.

A few kilometres out from camp I came suddenly upon a whole ruined village of stone houses of the ancient Eskimo type. I had already heard from the natives elsewhere that such were to be found in these parts, but had not seen any myself. No permanent winter dwellings had indeed been recorded from here, and it was now of the greatest importance to examine these, by way of supplementing our material from the excavations in the Hudson Bay district. Plainly, I could hardly have chosen a better spot.

A day or two after this discovery I made a short excursion to Nunariarsaq, an island off the southeast coast of Queen Maud Gulf. Here, in a little creek, I found a whole row of stone cairns, and on enquiry, found that they were of somewhat curious origin, being, indeed, monuments erected to the memory of the dead. It appears that some women had gone out spearing salmon on the ice while their husbands were away hunting caribou inland. The ice broke up suddenly and carried them out to sea, one only making her way back to land. Each of the men then built a monument "as a tribute of respect to the souls of the dead." I was surprised to find such an observance among a people who, as a general rule, do not even bury their dead, but lay them out on the bare ground.

One old man here offered me meat for my dogs if I could let him have some ammunition. This man, whose name was Amajorsuk, was the proud possessor of a wooden leg which he had made and fitted for himself. Ten years before, when guns were first introduced at Baker Lake, he had the misfortune to lose one foot by an accidental shot. He now went about with a kind of artificial leg made from the crosspieces of a sledge lashed round the thigh and padded with caribou skin below the knee, the whole ending in a "foot" of musk ox horn, which served its purpose excellently. Amajorsuk himself was not in the least disheartened by his handicap; he was indeed, a most cheery soul, and a skilful hunter as well. But it says much for the courage and endurance of these people, that a man should have gone through all the suffering and hardship the accident must have caused him in the first place, and then have learned to shift for himself and bear his part with the rest under such conditions.

On the 1st of July, Anarulunguaq and I set to
work on the ruins at Malerualik.   The natives there
by no means sympathized with our interest in these
remains, holding that such things were best left
alone.   Moreover, they knew we should have the
greatest difficulty in finding food here at this time of
year.   Already numbers had left for the interior,
where the fishing season was now about to begin.
By the 5th of July the place was deserted save for our
own little party.   My two hunters went out each day
after seal, while I grubbed about among the ruins.
By the 25th, the position had become critical.
Despite all our efforts, it was impossible to get meat
enough to feed our dogs as long as we remained
here.   Fortunately, however, Anarulunguaq and I
had worked hard at our excavations in the meantime,
and felt justified in shifting our quarters in search
of other folk and other fare.

With ourselves, my two hunters and their families,
we made quite a little caravan when we set off, taking
with us tents, sleeping bags and rugs, cooking utensils
and some extra footwear.   The dogs were called
into requisition this time as beasts of burden, and
their pack-saddles caused us some difficulty at first.
Once they have grown accustomed to the work however, dogs can easily carry a load of 25–30 kilos each
for a long day's march.

One day we came upon a huge flock of geese, moulting and unable to fly.   Being short of ammunition,
we let the dogs loose, and a moment later we had a
score of birds.

We were all suffering from want of fat with our food,

and the last remains of some old rotten blubber was looked on as a treat. Altogether, we were short of quite a number of things; we had no tea, coffee, sugar and no tobacco. Living as we did chiefly on raw meat, and going about with an aftertaste of suet or blubber in one's mouth, it was hard to be deprived of one's pipe at the end of the day. The only luxury we possessed was some saccharine; and with a make-shift herb that grows here and there we could turn out something the color of tea, and tasting of nothing particular.

On the 5th of August we reached Amitsoq, the principal fishing station. I had heard so much about it during the past two months, that the reality proved rather a disappointment. The whole en-campment consisted of but five poor tents, and the reports of the yield up to date were not encouraging; caribou few, salmon scarce, and no food for the dogs! We had come too early; the fishery would not begin till the 15th of August, and would be practically over by the end of the month.

We stayed here a week, during which time I wrote down over fifty of the native stories, and obtained a great deal of valuable information as to ancient cus-toms and ways. We managed to shoot six caribou, which gave an ample supply of meat for ourselves and the rest of the camp.

I have never in my life seen half-starved, wretchedly clad, chill-ridden people so cheerily heedless of their troubles, so full of fun and merri-ment under the most miserable conditions. Some of the children were positively in rags, their legs, arms and hands red and swollen with the cold, yet they played about as if unconscious of it all. The native idea of happiness in the Hereafter is a life where all is play. And they seemed to be well on the way to realizing it here, for men and women as well as children spent five or six hours of each day playing games. The work on which they relied for their daily sustenance was confined to three visits per diem to the salmon pool, each occupying perhaps ten minutes; and even this was more like a game than serious work, to judge from the laughter and fun that went on.

The salmon fishing was worked on a simple plan. The fish were found in a stream connecting two lakes; the stream was dammed and a shallow basin built with stones, leaving an entrance which was allowed to remain open all day until the signal was given; it was then closed, and the whole party, armed with fish spears, plunged in and set about spearing the fish, traps being set to catch any that might otherwise escape. Later on in the summer, or early autumn, the fish would be taken in such quantities that each family could, in the space of a fortnight, obtain something like a thousand kilos of excellent fish, which was stored for the winter.

It was extremely difficult to obtain fuel of any sort at Amitsoq. The Cassiope which is used in some parts is not found here, the nearest substitute being Dryas, which is moreover in bloom at this time of year. It is most difficult to keep alight, and one has to be constantly blowing it. It took Anarulunguaq five hours to cook a potful of fish and boil a kettle of water in this fashion. It is not surprising then that most prefer to eat their food raw. Raw meat tastes very nice really, but I never quite got accustomed to eating raw fish fresh from the water.

The fishing here often provides those reserves of food that may be indispensable in winter should the caribou hunting fail, and the place is regarded as sacred, just as are certain spots particularly frequented by the caribou. Strict rules had to be observed. Eating of marrow-bones, or fresh caribou brains, was forbidden; the heads, if brought to the spot, had to be picked clean and dropped in an adjacent stream where there were no fish. No needlework was to be done in the tents, nor might the men attend to their fishing gear there. No caribou skins old or new, might be worked on; not a tear might be mended nor a worn spot patched. Consequently, the whole party went about in their ragged last year's garments. The only kind of sewing allowed was for the mending of footwear, and the hide for this purpose had to be cut beforehand. This work, and the necessary repairs to fishing implements and gear had to be done at a particular spot away from the camp. Most of the party gathered here when not sleeping or at their games.

These games were of a very simple character, but served their purpose as a means of exercise and keeping warm. A favorite one was a mixture of hide-and-seek and "touch." Another was "keeping silence," the one who laughs first being given a comical nick-name which he is obliged to answer to for the rest of the day. Then there is the game of

"Bear" in which one player personates the bear, crawling about on all fours, while the rest dance about him and he attacks them as best he can. There was one game of ball which caused no end of fun and excitement. It is played by partners two and two against the rest, each of a pair trying to throw to the other. All is fair in this game, collaring, tripping, charging from beyond, and all is taken in good part. Young and old joined in the game, and once started, it would go on for the rest of the day and be started again the next. Husband and wife were generally partners; and it was really touching to see the affection between the pairs. I have rarely met with people where the men were so proud of their wives, the women on their part being tireless in their praise of their respective husbands.

A curious form of pastime, popular especially among the children, was the Tunangussartut, or "spirit game," which consists in "taking off" the seances of the angakoq, often in a really humorous manner. Spirits are invoked, imaginary enemies battled with and vanquished, exactly in the grown-up manner; the dread of evil powers is caricatured to the life, and prayers and spells uttered word for word as in cases of actual peril or distress. The whole thing was rank blasphemy; and yet the grown-ups looking on would gasp and rock and hold their sides with laughter, as if they found a certain satisfaction in watching their young hopefuls make fun of what to them was solemn earnest. And then perhaps, a few hours later, a sudden indisposition, or a bad dream, would call all the adults together in a real seance, none the less solemn now for the comic interlude just past. I asked one of my friends here how it could be that they were not afraid of incurring the anger of the spirits by these disrespectful harlequinades. But he answered that "of course" the spirits understood it was only in fun; and surely they knew how to take a joke! He seemed, indeed, astonished that anyone could raise the question at all.

On the 12th of August, to my regret, I felt obliged to take leave of my friends here and try hunting elsewhere. We divided our party into two, Anarulunguaq and I, with one of the hunters, returning to Malerualik, while the other, with half the dogs, went over towards Gjoa Harbor to see if better fortune might be had there.

We reached Malerualik once more on the 17th, and found the goods we had left there untouched—a matter by no means certain unless special precautions are taken to protect stores from being plundered by the various prowling beasts. It was good to see the sea again; and there was still some work to be done. Anarulunguaq and I had another spell at the ruins, but we were not suffered to go on very long. On the 25th of August, we had a gale from the north-west, bringing with it the first snow and frost. We had, however, got through most of the excavation work and collected a fine lot of material.

With the autumn now setting in, and in view of the indoor work I had still to do in writing out my notes and observations up to date, I decided that we had better build a stone house of the North Greenland (Cape York) type. Anarulunguaq and I set to work on this on the evening of the 29th, most of the building being done by Anarulunguaq, who is an expert at the work, while I brought up stone from the ruins. Among her people it is customary for the women to build the winter houses, while the men are out hunting in the autumn. By the 31st, we had the place complete save for the final dressing of turf that was to cover the rough stone. At this stage some old acquaintances appeared on the scene, Alorneq, Itqilik, and another named Oqortoq. They helped us with the finishing touches, and the same night we were able to serve up a modest banquet in our new quarters.

The talk soon turned to the subject of Miteq and his failure to appear. Oqortoq's wife was an angakoq of some note, and had moreover, a few days before, found a bit of lead on the shore of a stream. The lead had probably been dropped by some caribou hunter, but it was now regarded as a special token from the spirits, such as may sometimes be accorded to those specially favored. A great invocation was therefore held, resulting in the intelligence that Miteq was on his way home, and not far away; we were further informed that he had killed two bears on the way, and had encountered various difficulties, not specified.

This seemed encouraging, and likely enough but there was some doubt among the rest of the party even yet. It was openly asserted that we should never see Miteq again; he and his companion must certainly have been murdered long since by the Kitdlinermiut.

Our guests had come down to visit some caches they had laid down during the spring. On leaving, each of them presented me with a stick of tobacco; which, by the way, they had originally bought from me at our first meeting. I was the better able to appreciate the kindness of the gift in that I knew it amounted to half their own supply, and all three were ardent smokers.

Another commodity now running short with us was the very ordinary box of matches. Matches were frequently demanded in payment when I was buying amulets, and as the fresh supply Miteq was to have brought up had not yet arrived, we found ourselves now reduced to a ration of two matches per diem. Anarulunguaq managed, however, by keeping peat embers on the hearth from one time of using to the next. After all, one can always manage to get a light native fashion, though it savors somewhat of the stone age. More serious was the lack of ammunition for our guns, now that winter was close at hand.

The 3rd of September was fine, with a clear sky, a slight frost and a faint breeze from the west. Anarulunguaq and I were sitting outside the tent gazing out over the water in the quiet of the afternoon, when Anarulunguaq suddenly broke out excitedly:

"Look, look, what is that? I thought it was low water, and there is a reef I am sure was not there before. Look, it is moving!"

She pointed across to the low spit of land west of the island of Eta; and there sure enough was something dark in the water. It was a small canoe, making in towards us.   Kayaks are only used in fresh water lakes in this region, and are never seen out at sea. There were two men in this one; they could only be Miteq and his companion.   We had been looking out for them since the middle of June, and now that they were actually in sight it seemed to take our breath away.

I got out my glass; sure enough it was they.   And in less than an hour they had landed. We raced down to meet them long before they reached the shore, delighted to find them both alive and well, but eager to hear what news they brought; and what supplies.   Unfortunately, there was disappointment in store to temper the joy of our meeting. Miteq's first announcement ran:

"No ammunition, no tobacco, no tea, coffee, sugar or flour.   But," he added with a laugh, "we are thoroughly alive ourselves, and it might easily have been otherwise!"

The canoe grounded on the pebbles, Miteq sprang ashore and we embraced heartily.

His report may be given in brief.   On leaving King William's Land at the end of May, they had found the ice so impassable along the shores of the mainland that they had crossed over to Lind's Island, near Victoria Land, and thence to White Bear Point on the southern coast of Queen Maud Gulf.   On the way down to Melbourne Island they had twice encountered the Kitdlinermiut, who had given them a most hostile reception.   Only the women came down to meet them, the men lying in ambush close round, ready to fall upon them should occasion arise.

As a rule they managed to get on friendly terms, but in one or two places, the natives had been so surly and their behavior so suspicious that they judged it best not to sleep among them. They generally fastened the dogs in a circle round their tent, so as to be sure of being aroused in case of danger from any quarter. Our collections had been delivered safe and sound to the Hudson's Bay Company's representative at Kent Peninsula, but the trade in fox skins there had been so exceptionally heavy that season that the station had sold out of everything by the time they arrived. They had just managed to get enough ammunition to last them on their way back. The rivers flowing out into Queen Maud Gulf had broken up at the beginning of June, and they had had to borrow a canoe to get through. All their dogs had been left with some Eskimos near Ellice River, where they themselves had stayed a month waiting for the ice to clear sufficiently for them to proceed along the coast. As it was, they had only with the greatest difficulty managed to make their way down in the frail canoe.

Despite the bad news, we were of course only too glad to have them both back safe and sound. And I was greatly relieved to find that I should not be all alone among strangers without ammunition, for there would be a hard struggle now to keep our dogs. If we lost them, the sledge trip to Nome would be out of the question.

By this time the natives were beginning to find their way back to Malerualik and we had soon over a hundred souls in camp.   The caribou hunting was about to begin, and there was great excitement as to how it would turn out.

On the 15th of September, the advance guard of the caribou made their appearance.   There was a shout that echoed through the camp, and all turned out, to find the animals trotting down over the hills to the eastward.   At a distance, it looked like a great body of cavalry on the move, the herd advancing in line of 50 to 100 abreast, in steady formation down towards the ford at Eta.   The hunters snatched up their guns and hurried off, dropping down into cover immediately, among the little hummocks on the line by which the caribou must pass.   It was the first regular encounter of the season, and the unsuspecting beasts kept on at a steady trot towards the coast, until a deafening volley brought them up short. They stood as if paralyzed for a moment, and they gazed about helplessly in search of the invisible foe; this gave the hunters a fresh chance, and shot after shot rang out, the animals dropping on every side, and further confusing the rest, until the entire cavalcade broke up into scattered groups that dashed away headlong into the interior.

Miteq and I had taken no part in this battle, as we had only 75 cartridges between us, and I had no wish to see them wasted in the reckless firing that often takes place in the excitement of dealing with a mass of game at close quarters.   As it was, the total bag amounted to some 50 beasts, which had, I reckoned, cost from five to seven shots apiece; a poor result for the expenditure, compared with what might have been obtained under the circumstances. The Eskimos, however, accustomed to reckon with the slower and scantier yield of bow and arrow, would reckon it very satisfactory.

There was not snow enough on the ground to start sledging, and on the 18th, early in the morning, Miteq and I set off up country to go hunting on our own account. We came back the same evening with seven fine caribou—we had deliberately picked out the finest and fattest—a heavy load, but more than welcome.

It was on the 21st of September that the Great Event took place.

I was just walking up towards the tent when I noticed a stir among the others scattered about. Then suddenly all came pouring out from the tents, men, women and children, and a great cry of wonder went up:

"O—oh. . . . O—o—oh. . . . !"

For a moment all stood still as if rooted to the spot, then off they went again, hurrying down past me in great excitement. I thought at first it must be a new detachment of caribou in sight, and was prepared to give a curt refusal to anyone wanting to borrow my gun. Then one of the foremost hailed me, waving his hand in the direction of the shore:

"Look, look there!"

I turned and looked; and told myself it was nothing of the sort; I must be dreaming. A ship under full

sail making straight in towards us?   Who ever heard
of such a thing?   To the young folk gathered round,
agape with wonder, this was the Great Event of all
their lives.   A ship?   They had never seen a ship.
And see how it floated, that great thing!   And where
on earth could they have got all that wood?   Here it
came, actually moving, swimming on the water like
some great bird, yes, and with sails spreading out
above like huge white wings. . . !

In the midst of all this wonder and excitement, it
occurred to me that there would be ammunition on
board that ship—whose it was, or what its errand, I
did not trouble to think.

A pair of ski lashed together served as a flag-staff,
and in a moment we had hoisted the Danish flag and
the Union Jack over our dwelling.   An hour later the
vessel was at anchor close inshore, and a motor boat
came sputtering up to the beach with two white men
on board, who introduced themselves as Peter
Norberg of Hernoesand, Sweden, and Henry Bjoern
of Praestoe, Denmark.

After all, it is a little world!

They had come up to establish a station for the
Hudson's Bay Company in King William's Land.
The vessel was called *El Sueno* and had originally
been a private yacht stationed at San Francisco.
To our unaccustomed eyes, she seemed a very frigate;
though she was but 20 tons.   And in this cockle-shell
of a craft, without engines even, and with a heavy
boat in tow, Peter Norberg had forced a way through
the most difficult part of the old North-west Passage,
namely, Queen Maud Gulf, a piece of seamanship

the extent of which he himself was far from realizing. They had no charts, and no technical aids to navigation whatever, but as Peter Norberg very simply put it, both came of a seafaring race, the old viking strain had been turned to good account.

No fewer than forty vessels had taken part in the struggle for the North-west Passage. Roald Amundsen, with his little *Gjoa* was the first to win through; and here was Peter Norberg coming in second with a bit of a craft that could hardly be called a vessel at all, and had only been built for pleasure cruising round the Golden Gate.

Ten minutes later I was on board, with my teeth deep in an orange. A little later, I sat staring with wide eyes at a real cup of actual steaming coffee. There were such things as Bread, and Cheese, and Butter, on the table, but I did not touch them; being quite content to sit puffing great clouds of smoke. And having got used to the wonder of all this after a while, it seemed quite natural to be sitting on a box containing 5000 cartridges of the precise calibre we had been using; I listened calmly, was in a dream, to the promise of unlimited ammunition. . . .

Truly, a turn of events all on a sudden!

I gazed out through the open porthole; the snow was a glittering carpet of innumerable tiny crystals; and across it moved the caribou in their hundreds, trotting on all unaware towards death and destruction.

CHAPTER XVI

FROM STARVATION TO SAVAGERY

SHUT off from the rest of the world by ice filled seas and trackless wastes of vast extent, the little handful of people who call themselves the Netsilingmiut have been suffered to live their own life, such as it is, up to the present day uninfluenced by any form of alien culture. Their own enumeration of the various tribes belonging to their people is as follows:

The Arviligjuarmiut, in the neighborhood of Pelly Bay, numbering 32 men and 22 women; the Netsilingmiut proper,[1] from Boothia Isthmus, 39 men and 27 women; the Kungmiut, from the banks of Murchison River, 22 men and 15 women; the Arvertormiut from Bellot Strait and North Somerset, 10 men and 8 women, and finally, the Ilivilermiut of Adelaide Peninsula, 47 men and 37 women, making a total of 259.

From mid-July until December, these people live up in the interior, occupied in caribou hunting and salmon fishing; the rest of the year is devoted to seal hunting on the ice. The name Netsilingmiut, which

---

[1] In contrast to the Caribou Eskimos and the natives of the Hudson Bay district, the Netsilingmiut prounounce the letter "s" distinctly, as is evident from their songs and their names. Among the other tribes, the sound of "s" is not found, "j" or "h" being used instead.

THE VICTIM

All along the coast of Canada and Alaska steel traps are set in endless line, ready to snap up any foolish animal attracted by the smell of the bait. A white fox is shown caught in one of these.

means "Seal Folk" hardly derives from any special abundance of seal in their district, but is rather due to their having, after a previous period inland, moved down to the coast and taken up hunting there, in contrast to the Caribou Eskimo. This move would appear to be of comparatively recent date.

Though few in number, Netsilingmiut cover a territory of considerable extent, their hunting grounds amounting to some 125,000 square kilometres, which is three times the size of Denmark, and equivalent to the entire ice-free portion of Greenland.

I lived among these people for over six months, and had every opportunity of learning to know them intimately, being forced myself to return to altogether primitive conditions and share their lot in every way; a fact which was naturally conducive to mutual confidence.

There is hardly any country in the world more harsh and unfriendly than theirs, or more destitute of all that is generally regarded as necessary to mere existence. Winter begins in September and lasts till the middle of July. During the actual winter months they have to struggle for life against a temperature somewhere between minus 30° and minus 50°C. I visited them in April, and marvelled how they could keep up their spirits—find room, indeed, for fun and merriment—in their cold and comfortless dwellings. In May, the weather was but little better; certainly, it was a trifle less cold, but in return, the constant blizzards wrapped the whole poor encampment of snow huts in a flurry of snow; and as soon as the sun came out for a spell, its chief effect was to melt the roof over their heads.   But it did not seem to trouble them.   And I thought to myself that when summer came, it must make amends, and give them compensation for all they had so bravely and patiently endured; surely they must at some season or other absorb the warmth that even animals cannot do without.   The summer came, and I visited them up country at their salmon fishing.   It was not positively cold now, but the weather was by no means pleasant, being dull and chilly, with a constant wind; the snow had given place to rain, and the little tents made but a sorry shelter.   Nevertheless, the inmates were by no means depressed; on the contrary, they played games most of the day, going about in their wretched rags without a murmur at the stern tabu which forbade them even to make themselves new clothes or warmer sleeping rugs until they had shivered their way through the first of the snow right on into November.

And these step-children of Nature were by no means wretched in appearance; they were for the most part tall and strongly built; among the men, a height of 170 cm. was by no means uncommon. They were not only cheerful, but healthy, knowing nothing of any disease beyond the "colds" that come as a regular epidemic in spring and autumn.

A people must naturally be viewed in the light of their surroundings, and from what has already been said as to those of the Netsilingmiut, it will hardly be surprising to find the people themselves not only hardy and of great endurance, but with many harsh and forbidding customs savoring of the stone age.

The Netsilingmiut are remarkably well acquainted

with their country, both as regards its natural conditions and its history from early times. Though altogether unaccustomed to the use of pencil and paper they were able in a surprisingly short time to draw outline maps, with a very considerable amount of detail. The actual distances might not be quite exact, but every lake and island, every headland and bay was noted so carefully that one could easily find one's way by these maps in altogether new country.

Their own tradition holds that the Netsilingmiut immigrated at some distant date into the country they now occupy, driving out the original inhabitants. These, as in the Hudson Bay district, were called Tunit. It is so long since the Tunit hunted seal and whale in the land of the Netsilingmiut that everything has changed since then. Land and water were different; in that "the seas were deeper"[1] so that great sea beasts such as the whale could then come in to their shores, whereas now they are only found right up in Bellot Strait. Evidence of their former presence in these waters is seen in the many bones of whale found among the ancient ruined dwellings. And in support of the assertion as to change in the level of the sea, old men cited the finding of a whale skeleton far up inland at Saitoq, east of Shepherd Bay. Near the lake of Qorngoq also, in the same locality, many skeletons of white whales have been found, while farther inland again, near Lake Qissulik, there is a mass of driftwood, now so rotted by the weather that it crumbles at a touch. But the waters now are so shallow that not even the

[1] This is the Eskimo view. Actually, it is the land which has risen.

ribbon seal from Queen Maud Gulf pass in through Simpson Strait, and hunting of marine animals is restricted to the little common fjord seal.

The Netsilingmiut accounts of the Tunit supplement those we obtained in the Hudson Bay district about the aborigines there. And when, in the course of the summer, I was able to excavate and examine the remains of twelve winter houses at Malerualik, I found that this material also confirmed our theories as to the migrations of the Eskimo.

The ruined dwellings at Malerualik, comprising in all 65 houses built of stones and peat, are the first that have ever been investigated in this area, and therefore of the greatest importance as a link between our finds in Hudson Bay and Baffin Land on the one hand, and the collections afterwards made in the western regions of Alaska and East Cape.

Though the whales, as already mentioned, no longer penetrate into these waters, we found a considerable number of bones of whale used for building material in the dwellings of these old houses, and a great majority of the implements found were made from the same material. We obtained something over 200 items in this category, witnessing to a type of Thule culture somewhat more adapted to caribou hunting than in other places where excavations were made. These finds here were also rather more primitive, showing an earlier stage of development than the Naujan relics from Repulse Bay. It is thus also more nearly allied to the Alaskan form of culture than the other Thule finds.

The main bulk of the ruins lay distributed along

three separate lines, marking the site of former beaches, the highest being some 25 metres above sea level, at a distance of some 400 metres from the coast, suggesting that they must be at least as old as the ruins at Naujan.

As has already been indicated, there is no super-abundance of food in these regions. There are, of course, times when more game is killed than can be eaten at once, especially during the great caribou hunting season, in autumn, or when the salmon fishing in summer is particularly good. But on the other hand, we have to reckon with periods in winter when weeks may pass without any possibility of pro-curing food; it is therefore absolutely essential to have a store in reserve. Life is thus an almost uninterrupted struggle for bare existence, and periods of dearth and actual starvation are not infrequent. Three years before my visit, eighteen people died of starvation at Simpson Strait. The year before, seven died of hunger north of Cape Britannia. Twenty-five is not a great number perhaps, but out of a total of 259 it makes a terrible percentage for death by starvation alone. And yet this may happen any winter, when there are no caribou to be had. It is hardly surprising then to find canni-balism by no means uncommon. In citing a typical instance here, as showing the merciless nature of the struggle for existence, I give both facts and comment in the words of my informant, which express, I think, the typical native point of view. The speaker is one Samik, a good hunter and a respected angakoq.

"Many people have eaten human flesh. But never from any desire for it, only to save their lives, and that after so much suffering that in many cases they were not fully sensible of what they did.

"You know Tuneq, Itqilik's brother. You have met him, and his present wife, you have lived with them and you know him to be a cheery soul, a man who loves to laugh, and one who is always kind to his wife. Well, now, one winter many years ago the the hunting failed. And some starved to death and others died of cold, and the living lived on the dead. And all at once Tuneq went out of his mind. He said the spirits had told him to eat his wife. He began by cutting bits from her clothing and eating them, then more bits, till he had bared her body in several places. Then suddenly he stabbed her to death with his knife and ate of her as he needed and lived. But he placed the bones in their order as it is required to be done when anyone dies. . . .

"But we who have endured such things ourselves, we do not judge others who have acted in this way though we may find it hard, when fed and content ourselves, to understand how they could do such things. But then again, how can one who is in good health and well fed, expect to understand the madness of starvation? We only know that every one of us has the same desire to live."

The terrible uncertainty of life in these regions accounts to some extent for the prevalence of more or less superstitious rites and the use of amulets. The Netsilingmiut hold the same views on the subject of amulets as the Igdlulingmiut, but use them wholesale. One little lad of seven years old went about with no fewer than eighty sewn up in various parts of his clothing, which sadly hampered him in his play.

Perhaps the most striking evidence of the stern conditions under which these people live is afforded by their strictly economical attitude towards the business of childbirth. Girl children are invariably killed at birth unless previously promised in marriage and thus provided for already. And this is not from lack of feeling, nor from any lack of appreciation of woman's part in life, which is recognized as indispensable; it is due solely to a recognition of the fact that no breadwinner can hope to provide for a family numbering much beyond the necessary minimum. A girl is merely an unproductive consumer in the family up to the time when she is able to make herself useful; and as soon as she arrives at that stage, she is given in marriage, and her utility falls to the share of another household.

Every man knows that he can only reckon on a few years of active life as a hunter, unless he should happen to be endowed with a sturdier constitution even than his fellows. After a while he finds himself unable to compete. If he have sons, these will as a rule be able to help him when his own strength begins to fail; and it is thus an advantage to have as many sons as possible, staving off the evil hour when one literally feels the noose about one's neck. For it is a general custom that old folk no longer able to provide for themselves commit suicide by hanging. Life is short, and we must make the most of it—that is the crude moral of it all.   Moreover, it should be remembered that it takes three years at least before a child is weaned, during which period the mother does not as a rule give birth to others; parents can therefore ill afford to spend three years on a girl when they might hope to have a boy.

It has been generally believed that the Eskimos were a people with low birth rate as a whole.   This is only true to a certain extent; the long period of nursing accounts to a great extent for the length of time between births.

At Malerualik, in King William's Land, I went through the whole settlement, enquiring of the women individually how many children they had borne, and how many girls had been killed, noting carefully the names and numbers in each case. The result, from the list before me as I write, gives, for eighteen marriages, a total of ninety-six children of which 38 were killed at once as girls not previously provided for.   It is significant however, that of the 259 souls which make up the population of the Netsilingmiut, 109 are women as against 150 men.   Despite considerable fertility therefore, it is evident that the race is on the way to extermination if the girls continue to be thus summarily killed off at birth.

As an instance of their fertility I may quote a case which came to my knowledge.   Imingarsuk, aged about 60, whom I met at Committee Bay, had had 20 children; of these, 10 were girls killed in infancy, 4 died of disease, one son was drowned, leaving 4 sons and one daughter, whom I afterwards met, all fine healthy specimens of the race. I asked the mother if she did not regret the killing of the girls, but she answered, no, for if she had had to nurse all those girls, who were born before the boys, she would have had no sons at all. As it was, she loved her sons, who had secured relative comfort for herself and her husband in their old age, but had no sort of feeling for the infants killed, whom indeed she had barely seen. My list above quoted includes also two women with ten, two with eleven, and one with twelve births to their credit.

In the face of these hard conditions, the Netsiling-miut have developed a wonderful degree of ingenuity and endurance in the pursuit of that game on which their lives depend. Highest in this respect is their method of harpooning seal at the breathing holes. They rank first among all the tribes in this form of hunting, and their methods and apparatus are worth a brief description.

When the ice first forms, the seal noses and scrapes a small hole through which to breathe; the site is indicated by a slight rise, or bell-shaped protuberance of the ice above the rest. It is a comparatively easy thing to harpoon a seal at this stage, but the matter becomes vastly more difficult when the ice has thickened to some two or three metres, with a further layer of snow above. What exactly takes place may be seen from an account of a day's hunting.

Very early, before it is quite light, Inugtuk and I are roused from sleep, and a jug of boiling seal's blood is brought us. Still barely awake, we swallow the hot, thick soup with its abundance of blubber, knowing that we cannot expect to get another meal for the next ten or twelve hours. Then hurrying into our outdoor clothes, we join our companions, and the party, fifteen strong, sets out across the ice at a smart pace. It is bitterly cold, with a biting wind.

Each of us carries a bag slung from his shoulders, containing various minor requisites; the harpoon is carried in the hand. Dogs are used to pick up the blow holes by scent.

It took us three hours to find the first, which fell to the lot of Inugtuk. I remain with him, while the rest of the party scatter in various directions. Inugtuk now sets about his first preparations. First of all he cuts away the upper layer of snow, leaving the dome of ice exposed. Then, with an ice-pick at the butt end of his harpoon, he chips away at the fresh ice which has formed since the seal's last visit, scooping out the fragments with a spoon of musk ox horn. He then takes a "feeler," a long curved implement made of horn, and thrusts it down into the hole to ascertain the exact position of the bore, or vertical tunnel relative to the opening itself. This is a most important point, as the position of the seal when it comes up to breathe depends on this, and the direction of the harpoon thrust has to be determined accordingly. With the aperture immediately above the centre of the vertical shaft, a straight downward thrust will generally strike the animal, but where the aperture is a little to one side, there will be room for the harpoon to pass without touching. As soon as this has been ascertained, the snow is packed down

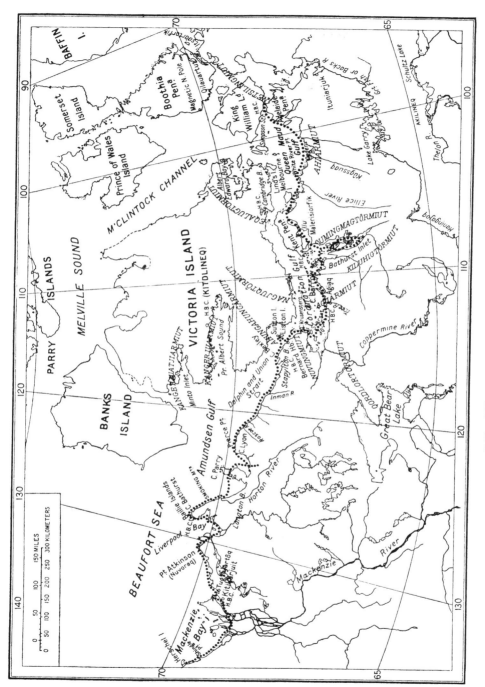

MAP: BAFFIN ISLAND TO MACKENZIE BAY

EQALUK AND HIS TWO WIVES, PAMIOQ AND AGSATOG

again over the ice, and a hole pierced straight through it with the harpoon so as to give a clear thrust when the moment arrives.

The next implement called into requisition is the "feather." This consists of a stiff sinew from the foot of a caribou, into which is fixed a piece of swansdown at one end, the other being forked, so that the forks catch on either side of the opening, leaving the swansdown indicator just far enough down the shaft to be still visible from above. As soon as the seal comes up and begins to breathe, the "feather" begins to quiver, and the hunter strikes.

The harpoon itself consists of a shaft with a loose head, a line being attached to the latter, so that on striking, the head becomes fixed in the body of the seal, and at the same time comes away from the shaft, when the animal is held on the line just as a fish on the hook. It is then drawn up to the hole again and killed.

As soon as all was in readiness, Inugtuk spread out his bag on the snow in front of the hole and stood on it. This partly to prevent the snow from creaking underfoot, and partly as a protection from the cold. And there he stood, like a statue harpoon at the ready, and eyes fixed on the swansdown just visible below. Hour after hour passed, and I began to realize what an immense amount of patience and endurance are required for this form of hunting with the thermometer at minus 50°C. Four hours of it seemed to me an eternity, but there are men who have stood for twelve hours on end, in the hope of bringing back food for the hungry ones at home.

We had just decided to give it up when we saw that one of the others a little way off had got a seal. As soon as he had hauled it up, we hurried over to him to take part in the "hunter's meal" a regular procedure almost in the nature of a sacrament. All kneel down, the successful hunter on the right, the others on the left of the seal. A small hole is cut in the carcase large enough to extract the liver and a portion of blubber, the opening being then carefully pinned up to avoid loss of blood. The liver and blubber are then cut up into dice and eaten kneeling. For myself, I always felt there was something touching and solemn about this ceremonial eating of the first meat on which men's lives depend.

Our total bag that day was one seal, and fifteen men were out for eleven hours to get it. But my comrades were only too thankful that they had anything to bring home at all, which is certainly not always the case. On the other hand, one may get three or four in a single day. But seal generally are scarce here. I reckoned out that the average haul per man would be about 10 to 15 seal from January to June. At a village with 10 families numbering 37 souls in all, the winter catch amounted to only about 150 seal. A skilful hunter in Greenland would have been able to get about 200 in the same time, which shows the enormous difference in the general conditions of life.

The mind of the Netsilik Eskimo is like the surface of one of these lakes with which his country abounds: easily roused, but soon calm again. But coolness is regarded as a virtue, and whatever misfortune may occur, a man is rarely heard to complain. The fact is noted, and regarded as inevitable: so it is, and it could not have been otherwise. So that the visitor dwelling among them for a while finds them living to all appearance in careless content.

Man and wife are comrades. The woman may have been purchased for a sledge, or a kayak; perhaps for a bit of iron and a few rusty nails; but she is by no means regarded as a chattel without feelings. Theoretically, the husband has the right to deal with her as he pleases; her very life is in his hands, but in point of fact she is not ill-treated in the slightest degree. She has her own position in the home, which is marked not merely by freedom and liveliness of manner, but also by some authority, especially among the older women.

Children are regarded with a touching devotion, and in times of dearth, the parents regard it as a matter of course that the little ones must first be fed, even though there be not enough for all. Children adopted into a family—bought for some trifle as a speculation—receive the same treatment in every way; the "orphan" type, the wretched, neglected, half-starved father-and-motherless child so common in Greenland, is here entirely unknown.

There is a regular division of labor: it is the man's business to procure food, while his wife attends to all the work of the house. Her work, moreover, is highly esteemed, and a good needlewoman is greatly respected by her fellows. She holds property in her own right; articles such as lamps and cooking pots, sewing requisites and other household goods make up her marriage portion, and she retains them when the marriage is dissolved. Divorce is common where there are no children, and a woman may be married seven or eight times before she settles down for good. Children are regarded by the parents as a great blessing, and serve to knit the two more closely together.

Polygamy exists, but is not common, owing to the scarcity of women. Where a man has more than one wife, it is always a sign of distinction and unusual skill in hunting. Jealousy is not unknown, but wives in one household generally get on amicably together. Polyandry also occurs; a woman may not infrequently have two husbands. A man, of course, is helpless if he has no one to make his clothes, and two friends will occasionally "go shares" in a wife. Such arrangements do not, however, turn out well as a rule, among young people at any rate, and not infrequently end with the killing of one of the men. A woman cannot on her own account invite a man friend to share her husband's rights in her; this is the husband's privilege alone.

"Changing wives" for a short time is of common occurrence. The man's position is altogether one of considerable freedom, and it is regarded as perfectly natural that he should have intercourse with other women as often as any opportunity occurs. Consequently, a woman left alone while her husband is out hunting is exposed to some risk from the advance of other men; should she give way to any such, she will as a rule be punished by her husband. On occasion, however, it is the co-respondent who is called to account, the matter being settled by a bout at fisticuffs. All the men are practised boxers.

The freedom thus claimed by the man in the marital relation is by no means extended to the woman, who in this respect is considered her husband's property. Changing wives is effected without the least regard to the feelings of the respective wives, who are not consulted in the matter at all. Even where a woman definitely wishes to remain "faithful" to her own spouse, her constancy would not only be unappreciated, but would be regarded as disobedience, and punishable as such. It is indeed regarded as a sin: "the spirits do not like it."

Natural desire and economical necessity, combined with the fact that there are not enough women to go round, give rise inevitably to keen competition among the men, as well as to quarrels, not infrequently with a fatal termination.

In earlier times, there was also continual war with other tribes, and there are many stories of killing and even massacre. Since the coming of the white men to the Hudson Bay district, there had been peace with the tribes to the eastward, but relations with those on the west, especially in Victoria Land, were still somewhat strained. And to this day it is customary for sledge parties approaching a village to halt some distance off and send forward a woman as a herald of peace. During my stay among the Ilivilermiut I happened to hear one of the natives there giving an account of an encounter with the Kitdlinermiut which was the more valuable as the man was not speaking to me at all, but addressing himself to his own companions.   The speaker was one Nakasuk, from Adelaide Peninsula, and his account was as follows:

"Many came out towards me.   But without showing sign of fear I drove straight in among them and said:

"'Well, it is only me; and I am nobody much.   If those here wish to kill me, it may be done without much risk, for there is none who would care to take vengeance.'"

"This was received with laughter, and one of the strangers stepped forward to my sledge and said:

"'Are you afraid?'"

"I answered: 'I am past the age when one is afraid of others.   I have come alone into the midst of your camp, as you see; if I had been a coward, I should certainly have stayed at home.'"

"These words were greeted with much approval, and an old white-haired man gave me their welcome. He said:

"'You are a man, and you speak with the words of a man.   You may stay among us without fear.   No one will harm you.'"

The said Nakasuk, it should be noted was a man of middle age, with two wives and several sons, and a man of no little importance among his own people; actually, then, neither so old as to count life worthless himself, nor so insignificant that none would care to avenge his death.   But the little dialogue is eloquent of the general feeling between one tribe and another; it does not do to regard strangers as friends.

I had, indeed, later on, abundant evidence that caution in such respects was needed. At a little settlement called Kunajuk, on the Ellice River, I questioned each of the men as to whether they had taken part in or been subject to acts of violence. The results are set out as follows: and it should be noted that in nearly every case the victims were of the same tribe; the motive was invariably some quarrel about a woman.

Angulalik had taken part in a murderous affray but had not himself killed any one.

Uakuaq had killed Kutdlaq in revenge for the latter's killing of Qaitsaq.

Angnernaq had two wives. One had been stolen away from him, but he had not yet taken vengeance.

Portoq had carried off the wife of a man who had not yet taken vengeance.

Kivggaluk had lost his father and brother—both murdered.

Ingoreq had attempted to murder two women, but failed.

Erfana had killed Kununassuaq, and taken part in the killing of Kutdlaq.

Kingmerut had killed Maggararaq and had also taken part in a murderous attack upon another man.

Erqulik stated that two attempts had been made to carry off his wife, both without success.

Pangnaq, a boy of twelve, had shot his father for ill-treating his mother.

Maneraitsiaq had shot a man in a duel (with bow and arrow) but had not killed him.

Tumaujoq had killed Ailanaluk in revenge for the murder of Mahik.

One may often hear people who know nothing of the life of "savage" tribes suggest that these should be left to live in their own way and not have civilization forced upon them. My own experiences in these particular regions have convinced me that the white man, though bringing certain perils in his train does nevertheless introduce a gentler code, and in many ways lightens the struggle for existence.

On the other hand, one must not judge these children of nature too harshly. They are, in fact, still in but an early stage of evolution as human beings. And we should bear in mind that life in these inhospitable regions, exposed to the cruelest conditions and ever on the verge of extermination is not conducive to excessive gentleness.

CHAPTER XVII

BY the end of September we were ready to start sledging again. A week sufficed to procure the caribou meat needed for our stay and for the journey. We had built two light sledges of the Greenland type, with iron runners, for this autumn work, as the long Hudson Bay sledges with peat-and-ice shoeing would be useless on the soppy new ice of the autumn, when there is no snow. The work was soon done, and we were now only waiting for the ice to come. We were, to tell the truth, impatient to make a start on this new stage of our journey, which should, in the course of the spring, carry us into civilized regions once more. Meantime, we occupied ourselves with short excursions in the neighborhood. I had by this time completed my work as far as the folklore department was concerned, and was able now to turn my attention to a project I had long had in mind, and which, I am happy to say, proved successful.

It was, as many of my readers are doubtless aware, in the region of King William's Land that one of the greatest tragedies in the whole history of Arctic exploration took place. In the year 1845, John Franklin sailed from England with two fine ships, the *Erebus* and the *Terror*, with crews totalling 129 officers and men. The object of the expedition was to find and traverse the North-west Passage, the great sea-route then supposed to connect the Atlantic with the Pacific. But instead of an open channel, they found only straits and sounds blocked with heavy ice. After one winter spent under these conditions, the ship was beset, and had to be abandoned; and an attempt to find a way back to civilization via the Great Fish River resulted in the death, after terrible sufferings, of all those who had not previously perished of disease. Numerous relief and search expeditions were sent out, but it was many years before definite information was obtained, through the Netsilingmiut themselves, as to the fate of the unfortunate explorers.

I have already mentioned meeting, while at Pelly Bay, a native named Iggiararsuk, whose parents had come in contact with members of the Franklin Expedition. And now, here at Malerualik again, I found that several of the older men were able to communicate interesting details as to what had taken place on that occasion. I made careful notes of all they had to say; the account given below is in the words of Qaqortingneq himself. One feature common to all the accounts, which struck me as curious at the time, was the comparative indifference of the narrators to the tragic element in the story; the point that seemed to interest them most was the ignorance that prevailed in those days among their own people as to white men generally, and their goods and gear in particular as viewed in the light of the narrators' own superior knowledge. This was drawn upon to the utmost as a source of comic relief.

I have here omitted the numerous Eskimo names, for the sake of brevity: Qaqortingneq always insisted on giving the names of all concerned, as evidence that his story was to be relied on.

Qaqortingneq's account, then, is as follows:

"Two brothers were out hunting seal to the north-west of Qeqertaq (King William's Land). It was in the spring, at the time when the snow melts about the breathing holes of the seal. They caught sight of something far out on the ice; a great black mass of something, that could not be any animal they knew. They studied it and made out at last that it was a great ship. Running home at once, they told their fellows, and on the following day all went out to see. They saw no men about the ship; it was deserted; and they therefore decided to take from it all they could find for themselves. But none of them had ever before met with white men, and they had no knowledge as to the use of all the things they found.

"One man, seeing a boat that hung out over the side of the ship, cried: 'Here is a fine big trough that will do for meat! I will have this!' He had never seen a boat before, and did not know what it was. And he cut the ropes that held it up, and the boat crashed down endways on to the ice and was smashed.

"They found guns, also, on the ship, and not know-ing what was the right use of these things, they broke away the barrels and used the metal for harpoon heads. So ignorant were they indeed, in the matter of guns and belonging to guns, that on finding some percussion caps, such as were used in those days, they took them for tiny thimbles, and really believed that there were dwarfs among the white folk, little people who could use percussion caps for thimbles.

"At first they were afraid to go down into the lower part of the ship, but after a while they grew bolder, and ventured also into the houses underneath. Here they found many dead men, lying in the sleeping places there; all dead. And at last they went down also into a great dark space in the middle of the ship. It was quite dark down there and they could not see. But they soon found tools and set to work and cut a window in the side. But here those foolish ones, knowing nothing of the white men's things, cut a hole in the side of the ship below the water line, so that the water came pouring in, and the ship sank. It sank to the bottom with all the costly things; nearly all that they had found was lost again at once.

"But in the same year, later on in the spring, three men were on their way from Qeqertaq to the southward, going to hunt caribou calves. And they found a boat with the dead bodies of six men. There were knives and guns in the boat, and much food also, so the men must have died of disease.

"There are many places in our country here where bones of these white men may still be found. I myself have been to Qavdlunarsiorfik [a spit of land on Adelaide Peninsula, nearly opposite the site where Amundsen wintered]; we used to go there to dig for lead and bits of iron. And then there is Kanger-arfigdluk, quite close here, a little way along the coast to the west.

"And that is all I know about your white men who once came to our land, and perished; whom our fathers met but could not help to live."

One day just before the ice had formed, I sailed up with Peter Norberg and Qaqortingneq to Qavdlunarsiorfik, on the east coast of Adelaide Peninsula. And here, exactly in the spot indicated by the Eskimos, we found a number of human bones, unquestionably the last mortal remains of Franklin's men. Some scraps of clothing and footwear scattered about the same spot showed that they were those of white men.

We gathered the poor remains together and built a cairn above them, hoisting two flags at half mast above; their own and ours. And without many words we paid the last honors to the dead.

Here on this lonely spit of land, weary men had toiled along the last stage of their mortal journey. Their tracks are not effaced, as long as others live to follow and carry them farther; their work lives as long as any region of the globe remains for men to find and conquer.

Our first encounter with a fellow human here was not exactly cordial to begin with, but characteristic of these people in their normal relations with other tribes. I was out reconnoitring, when I caught sight of a young man fishing for cod through a hole in the ice. The moment he sighted me, he snatched up his line and scuttled off to the shelter of a rock, whence he presently reappeared with a fine new magazine rifle of the lastest model, evidently ready to make short work of me at the slightest sign of danger. It did not take long, however, to convince him of my complete friendliness as far as he was concerned, and we were soon laughing heartily at the misunderstanding. And he took me along to his village and introduced me almost as if we had known each other for years. From the appearance of the hut and its furnishings it was plain that we were not far from a trading station. Fine woollen blankets of the Hudson's Bay Company's best were spread about among caribou skins more suited to the climate; enamelled ironware had taken the place of the carved and blubber-polished vessels made from driftwood; there were aluminium cooking pots instead of the heavy stone utensils, and even the soapstone lamp, a handsome article in itself, was here replaced by a glittering tin contrivance out of a shop.

On the sleeping place sat a young woman cross-legged, her magnificent caribou furs partly covered and utterly effaced by a horrible print apron. Her hands were covered with cheap-jack rings, a cheap cigarette was held between two fingers, and she breathed out smoke from her nostrils as she leaned back with the languid insolence of a film star and greeted us with a careless "how do you do."

I thanked my lucky stars at that moment that I had visited King William's Land at least before the trading stations had got hold of it; while there was still some native life and folklore left to explore.

HONOR TO THE DEAD

Cairn built above remains of human bodies from the Franklin Expedition which we found in this region.

LEO HANSEN, THE FILM PHOTOGRAPHER

CHAPTER XVIII

AN EXUBERANT FOLK

ON a fine afternoon—it was the 14th of November—just as the chill autumn sun was slipping below the horizon, I drove into the little trading station, which is built in a sheltered creek just at the mouth of Arctic Sound. And here a pleasant reception awaited me, in that I found two fellow-countrymen.

The station was in charge of Mr. H. Clarke, who was, moreover, entrusted with the organization of all the new stations east of Baillie Island. And his assistant was a Danish trapper named Rudolf Jensen, who had been working on his own account for some twenty years in the region of the Mackenzie River delta, and was now engaged in the Company's service. Even more pleased was I to find Leo Hansen, the film photographer who had come up to meet me and share our final spurt through the third and last winter of the expedition. I had written home from Repulse Bay in January, 1923, asking my Committee to send out a film photographer, as I felt convinced that motion pictures would be a valuable addition to the other material we were collecting. He had made an adventurous journey on his own account, first from Copenhagen to New York, then across Canada to Vancouver; from there on board the Hudson's Bay Company's steamer *Lady Kindersley* northward via Point Barrow and Herschel Island to the little trading station at Tree River, in Coronation Gulf, and thence finally to Kent Peninsula by the little schooner that plies, during the brief arctic summer, between the small outlying stations towards Victoria Land. He had brought his technical impedimenta through without mishap, and was eager to get to work.

In any case, we could not afford to make any long stay here; winter and darkness were upon us, and we could not reckon on light enough for motion pictures in December. By the time it was light again in March, we should be well out of the North-west Passage country, among the semi-civilized Eskimos of the Mackenzie Delta; it was essential therefore to make the most of our time now.

The natives here are generally known as Kitdlinermiut; that is, among the other tribes to the eastward. And the use of the word, which means "frontier" or "boundary," among the tribes to the south may doubtless be taken as suggesting that the Kitdlinermiut are "the people farthest to the north." They constitute, as do the Netsilingmiut, one tribe, all the members of which are acquainted, and often meet at the various hunting grounds, but certain subdivisions are reckoned with, according to locality.

There are the Eqalugtormiut, or People of the Rich Salmon Rivers, from the neighborhood of Cambridge Bay in Victoria Land, numbering 98 souls, of which 54 are men and 44 women; the Ahiarmiut, or People Living Away to One Side, on the shores of Queen Maud Gulf, numbering 116, of which 70 are men and 46 women. (The Netsilingmiut call them Asiarmiut, but their own pronunciation of the name is as given above). Then there are the Umingmagtormiut, between Kent Peninsula and Bathurst Inlet, total 50, of which 27 are men and 23 women; and finally the Kiluhigtormiut, or People at the Base of the Deep Fjord, from Bathurst Inlet, numbering 113, of which 68 are men and 45 women. It will be noticed that there is throughout a surplus of men, this again being due to the killing of girl children at birth.

The natives of Victoria Land live mainly by caribou hunting and salmon fishing in summer and autumn. Seal hunting is carried on from the ice between Kent Peninsula and Victoria Land, sometimes extending more to the westward, linking up with the Kiluhigtormiut at Bathurst Inlet, sometimes more to the east, meeting the Netsilingmiut in the neighborhood of Lind Island. The Ahiarmiut also move up to the north-eastward in the spring.

These Ahiarmiut are undoubtedly the most nomadic of the Eskimo tribes, and thus the most skilful and hardy travellers. They will sometimes spend the summer right over in Victoria Land, at Albert Edward Bay, at other times penetrating far into the interior of the mainland, taking part in the great trading assemblies which, prior to the formation of the trading stations, were regularly held in the Akilineq hills, right up in the Barren Grounds. On these occasions they would even journey as far as the forest belt, to procure timber for kayaks and sledges. They are regarded as not only the most skilful, but also the most warlike of the tribes. And their numbers, 70 men against 46 women, also suggest that the reputation is not undeserved, since there are as a matter of fact, more girl children born than boys. At any rate, the dearth of women would be a constant source of strife among themselves, and a constant incitement to the carrying off of women from other tribes.

The Umingmagtormiut live in close contact with the people from Bathurst Inlet, having at certain times of the year the same hunting grounds for seal, and separating only in the spring, when they move up country for the caribou hunting, from May to October. They make for Hope Bay, where the country is hilly, and was once rich in musk ox— hence the name. There are still plenty of caribou in these regions. Only last summer the herds passing Ellice River were so enormous that it took them three days to cross the delta, though the animals were always on the move. The Umingmagtormiut however, profited little by this abundance, as owing to the use of firearms following on the establishment of the trading station at Kent Peninsula, hunting had been carried on to such effect that the caribou no longer dared to cross into Victoria Land or scatter westward as they had done formerly.

The failure of the caribou hunting is a serious matter in a district where so much depends on it. Kent Peninsula itself is well on the way to becoming depopulated.

I had now to choose a field of work for myself from among these various peoples. I was at first chiefly inclined to visit the Eqalugtormiut, but as both Stefansson and Diamond Jenness had already been in Victoria Land, and had described some of the tribes farther to the north-west, I decided finally to patronize the Umingmagtormiut, who were at that time to be found on a small island not far from Kent Peninsula, where they were making preparations for the winter sealing. Here, at any rate I should be among people whom no previous explorer had described.

On the 22nd of November we reached Malerisiorfik, where they had built their camp of snow huts under shelter of a hill. There was a howling blizzard on, but all the men at once turned out to build a hut for us, while the women looked after Anarulunguaq, who was naturally a source of interest. Meat and fish were brought us in abundance far exceeding our present needs; indeed our reception from the first was typical of the unstinted hospitality with which we were treated throughout.

I had not been long among the Umingmagtormiut before I realized that there was a great difference between them and those I had just left farther to the east. A notable feature was their lively good humor and careless, high-spirited manner; we found it necessary, indeed, to check one or two of the more exuberant souls. It is perhaps this trait in their character which has led the other, milder-mannered tribes to fear the Kitdlinermiut. Certainly they had some reason to be proud of them-

selves, for they were greatly superior in many
respects to other natives I met with in Canada.
Little details such as the careful ornamentation of
their hunting implements, especially their bows and
arrows, showed that they had a sense of something
beyond mere hand-to-mouth necessities. Their
cleanliness and orderliness were remarkable, and their
dress, despite the shortage of material, neat almost to
the point of elegance. The women were very clever
with their needle, and paid far more attention to the
decorative side of their dressmaking than did the
Netsilingmiut and Hudson Bay natives. I found
here, moreover, an institution which I had not
previously met with, to wit, that of something
approaching "Sunday clothes"; they had special
sets of garments only worn on special occasions, at
festivals in the great dance hall.

It was not altogether easy, among these kindly
and cheerful souls, to secure the necessary quiet
and relative privacy for my particular work. Our
hut was always full of visitors, and as they all talked
at once, writing was done, to put it mildly, under
difficulties. Both men and women seemed to be born
traders, with a positive passion for bargaining; it
was more than a form of sport with them, it was
really an art. This was useful to us of course, in
as far as it enabled us to add to our ethnographical
collections, but on the other hand, it was not long
before we had bought as much as we felt we could
afford. Our friends here were not over-modest in
pricing their goods. Twenty-five dollars they considered a reasonable figure for a newly killed seal; and

when this was rejected, they would ask for something odd as an alternative; as for instance "the one half" of my rather expensive prism binoculars. They would give away all sorts of things, such as food and even clothing, in the most generous fashion; but as soon as it came to anything in the nature of a deal, their ideas of value were the more extravagant. Fortunately for me, the one thing on which they seemed to set no value at all was their time; and a few comparatively trifling presents were reckoned ample return for whole days of interviewing and interrogation as to implements, culture, ceremonies and belief, and folklore generally.

A detailed account of the manners and customs of the Musk Ox People would necessarily involve much repetition of matter already noted in connection with the other tribes. I will here give briefly some of the more characteristic features which distinguish them from the rest.

They are to begin with the most poetically gifted of all the tribes I met with, and their songs are not restricted to epic and narrative forms, hunting achievements and the like, but include also more lyrical elements in which feeling and atmosphere predominate. Their artistic temperament is reflected, moreover, in their actions, which do not always agree with the white man's ideas of morality. Before passing on to a consideration of their qualities as singers, poets and hunting companions, I will endeavor to show how they are regarded by the Canadian Mounted Police, who once had a patrol up here.

In 1913, two American scientists, Radford and Street, made a sledge trip through the Barren Grounds to the shores of the Arctic. At the base of Bathurst Inlet, wishing to engage assistance for the next stage of the journey, they came into conflict with the natives, with the result that both men were stabbed to death. Radford is described as an excitable person, who thrashed one of the natives for refusing to accompany them, and thus doubtless brought the disaster upon himself. It is not least interesting here to note the account given by the leader of the police patrol as to the Eskimos of Bathurst Inlet. He did not meet the actual murderers himself, but only some others of their tribe and these he characterizes as born thieves, terrible liars and altogether unreliable; indeed he would not be surprised to hear of more murders before long, as any one of them would sell his soul for a rifle.

Oddly enough, Leo Hansen and I had, while at Malerisiorfik, lived for nearly a month with two of the wanted murderers, Hagdlagdlaoq and Qanijaq, the latter, indeed, being our host for part of the time. And we found them both kindly, helpful and affectionate; thoroughly good fellows, all round. It must always be borne in mind that these people take an entirely different view of human life from that which obtains among ourselves.

Mr. Clarke and I once made enquiry among the inhabitants of one encampment, and found that out of fifteen families, there was not a single full-grown man who had not been in some way involved in the killing of another. As I have already noted among

ARCTIC COD

The small arctic cod is found in great numbers round Kent Peninsula, and is used for winter stores as well as for feeding the dogs. The cod is supposed to have an immortal soul which returns to the sea when the body has been eaten. If the fish are laid out in a circle with heads facing inwards toward the hole in the ice, the fisherman will be standing in the middle of a shoal; the cod keep on coming back to be caught on the hook anew.

SETTING OUT IN SEARCH OF A NATIVE VILLAGE

the Netsilingmiut, the man who has killed another is by no means necessarily a bad man on that account; on the contrary, such may often prove to be among the most skilful and useful members of their own little community, whose help and guidance and example are invaluable to their fellows.

At the beginning of December, Netsit, a young Eskimo, expert in folk tales, went off with me on a little journey to visit a camp in Bathurst Inlet, where men were getting ready for the seal hunting. Bathurst Inlet is a great fjord, with mountains on either side, a welcome relief after the monotonous lowlands to the east. The country here reminded me of Greenland but was somehow colder and harsher.

Netsit and I did not talk much on the way; there was nothing to make us communicative in our surroundings, and we had hardly got to know each other as yet. At the end of the first day's run, we found a comfortable snowdrift, and proceeded to build ourselves a hut for the night.

I had with me a few cigarettes, which I kept for special occasions, and this evening, after a meal and a cup of coffee, felt inclined to indulge. I therefore lit a cigarette and gave one to my companion. To my surprise, he did not light up himself, but packed the cigarette carefully away in a piece of rag.

Our snow hut would not perhaps have been considered specially warm and cosy by any save those who had like ourselves been thrashing for ten hours against a bitter wind. But as it was, the tiny blubber lamp seemed to shed a cheerful golden glow all about us; we felt in the mood for a little entertainment.

We made an extra cup of coffee, and I suggested that
Netsit should tell a story or so.   To make ourselves
thoroughly comfortable before starting, we gave the
hut a good coating of loose snow to caulk any possible
leaks, sealed up the entrance so that not a breath of
air could get in, and then settled down in our sleeping
bags, entertainer and audience ready to drop off as
soon as either wished.

Here is one of his stories.

Two men met while out hunting.   One of them had
caught a wolf in a trap, and the other had shot a
caribou with his bow and arrows; each had the skin
of his beast slung over his shoulders.

Said one: "That is a very fine caribou skin you
have there."

And the other answered: "That is a very fine
wolf skin you have there."

And then they fell to talking about the skins, and
the look and the state of them; and at last one said:
"There is more hair on the caribou skin."

"No, no," answered the other, "the wolf has more
hair than the caribou."

And they grew so excited over this question that
the two of them straightway sat down where they
were, and the man with the caribou skin began counting the hairs in it, pulling them out one by one.   And
beside him sat the man with the wolf's pelt, counting
hairs in the same fashion, pulling them out one by one.

But we all know that there are a terrible number of
hairs in the coat of wolf and caribou, if we once start
counting them one by one.   And it took them days.
Day after day the two of them sat there, pulling out
hairs and counting, counting. . . .

And each held that his own had more than the
other's.

"The caribou has more than the wolf," said the one.

"The wolf has more than the caribou," said the other.

And neither would give in, and at last they both died of hunger.

That is what happens when people busy themselves with aimless things and insignificant trifles.

I listened with interest to one story after another, and Netsit, encouraged by my appreciation, went on untiringly. He told a host of stories that evening. Of the Boy who lived with a Bear, The Bear that turned into a Cloud, The Eagle that carried off a Woman; The Woman that would not Marry and Turned into Stone; Navarana, the Eskimo Girl Who Betrayed her People to the Indians; The Man who made Salmon out of Splinters of Wood; and The Inland-dweller with a Dog as Big as a Mountain—and so on and so on. Many of them were but different versions of stories current in Greenland, and one little fable I remembered distinctly having heard almost word for word years ago at my own place in Thule. This uniformity is the more remarkable when we reflect that there has been no sort of intercourse between the two peoples for at least a thousand years.

Another odd little fable is worth noting, not least for the narrator's comment. It is one of the old stories of the Fox and the Wolf.

A fox and a wolf met one day out on a frozen lake.

"I see you catch salmon, Fox," said the wolf. "I wish you would tell me how you manage it."

"I will show you," said the fox. And leading the wolf towards a crack in the ice, it said:

"Just put your tail right down under the water, and wait till you feel a fish biting; then pull it up with a jerk."

And the wolf put its tail down through the ice, while the fox ran off and hid among some bushes on the shore, from where it could see what happened. The wolf stayed there, with its tail in the water, until it froze. Then too late it realized that the fox had been deceiving it; there was no getting the tail free, and at last it had to snap off the tail in order to free itself. Then following on the track of the fox, it came up, eager for revenge. But the fox had seen the wolf coming, and tore a leaf from the bushes and held it in front of its eyes, blinking and winking all the time against the light.

Said the wolf: "Have you seen the fox that made me lose my tail?"

Said the fox: "No, I have had a touch of snow-blindness lately, and can hardly see at all." And it held up the leaf and blinked and winked again.

And the wolf believed it, and went off on the track of another fox.

This seemed an odd sort of ending, and I said as much. "What is it supposed to mean exactly?" I asked.

"H'm, well," answered Netsit, "we don't really trouble ourselves so much about the meaning of a story, as long as it is amusing. It is only the white men who must always have reasons and meanings in everything. And that is why our elders always say we should treat white men as children who always want their own way. If they don't get it, they make no end of a fuss."

I left it at that.

CHAPTER XIX

THE PLAY OF SPIRIT

WE started out again the following morning before
it was light. When we had been driving for a
couple of hours, a little interruption took place, which
rather mystified me at the time. We were driving
across a big fjord, more than 60 km. wide at this
part, and were just passing a steep rocky island, that
stood out in the gloom like a huge black monument
against the white snow. Suddenly Netsit begged me
to halt for a moment. I held in the dogs as well as I
could, and he proceeded to climb the mass of rock.

He stopped some distance up, and knelt down;
there was barely light enough to make out what he
was doing. I saw him digging a hole in the snow
with his knife; then he took out the cigarette I had
given him the night before, placed it, with a couple of
matches, carefully in the hole and covered all over
with snow once more. Through the howling of the
gale I could hear him reciting something, ending up
with a few words to call attention to the valuable gift
he had just deposited in the snow. I wrote down the
earlier part afterwards: it was as follows:

> Big Man, big Man,
> Make smooth your big hands
> And your big feet,

Make them swift-running
And look far ahead.
Big Man, big Man,
Smooth out your thoughts
And look far ahead.
Big Man, big Man,
Let fall your weapons now.

Then he came running back to me and we continued our journey.

What had happened, as I afterwards found, was this. He had been paying a visit to the grave of his father, Ilatsiaq, who had been a great wizard in his time. Netsit thought that the gift of so unusual a luxury as a cigarette would surely have power to call up the soul of the dead man, and secure his protection for us against the troublesome weather we were having. It is generally held that the souls of the dead remain, for the first few years after death, in the vicinity of the grave. "Grave," however, is hardly the proper word in this case, as no grave is dug, the bodies being simply laid out and left to the mercy of prowling beasts. The immortal soul, however, can look after itself, and needs no shelter.

The verses noted above were a formula designed to propitiate the spirit of the departed. They have been handed down from very ancient times for use on special occasions, and are supposed to be highly effective.

And certainly, in our case, it appeared as if the lamented Ilatsiaq had appreciated his cigarette. For on the following morning, on cutting a hole in the side of our hut to see what the weather was like, we found to our delight that it was a fine, calm, frosty day.

Two more of the same sort followed, with delicious rest at night in fresh snow huts, and we reached the base of the fjord, where the "band of murderers" were understood to be. On the third day, about noon, we came upon three sledges loaded up with firewood, in charge of a party of boys and girls. The young people answered our greetings cheerfully, and informed us where the village lay; it was a big one, by their account: "Inuit amigaitut"—a whole world of people, they said. And soon, for the first time in many long weeks, we were driving down a regular track worn deep by the passing and repassing of many sledges.

The place was, certainly, a big one by Eskimo standards: over thirty huts stood grouped round the sides of a natural amphitheatre, and in the midst, one glittering white hall bigger than all the rest. This was the Dance-house, Temple, and centre of festivities and solemnities generally; built out of a snow drift in the waste, by these ruffians of sinister repute.

Smoke rose from the chimneys—yes, there were chimneys, ugly black things sticking up brutally through the white snow roofs from the patent stoves within; spoiling the picture no doubt, but a welcome sight to the half-frozen traveller for all that.

The place seems quite a metropolis after what we have been accustomed to for months past; and when the inmates come tumbling out of their burrows we find ourselves in the midst of a crowd. And a

very noisy, boisterous crowd, though good-humored
enough when one knows how to deal with them.
The natives here are by no means the shy and peaceable creatures that one finds in Greenland. They
are accustomed to treat visitors without ceremony,
and see no reason to alter their ways for a white man.
Indeed, the appearance of one all alone seems to be
taken as an excellent opportunity for a little rough
horseplay.

One of them tries to take my pipe out of my mouth
—but very soon learns he had better not! Another
pulls at my tunic, a bob-tailed arrangement of the
Cape York type; but soon finds out his mistake.
And when I begin unloading, preparatory to feeding
my dogs, the women come pressing forward and
begging for blubber. Their own seal-hunting season
has not yet begun, and the fresh, pink blubber in
hard-frozen slabs makes their mouths water. I had
to keep them back.

"Do you think I have come all this way to feed
you with blubber? This is for my dogs; and you
have men enough to look after you. Why don't you
start getting seal for yourselves if you are so anxious
for blubber?"

There was a general laugh at this. But I was alone
against the crowd of them, for Netsit was their kinsman more than my companion, and looked on highly
amused at it all.

"Who are you? Are you a trader come to buy
foxes?"

"I have come to have a look at *you*, and see what
you are like inside!"

At which they laugh more uproariously than before. But one of the elders answers, a little hesitatingly, not knowing whether to take my words in jest or earnest:

"H'm. Well, you will find all manner of folk here. Some of them are quite nice to look at, but most are ugly, and you will find little pleasure in looking at their faces."

All this was very amusing as far as it went.

I realized, however, that it was essential to show them a bold front, if I wished to keep them in hand, and therefore came straight to the point.

"I have come to you alone, though ill things are said of you in other parts. It is not many years since two white men were killed here; and the Police do not speak well of you to travellers. But I am not afraid of meeting you alone, as you can see."

"It was not our fault! It was the white men who began the quarrel. We are peaceable enough, only somewhat given to fun; fond of singing and laughter, and with no evil thought as long as we are not afraid. You are our friend and need fear no harm."

Certainly, they did their best now to set me at my ease. I was led to a snow hut in which quarters had been assigned to us both. Our hostess, Qernartoq, received us with the greatest hospitality; though I afterwards learned that her husband had been killed by Netsit's father! This however did not appear to affect our friendly relations in the least.

I had put on my sternest manner in order to keep the more impertinent at a distance. But I could not keep up the pose very long. A woman came up to me, and placing one hand on my shoulder, looked me full in the face and said:

"Tell me, stranger; are you the sort of man who has never a smile for a woman?"

I laughed aloud; I could not help it. And with that the ice was broken all round.

I spent the first few hours going visiting from house to house. All were of the same type, fine large snow huts, but altered out of all recognition as Eskimo dwellings by the metal stoves and their long chimney pipes sticking up through the roof. They used brushwood for fuel, which sent out a powerful heat, but the snow roof was so cleverly constructed that it hardly dripped at all. Here and there one might find a hole melted through, but the draught was pleasant rather than the reverse.

In the evening there was an entertainment in the dance house, which was big enough to hold sixty with ease. It was built of snow like the rest, only on a larger scale. Niches were cut in the walls half way up, and small blubber lamps placed in these, throwing a weird light over the assembly. In the middle of the hall stood the leader of the revels with a huge drum in his hand, and round him the men and women constituting the chorus. The drum is held in the left hand; and consists of a whole caribou hide stretched on a thick wooden hoop; its weight alone is no trifle, and it needs considerable physical strength to take the part of drummer, dancer, and leader of the chorus all at once, often for an hour or more at a time. The dancing, which consists of hops and leaps and writhings of the body, steadily accompanied by the drum, is likewise exhausting, and the performers are limp with heat and exertion when their "turn" comes to an end.

Everything is done to make these entertainments in the dance hall as festive as possible; both men and women wear special costumes, gaily decorated with patterns of fine white skin. The men fasten white ermine on back and shoulders, the tails fluttering as they move; both men's and women's boots are beautifully embroidered in white and red. The headdress is a kind of patchwork helmet, with the beak of a loon sticking up like a spike on top.

I had never heard spirit songs delivered by a chorus before, and a few of those peculiar to this tribe were included in the programme "by request." Later in the evening, songs of recent date were given, turn and turn about with "classics" by the ancient masters. I managed later to write down the text of all these songs, of which a few are here given. It should be noted, however, that when sung, the same lines are constantly repeated, so that a text of but a few verses may last half an hour or more.[1]

SPIRIT SONGS

I

Spirit from the Air,
Come, come swiftly hither,
Thy wizard here
Is calling thee.

[1] I took out a phonograph with me from Denmark with a view to recording the melodies of native songs; unfortunately, however, an essential part of the mechanism was lost early in the expedition, and could not be replaced.

Come and bite ill-luck to death,
Spirit from the Air
Come, come swiftly hither.

I rise,
Rise up amid the spirits,
Wizards help me,
Lift me up amid the spirits.

Child, O Child, great Child,
Rise up and come hither
Child, Child,
Great Child.   Little one,
Rise up among us!

II

The little seamew
Hovers above us,
Staring and scolding.
Its head is white.
Its beak opens gaping,
The little round eyes
See far, see keenly.
Qutiuk, qutiuk!

The little tern
Hovers above us;
Staring and scolding.
Its head is black.
Its beak opens gaping,
The little round eyes
See far, see keenly.
Iyoq—iyoq!

The big raven
Hovers above us
Staring and scolding.
Its head is black.
Its beak is sharp, as if it had teeth.
Qara—qara!

III

Whither is my soul gone?
Let me fetch thee, let me fetch thee!
It is gone to the southward of those
Who live to the southward of us.
Let me fetch thee,
Let me fetch thee!

Whither is my soul gone away?
It is gone to the eastward of those
Who live to the eastward of us.
Let me fetch thee,
Let me fetch thee.

Whither is my soul gone away?
It is gone to the northward of those
Who live northward of us.
Let me fetch thee,
Let me fetch thee!

Whither is my soul gone away?
It is gone to the westward of those
Who live westward of us.
Let me fetch thee,
Let me fetch thee!

IV

I will visit
Unknown woman,
Search out hidden things
Behind the man.
  Let the boot-thong hang loose—
Seek thou under man
And under woman!
Smooth out the wrinkled cheeks,
Smooth wrinkles out.

I walked on the ice of the sea,
  Seal were blowing at the blowholes—
Wondering I heard
The song of the sea
And the great sighing of the new-formed ice.
Go, then, go!
Strength of soul brings health
To the place of feasting.

A Dead Man's Song

(Aijuk's song, dreamed by Paulinaoq.)

I am filled with joy
Whenever the dawn rises over the earth
And the great sun
Glides up in the heavens.

But at other times
I lie in horror and dread
Of the creeping numberless worms
That eat their way in through hollowed bone
And bore eyes away.

In fear I lie, remembering:
Say, was it so beautiful on earth?
Think of the winters
When we were anxious
For soles to our footwear
Or skins for our boots:
Was it so beautiful?

In fear and in horror I lie,
But was I not always troubled in mind,
Even in the beautiful summer,
When the hunting failed,
And there was dearth of skins
For clothing and sleeping?
Was it so beautiful?

In fear and in horror I lie
But was I not always troubled in mind
When I stood on the sea ice
Wretched beyond measure
Because no fish would bite?
Or was it so beautiful
When I flushed with shame and dismay
In the midst of the gathering,
And the chorus laughed
Because I forgot my song and its words?
Was that so beautiful?

Say, was it so beautiful on earth?
Here, I am filled with joy
Whenever the dawn rises over the earth
And the great sun
Glides up in the heavens.

But at other times
I lie in horror and dread
Of the creeping numberless worms
That eat their way in through hollowed bone
And bore eyes away.

AN OLD SONG OF THE SUN AND THE MOON AND THE FEAR
OF LONELINESS.

There is fear
In the longing for loneliness
When gathered with friends,
And, longing to be alone.
Iyaiya-yaya!

There is joy
In feeling the summer
Come to the great world,
And watching the sun
Follow its ancient way.
Iyaiya-yaya!

There is fear
In feeling the winter
Come to the great world
And watching the moon
Now half-moon, now full,
Follow its ancient way.
Iyaiya—yaya!

Whither is all this tending?
I would I were far to the eastward.
And yet I shall never again
Meet with my kinsman.
Iyaiya-yaya!

The northern lights had spread a belt of wonderful living color over the hills behind the village. And as I walked back to my hut, with the songs still ringing in my ears, I could not help feeling a sympathy, almost a tenderness, for these wild simple folk. Bandits and murderers? I could not feel them so. They had received me with the utmost hospitality, and done all in their power to please and entertain me. And these songs of theirs, their harmless fun, and a wistful sense of beauty, of loneliness, all struggling for expression, showed them rather as children in the wide strange world; at least as human beings like ourselves.

CHAPTER XX

I HAD now enough material for a whole monograph on the Musk Ox People. There were the four main sections: the Willow-folk or Caribou Eskimo, the Hudson Bay tribes, the Netsilingmiut or Seal Eskimo, and now the Musk Ox People. It remained to procure supplementary material from the western tribes of the Mackenzie Delta, Alaska, Bering Straits and Siberia. The country between—that is, the coast from Bathurst Inlet to Baillie Island—had been visited and described by Stefansson's Expedition during his first visit to these regions, and later by Dr. Diamond Jenness, Ethnographer to Stefansson's last Expedition, the so-called Canadian Arctic Expedition, 1913–18. Few have understood the Eskimo so well as Stefansson, or had the power of living their life and entering into their way of thought; and no modern writer has given a more thorough and detailed description of an Eskimo tribe than Jenness. I could therefore with an easy conscience pass lightly over this section.

From my last field of work to the next was a distance of something like 2200 kilometres, which had to be covered as rapidly as possible, though at the same time I should have to make halts on the way, and form some acquaintance with the natives for purposes of comparison.

We divided the dogs into two teams, small teams they were, considering our load. I and Anarulung-uaq had to make do with six of the best animals, taking, however, the smaller of the two sledges, and a comparatively light load, of some 300 kilos. Miteq had ten dogs, and was to drive Leo Hansen with his camera and other impedimenta, their load amounting I should say to something approaching 500 kilos. Thanks to the invaluable method of ice-shoeing, however, we were able from the first to travel at a fine smart pace, which brought us through well up to time.

We started in a smother of snow, that drove right in our faces, with the thermometer at minus 42. Our first objective was Malerisiorfik, where we had to pick up some of our effects left there from our previous visit. Here we were stormbound, but managed to get away on the 18th of January, though it was still snowing hard. On the 21st we rounded Cape Barrow, and after following the coast—low granite rock for the most part—for a few hours, we shaped our course for a high, steep promontory some distance ahead. Before we reached it, however, a fog came down and we were beginning to feel thoroughly lost, when the dogs got scent of something, and about three o'clock we drove into a village out on the ice, and were received with great friendliness. The place, we were informed, was called Agiaq, and the people styled themselves Agiarmiut; there were 46 of them in all, 25 men and 21 women.

Our recent experiences had led us to adopt a certain reserve as a protection against the exuberance of the native welcome; here, however, we were pleasantly surprised to find our hosts quiet and modest almost to the verge of shyness. We found a snowdrift close handy, and managed, with their help, to get a hut built just in time, for it was growing dark, and there was a blizzard coming up. It came; and kept us hung up there from the afternoon of the 22nd until the 26th. All that time we were literally imprisoned in our snow hut, which threatened every now and them to fall to pieces or be torn away by the gale, as the snow from which it was made had been too soft to start with, but we had not had time to pick and choose. We had to dash out every now and then to patch up a threatened spot, and it was no easy matter in such a storm. The blocks we cut crumbled between our fingers.

During these four days, anyone who came to visit us had to come armed with a snow knife in case of getting lost; it was only a matter of five minutes from their huts to ours, but all the same, a man might go to his death. Despite the risk, we had a constant stream of visitors, men, women and children, including infants in arms, or in the amaut that answers to it. And I found myself once more admiring the manner in which these people adapt themselves to their surroundings. Just fancy—you go off to visit a friend who lives five minutes' walk from your door. If you lose your way it is death; unless you have your snow knife, which of course you are not foolish enough to leave behind. Armed with this, you have only to build yourself another little house by the roadside, and here you can settle down in safety, if not in comfort, until the weather clears. People at home might think it a troublesome way of going visiting; but here it is considered all in the day's work, or the day's play, and all adds to the excitement of the visit.

On the third evening we were formally invited to a spirit seance in one of the huts. The invitation was issued by one Kingiuna, a typical blond Eskimo, with a bald head, reddish beard, and a touch of blue about the eyes. We were given to understand that the stormchild, Narsuk, was angry, and it was proposed to ascertain if possible what had been done to offend him, with a view to propitiation, that the storm might be called off.

It took us something like half an hour, I really believe, to cover the half kilometre we had to go, so fierce was the storm. When at last we arrived, we found ourselves in a snow hut some 4 metres by 6, but so high that the roof had to be supported by two long pieces of driftwood, that looked most imposing as black pillars in this white hall. There was ample room for all; and the children, who had been brought along by their respective parents, played hide and seek round the pillars while the preparations were being made.

These preparations consisted mainly of a banquet, the menu comprising dried salmon, blubber, and frozen seal meat, the last served up, not in joints, but in whole carcases, from which slabs were cut with axes. This frozen meat has to be breathed on at every mouthful, to take the chill off; otherwise it is apt to take the skin off one's lips and tongue.

"Fond of eating, these people," whispered Miteq, with his mouth full of frozen blood, "stand anything; and make great festivals anywhere."

And indeed it needed a good digestion to tackle the food, as it needed cheerful courage to feast under such conditions.

The officiating angakoq was one Horqarnaq, a young man with bright, intelligent eyes and little hasty movements. He looked the picture of honesty; and it was perhaps on that account that it took him so long to get into a trance. Before starting, he explained to me that he had not many helping spirits. There was the ghost of his dead father, with *his* helping spirit, a kind of ogre out of the stories, a giant with claws that could shear through a human body; then there was a figure he had carved for himself out of soft snow, in the shape of a human being; this spirit always came at his call. A fourth mysterious helper was a red stone called Aupila-languaq, which he had found once when out caribou hunting; it looked exactly like a head and neck together, and when he shot a caribou close by, he made a necklace for it from the long hairs of the caribou's neck. In this way he made his helping spirit an angakoq itself, and thus doubled its power.

These were the spirits he was now about to invoke. And he began by declaring very modestly that he knew he could never do it. The women stood round encouraging him with easy assurance.

"Oh, yes you can; it's easy for you because you are so strong."

But he went on repeating the same thing: "It is difficult to speak the truth; it is a hard thing to call forth the hidden powers."

For a long time matters remained like this, but at last he began to show signs of the approaching trance. Then the men joined the circle, pressing in closer around him, and all shouted encouragement, praising his strength and spiritual powers.

The wizard's face is strained, his eyes are wide open, as if staring out into a vast distance; now and again he swings round on his heels, and his breath comes in little jerky gasps. He seems hardly to recognize those about him.

"Who are you?" he cries.

"We are your own people."

"Are you all here?"

"Yes; all but those two who have gone on a journey to the eastward."

But he does not seem to hear, and asks again and again:

"Who are you? Are you all here?"

Then suddenly he fixes his gaze upon Miteq and myself, and he cries:

"Who are the strangers?"

"They are men travelling round the earth; men we are glad to see. They are friends; and they too would gladly hear what wisdom you can give us."

Again he goes round the circle, looking into the eyes of each as he passes, they stare wildly around,

and at last, in the despairing voice of one who can do
no more, he cries, "I cannot, I cannot!"

Then comes a gurgling sound, interpreted as
meaning that a helping spirit has taken possession of
his body.   He is now no longer master of himself, but
dances about among the rest, calling on his dead
father who is become an evil spirit.   It is only a year
since his father died, and the widow, who is present,
groans aloud and endeavors to comfort her son in his
frenzy, but the rest will not have it; he is to go on, go
on, and let the spirit speak.

He then mentions several spirits of the dead, that
he sees before him among the living audience.   He
describes their appearance, this old man and that old
woman whom he himself has never seen, and calls on
those present to say who they are.

The audience are at a loss; there is a moment of
silence, then a whispering among the women; one
mentions hesitatingly this name or that.

"No, no, that is not right."

The men look on in silence, the women growing
more excited, all save the widow, who sits weeping
and rocking from side to side.   Then suddenly an
old woman who had been silent up to now, jumps
up and utters the names that none as yet have dared
to mention; a man and a woman from Nagjugtoq,
who died quite recently.

"Qanorme."

"Qanorme!"

"They are the ones," cries Horqarnaq in a strange
gasping voice, and a feeling of dread takes possession
of all at the thought of those now spirits who but a

few days before were living and moving among them in the flesh. And to think it was they who were causing the storm. The terror spread through the house; the mystery of life hung heavy upon all; here were happenings beyond their understanding.

Outside the storm was raging in black darkness, and even the dogs, who are not allowed inside the houses as a rule, are suffered now to seek shelter and warmth. A man and a woman, who live next door, but had lost their way, come in with mouths and eyes choked with snow. It is the third day of the storm. They have no meat for tomorrow, no fuel; and the threatening disaster seems all at once nearer and more real. The storm child is wailing, the women are moaning, the men murmur incomprehensible words.

After about an hour of shouting and invocation of unknown forces, the seance takes a new turn. To us, who have not previously assisted at a taming of the storm-god, the next development is horrible to see. Horqarnaq leaps out and flings himself upon poor inoffensive old Kingiuna, who was singing a little hymn on his own account, grabs him by the throat with a swift snatching movement, and flings him backward and forward among the rest. This goes on for some time; with hoarse gasps from both men at first; but after a while Kingiuna chokes, and can utter no sound save a faint wheezing; then all in a moment he too seems to fall into a trance. He makes no resistance now, but suffers himself to be swung this way and that; Horqarnaq drags him about the place, heedless of any risk to themselves or the rest. Some of the men place themselves in front of the lamps, to guard against accidents, the women drag their children up out of the way—and so the ghastly play goes on, until Horqarnaq, himself exhausted, or satisfied that he has done enough, drops his victim in a heap on the floor.

Thus the wizard battles with the spirit of the storm—a fellow-man being made to represent it. Finally, he stoops down over the still unconscious Kingiuna, and fixing his teeth in his neck, shakes him viciously, as a dog shakes another beaten in fight.

Then he continues his wild capers, the rest looking on in silence, until at last the frenzy seems to die out, and he kneels down beside his victim stroking the body to bring it back to life. Slowly the other awakens, and rises unsteadily to his feet, but he is hardly up before the wizard is upon him once more, and the whole dreadful business is repeated until Kingiuna again lies helpless and insensible as before. Yet a third time he is "killed" in this horrible mummery; that man's mastery of the elements may be established beyond question. But when he comes to life for the third time, it is Horqarnaq who collapses, and Kingiuna now takes the active part. The old fellow, with his unwieldly bulk, seems unfitted for anything but a comic part, yet the wild fierce look in his eyes, and the horrid bluish tinge that has not yet faded from his face, are impressive enough; he looks like one dragged back from the clutches of death. All step back involuntarily as with his foot on Horqarnaq's chest he tells what he sees. With fluent speech and a voice quivering with emotions he begins:

"The heavens are full of naked beings rushing through the air. Naked men and women, rushing along and raising the storm, raising the blizzard.

"You hear it? A rushing as of the wings of mighty birds, up in the air. It is the fear of naked beings, the flight of naked men.

"The spirit of the air drives forth the storm, the spirit sends the whirling snow out over the earth, and the helpless storm-child, Narsuk, shakes the lungs of the air with its weeping.

"Hear the crying of the child in the shrieking of the storm!

"And see now—there among the hosts of naked ones in flight is one, a single figure, a man pierced all into holes by the wind. His body is but a mass of holes, and the wind howls through them—Tchee-u-u-u; tchee-u-u-u. Hear! He is the mightiest of them all.

"But my helping spirit shall bring him to a stand; bring all to a stand. Here he comes, striding down sure of victory towards me. He will conquer, he will conquer—Tchee-u-u-u, Tchee-u! Hark to the wind! Hist! hst, hst! See the spirits, the storm, the wild weather, rushing by above us, with a sound as the wings of mighty birds!"

At these words Horqarnaq gets up from the floor, and the two wizards, their faces now transfigured after what has passed, join in a simple hymn to the Mother of the Sea:

Woman, Great Woman down there!
Turn it aside, turn it aside from us, that evil!

Come, come spirit of the deep,
One of thine earth-dwellers
Calls upon thee;
Prays thee to bite our enemies to death,
Come, Spirit of the Deep!

As soon as the two had sung it once, all present joined in a wailing, imploring chorus; they had no idea of what they were praying to, but they felt the power of the ancient words their fathers had sung. They had no food to give their children on the morrow; and they prayed the powers to make a truce for their hunting, to send them food for their children.

And so great was the suggestive power of what had passed, in this wild place too near to the elemental forces, that we could almost see it all; the air alive with hurrying spirit forms, the race of the storm across the sky, hosts of the dead whirled past in the whirling snow; wild visions attended by that same rushing of mighty wings of which the wizards had spoken.

So ended this battle with the storm; a contest between the spirit of man and the forces of nature. And those present could go home and sleep in peace, confident that the morrow would be fine.

And in point of fact, so it proved. Through dazzling sunlight over firmly packed snow we drove off on the following day, arriving in the afternoon at Tree River, where there is a station of the Hudson's Bay Company and a police post of the C. M. P. We were very kindly received by the Company's representative, Mr. MacGregor, with whom we stayed for two days.

THE RETURN OF THE SUN

Sunrise over the North-west Passage near Kent Peninsula, January. Darkness is now at an end, and the long sledge journeys can begin.

THE HUNTING CAMP NEAR BERNARD HARBOR

A farewell banquet was given in our honor. All wore "evening dress," special costumes reserved for occasions of ceremony. The illustration shows a scene from the vocal entertainment which started in the morning and lasted until the following day. In the foreground, the leader wearing a "spiked helmet"—the spike is the beak of a loon. The chorus of men and women gathered round him.

Tree River is a pleasant little place, set in beautiful hills. No natives lived here except an old couple who were to be taken down to Herschel Island as witnesses in a murder case. Murder unfortunately is not rare in these regions, and Tree River, peaceful as it seemed, had a year or so before been the scene of dramatic events.

Five people had been murdered near Kent Peninsula, the original cause of the trouble being that one of the attacking party wanted to steal another's wife, who, however, was killed in the struggle, together with her husband, the defenders making so stout a resistance, that the assailants found themselves at the finish fighting for their lives. Among them were two young men one Alekamiaq, only 16 or 17 years old, the other, Tatamerana, but little older. They were captured by the police, but Alekamiaq managed to shoot the corporal who arrested him, together with a trader living near. Before he could escape however, two sledges from a neighboring settlement came up; and he was taken off at once to Herschel Island, the chief police post of the district. Here he and Tatamerana lived for a couple of years, acting as a kind of servants to the police, while they were waiting to be tried. They were allowed to move about freely among the other natives and the white men; no one felt any fear of them; they were indeed rather liked in the place.

It was a lengthy and difficult business to get the two murderers hanged. Judges, advocates, and witnesses had to be brought from a long distance. The murder of the two white men took place in 1922 and it was not until last winter—in February if I remember rightly—that the murderers were hanged.

The trial with its ceremonial made no great impression on them; they seemed to have an easy conscience in the matter. Both men were condemned to death; but the sentence had first to be confirmed by the supreme authority in Canada. At last one evening, when they were busy making salmon nets, they were informed that they were to be hanged at three the next morning. Young Alekamiaq received the information with a smile; Tatamerana asked huskily for a glass of water, but as soon as he had drunk it he was himself again, and ready to meet his fate. Just before going to execution, they gave the Police Inspector's wife some little carvings of walrus tusk, as souvenirs, to show they bore no ill will against the police. Both met their death calmly and without sign of fear.

I was informed that this execution had cost Canada something like $100,000; among other expensive items being the cost of the executioner, who had to be brought up and kept there all the winter, as none of the Police themselves would have any hand in this part of the work.

One of the two criminals had an old father living at Kent Peninsula, who, learning that his son was to be sent to the eternal hunting grounds, decided that he could not let him go alone. And after three attempts, he managed to kill himself, fulfilling what he conceived to be his duty to his son.

CHAPTER XXI

AMONG THE BLOND ESKIMOS

ON the 28th of January we left our kindly hosts at Tree River and crossed over Coronation Gulf to Cape Krusenstern. The wind was like cold steel, and the snow drove right in our faces. It is costly travelling on a day like this, as one cannot avoid getting frost sores in the face, and these are a constant source of trouble and annoyance throughout the rest of the winter. We reached Cape Krusenstern on the 30th after a struggle with pressure ridges and fantastic barriers of ice, through all of which to our surprise, the ice shoeing held. The natives here came literally tumbling over us, in the most unceremonious fashion; some of them scrambled up on to our sledges, and I was amused to see them sitting there with their harpoons, looking like halberdiers on guard. They somehow got the idea that Leo Hansen was a very great personage whom we were escorting into the white men's country, and as we approached their village, the ones who had met us first shouted out without the least reserve the most amusing remarks about ourselves, telling the others to come and look at the new sort of travellers they had found. They must be something very odd, for they did not appear to be either traders or police!

It never seemed to occur to them that we could understand what they said, and they commented frankly on my big nose and Anarulunguaq's fat cheeks. Our dresses, appearance and equipment were criticized in like fashion, exactly as if we were a travelling circus making entry into some village miles from anywhere.

I stood it for a while, and then gave them, briefly but pithily, my own opinion of *their* manners, appearance and order of intelligence, more particularly their simplicity in taking it for granted that we could not understand them. There was a moment of dead silence when I had finished; all stared at us with eyes and mouths agape, then gave vent to a howl of laughter. They were not accustomed to meeting white men who understood their language. But the mistake left no ill-feeling; on the contrary, we were friends at once. We stayed here a day, and I went through my regular list of questions, which, from long practice, enabled me to get quite a lot of information, while Leo Hansen was busy with his pictures.

On the 1st of February we arrived at Bernhard Harbour, where the Hudson's Bay Company has a station. Their representative here proved to be a fellow-countryman of mine, Peder Pedersen, of Loegstoer, who had left Denmark 42 years before and spent about a generation in the Arctic. He received us with the greatest cordiality, and though he spoke Danish with some hesitation at first, it was not long before it all came back to him.

We were now anxious to get through to the

OUR HOST, QANIGAG, A TYPICAL SPECIMEN OF THE "BLOND" ESKIMO OF THESE
REGIONS

Mackenzie Delta without delay, and therefore put in a couple of days here getting a tent made; a double tent which we could easily warm. Single tents are useless in extreme cold, as a layer of rime forms on the inside and lets loose a shower of frost as soon as the canvas is touched.

Bernard Harbor was at one time the headquarters of the Canadian Arctic Expedition under the capable leadership of Dr. Martin Anderson. I could therefore with an easy conscience deal summarily with this district, as ethnographical studies had already been systematically carried out by my predecessors. I contented myself therefore with going through the afore-mentioned list of questions, which gave me all I needed for comparison with my notes from elsewhere. We then hurried out to a big hunting camp near Sutton and Liston Island, which the Eskimos call Ukatdlit, in Dolphin and Union Strait. I stayed here a week and brought my journals up to date.

The Eskimos of these regions, like those farther east, have no regular chiefs, but each settlement has one man who acts as a sort of general adviser and leader in common undertakings. The leading man here was Ikpakhuhak, who, with his jovial wife Hikilaq, is described at length in Diamond Jenness' excellent work *The Life of the Copper Eskimos.*

The encampment consisted of twenty large and roomy snow huts, and was built near a small island called Ahongahungaoq, whence the people called themselves Ahongahungarmiut; they numbered 83 souls, of which 46 were men and 37 women; a considerable population for one village in these regions. Most of them were from Victoria Land where they had lived until recently under the name of Puivdlermiut, but owing to the gradual thinning out of the game in those parts, they had moved across to the mainland, hunting the territory between Great Bear Lake and the coast north of Stapylton Bay. My actual hosts belonged to this contingent; but there were also representatives of the original mainland tribes, and others again from Prince Albert Sound and Minto Inlet, so that I had here an excellent opportunity of collecting information from a considerable area at one spot, and was saved the necessity of visiting Prince Albert Sound.

The camp here, at Dolphin and Union Strait, marks the boundary of the so-called eastern Eskimos, the whole range of country between Inman River and Baillie Island being inhabited only by trappers or immigrant Eskimos from Alaska. At Baillie Island we have the beginning of an entirely new Eskimo culture, closely associated with hunting by sea, and consequently superior in material respects, while the natives to the eastward are still only in the initial stages of development to the coastal form, and are in fact very nearly allied to the Caribou Eskimos.

Nearly all movement among the Eskimos of the North-west Passage seems as far as tradition serves, to have run in an easterly direction, and occasionally by certain definite routes to the southward, where the diffierent tribes exchanged needful commodities. There is no record of any journeys to the west, toward Cape Bathurst, and all that was known about the country on the west was that it were said to be inhabited.

The whole of the area here described had a special source of wealth in the deposits of pure copper, which are found at Bathurst Inlet and in parts of Victoria Land, especially Prince Albert Sound. This copper was used for making knives, ice-picks and harpoon-heads, which were of great value when trading with other tribes. Diamond Jenness has therefore rightly grouped all these tribes under the name of Copper Eskimos.

These are the same people who suddenly sprang into fame some years back as the "blond Eskimos." They were discovered in 1905 by a Danish adventurer named Klinkenberg, who, setting out from Herschel Island in a small schooner, was driven out of his course and landed at a spot which later proved to be Minto Inlet. On his return, he told of a strange people he had met, who spoke the Eskimo tongue and lived in the Eskimo fashion, but in appearance looked exactly like Scandinavians. Klinkenberg's report led Vilhjalmur Stefansson, with the zoologist Dr. Martin Anderson, to set out on a new expedition, lasting from 1908–12, and described in his book *My Life with the Eskimos*.

In the year 1910 Stefansson had his headquarters at Langton Bay, and travelled eastward, accompanied by the Eskimo Nakutsiaq, until he encountered natives near Cape Bexley. And here a curious thing happened. The people here took him for an Eskimo himself, because he spoke the Eskimo tongue, altogether heedless of his appearance, which of course was that of a white man. When he asked them how it was they could not see at once that he was not an

Eskimo they answered that he did not look very much different from some of the Eskimos of Victoria Land where it was very common to find people with grey eyes and fair hair and beard. Stefansson then at once determined to visit a particular spot indicated, and his observations led him to formulate a theory that some of those Norsemen who had been last heard of in Greenland might possibly have made their way to these regions, and intermarried with the Eskimos there.

I admit that we do find, among the Copper Eskimos as well as among those farther east towards King William's Land, a surprisingly large number of types differing in appearance from the ordinary Eskimo; this however, is hardly sufficient to support a hypothesis which claims them as descendants of Norsemen from Greenland. Stefansson suggests that the distance from Greenland to Victoria Land is no hindrance. To this I cannot agree. The ancient Norsemen were great sailors, and did get far to the north with their vessels, but they were hardly well enough up in sledge travelling for such a journey. The last certain record of their movements to the northward is the runic inscription at Upernivik. And without a thorough knowledge of the methods of travelling in the Arctic, the distance between Greenland and Victoria Land becomes a very serious obstacle. Distance is after all a question of transport facilities; and the fate of the Franklin Expedition and the many which followed it afford the best proof of how impossible it would have been for the Norsemen to navigate in these regions. And finally, if any did come, it must have been more than a single vessel or so driven out of its course; it would require an extensive systematic immigration to set and leave its mark upon the native population so as to endure through all these years.

Moreover, we have to consider the evidence of tradition. It is hardly imaginable that such an event should have been utterly forgotten among the natives themselves, even after the lapse of a thousand years. There are many stories still current among the Eskimos in Greenland as to the Norsemen and their conflicts with the natives. The blond type is not peculiar to Victoria Land, but is found also in King William's Land and on the Great Fish River; even among the Musk Ox Eskimo I found some with the same reddish or brownish hair and grey or almost blue eyes, and a remarkably strong beard, which last is unusual among the Eskimos generally. And there was no tradition among any of these people as to any foreign blood. I am convinced that these peculiar types are the result of purely biological conditions, which are altogether accidental, and for which no rule can be established.

On the 15th of February we bade farewell to our friends here. There had been excellent sealing for the past month, the finest indeed we had seen, a single day sufficing for the capture of as many seals as would have been taken in a whole month among the Netsilingmiut to the eastward. It was not that the natives here were more than commonly skilful, but the waters here in Dolphin and Union Strait, where the ice is cut about by the currents, seem to be a general meeting place for the seals both from east and west.

With heavy-laden sledges we set out on the 900 km. run to Baillie Island.

We had met at Bernhard Harbor a young trapper named Lyman de Steffany, and afterwards his brother Gus, who lived some distance further west. Both were excellent hunters and drivers, and we were glad of their assistance. Leo Hansen had hurt his shoulder in struggling with the heavy Hudson Bay sledge, and one arm was useless for some time; indeed it was only by a stubborn effort that he was able to go on. The aid afforded us by the two brothers on the journey was thus doubly welcome, and the fortnight we spent travelling in their company was one of pleasant companionship throughout.

The coast we had now to follow to the northward was for the most part dull and monotonous; it was low-lying country, in many places merging imperceptibly into the tumbled ice and pressure ridges off the shore, and only broken here and there by steep sandstone rocks often hollowed into fantastic caves that afforded a welcome shelter. The ice off shore was good, and when we wanted fresh provisions we had as a rule only to drive out some ten kilometres where seal could be had without difficulty in the patches of open water. We were loth to waste time on such excursions however, and only turned aside when forced to it. At one place we encountered a solitary Swede, Kalle Lewin, of Kalmar, who quoted Frithiof's Saga with true patriotic enthusiasm, in the intervals of gloomy prophesyings as to the prospects of fox in the coming season. A day's journey farther north, at Pierce Point, in the most beautiful part of the country, amid arches and monuments of ice-embroidered sandstone, we met another trapper named Bezona, said to be an Italian nobleman who had come to the Arctic in search of an Eldorado—up to date without success.

At Cape Lyon we encountered the first Eskimo immigrants from Alaska, who, like the white trappers, were now seeking their fortune in the country of their "wild" tribal kinsmen. They were extremely hospitable, spoke fluent English, and soon proved to be thoroughly businesslike. We did not take long to discover that we were in the land of the Almighty Dollar. A joint of caribou meat such as would have been given us freely as a token of welcome among the tribes farther east, here cost $8, and when we wanted a man and a sledge to help us one day's journey on ahead, as Leo Hansen was still laid up, the price asked for this was $25.

We thought perhaps, for a moment, with regret of the kindly folk we had left, who would have helped us on our way for a week and been only too pleased, without any question of payment. But the principle here was unquestionably right; the Eskimos had now to compete with the white men, and if they were to make ends meet, it was necessary to ask a fair payment for services rendered. We were strangers, merely passing through the country, and had to pay our way.

During the further stages of our journey westward we put on the pace, doing 50 or 60 kilometres per day. This meant that the dogs had to trot, and we ourselves to run beside the sledges, which was perspiring work, but gave one splendid rest at night.

On the 9th of March we halted for a spell at Cape Parry, where lived the trapper, skipper and adventurer Jim Crowford. We got in to his place in the evening, just as the setting sun lit up his little schooner, as she lay icebound, and the corrugated iron hut he had built at the foot of a cliff. It looked chilly enough in itself, but there was smoke rising from the chimney, and it was not long before we were seated at a meal like old friends, listening to our host's account of his adventures in the gold rush of 1900.

On the 15th of March we reached Horton River, where there is an old Eskimo settlement named Idglulualuit; the widow of a well-known German whaler, Captain Fritz Wolki, lives here. We entered a house where everything was so neat and clean and orderly that we instinctively walked on tiptoe, and found three taciturn women who regaled us with roast ptarmigan—dainty and appetizing as could be.

Next day we encountered a natural phenomenon, and camped for a spell to take some pictures, though we could only stay a few hours. We had reached the Smoking Mountains. Long ago, perhaps a hundred years or more, some subterranean deposit of coal here caught fire, and the smoke is still pouring out from ten different hills. In the strong sunlight, they seem wrapped in halos of greyish blue smoke, that oozes out from every crack and crevice in the sides. Here and there among the hollows, white

NEAR PIERCE POINT

A mass of rugged headlands jutting out into Amundsen's Gulf. We passed some enormous sandstone caves on lonely islets, like ice-clad portals opening on to the frozen sea. The storms of autumn had flung endless breakers over them, and huge icicles now glittered in the sunlight with all the colors of the rainbow.

THE SMOKING MOUNTAINS, NORTH OF HORTON RIVER

vapors pour forth like the smoke from sacrificial fires, carried by the wind over to the mighty barrier of snow-covered pressure ridges that runs along the shore. It is a fight between fire and cold, and the cold is the stronger. Even the smoking mountains themselves are covered with snow; only the black sand on the front of the slopes, wrapped in smoke, is warm and moist. Ahead of us as far as the eye can reach, lay the frozen sea, glittering in the sunlight, smiling in its majesty as if in scorn of the fire demons and their vain pyrotechnics in the bowels of the earth.

CHAPTER XXII

TRADE AND PROSPER

ON the 17th of March we reached Baillie Island, where the Hudson's Bay Company has a station, in charge of our fellow-countryman Henrik Henriksen. I need hardly say that he at once invited us to share his comfortable quarters.

The first part of our journey was thus at an end. I was now among new tribes, the Mackenzie Eskimos.

It was like coming into new country altogether. We had been accustomed to living among people who lived chiefly on land game, and only hunted seal from the ice. Here we found ourselves among folk who won their food from the open sea, and spoke a language which was almost exactly like that of the Eskimos in Greenland; they talked of whale and white whale, seal and ribbon seal, which were hunted in kayaks or umiaks. And these umiaks were exactly like those used in Greenland; it was a pleasure to us to see the well-known lines, coming as we did from among people to whom the very name of Greenland was unknown.

The little white snow villages that we had grown so familiar with were here replaced by log huts, or houses built of wood or peat, the arrangement entirely corresponding to that common in Greenland, so that my two Greenlanders opened their eyes and

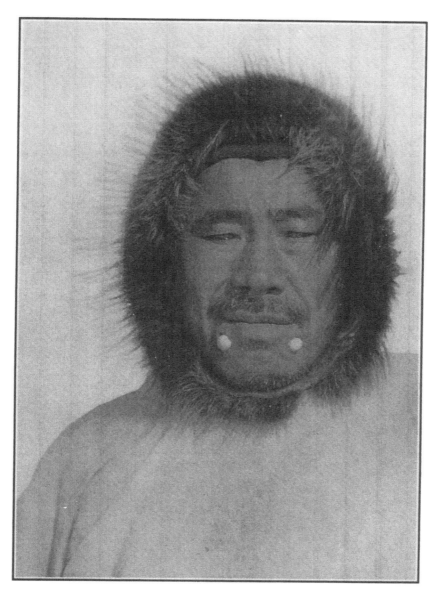

ANGUISINAOQ, MY STORY-TELLER FROM BAILLIE ISLAND

One of the old school, as shown by the labrets, or lip ornaments, which he still wears. These are made of mammoth tusk, white quartz, nephrite, granite or slate, and thrust through a hole in the lip. In former times, they were worn by all the men between the Mackenzie River and the Yukon.

thought they were nearly home again, though they had now for three years been moving farther and farther from their own country.

This was our first impression, but on closer acquaintance we found things very different from what we knew. The Mackenzie River had been the great source of culture, and just as its mighty currents had torn up whole forests by the root and spread the timber far along its shores, so also it had torn up the Eskimo culture from its old surroundings and created a transition form, in the midst of which we found ourselves now. Hunting by sea was no longer the one thing needful. The pursuit of gold and money values had revolutionized everything. The Hudson's Bay Company was no longer the only source and centre of trade; independent traders came down the rivers buying up skins for cash, and the competition between them sent prices up to such a degree that the Eskimos in this rich fur country found themselves wealthy men all of a sudden. And accustomed as they were to reckon from hand to mouth, or at most in terms of a single year's supply of food, their ideas of foresight went no farther than the laying by of a store of meat for the winter; they were all skilful hunters, and it was easy for them to procure, and dispose of, the coveted skins; which they did without any consideration for the future or their old age.

Consequently, we found ourselves now among a people highly paid and independent in proportion. The price of a white fox was $30, and many could be caught between November and April, in addition to the other sorts of fox, and other fur-bearing animals. The Eskimo hunters were no poor savages in kayaks; they owned schooners and called one another "Captain." A schooner of the flat-bottomed type such as is used in the deltas of great rivers could be bought for $3000, but there was not much occasion to use it after all. One could go visiting up and down the coast in summer, or take a sort of fashionable holiday "yachting" after the fur season was over; for hunting proper they used the cheaper and handier umiak, or whaleboats. Most of the schooners of course had motor power, and machinery in general was used as far as possible. The women, whose deft fingers had been wont to compass unaided the making and decorating of clothes, now used sewing machines. Men and women alike had learned to write; and the men, to be in the fashion, bought typewriters, though their correspondence was hardly enough to give them any great practice in the use of them. Safety razors were in general use, and cameras not uncommon. The old blubber lamps, excellent for their purpose, were now sold to tourists as curiosities (price $30), and gasoline or kerosene lamps were used instead.

I felt, indeed, something of an old fossil myself at first, among all these smart business folk; legend and myth and ancient traditions were things they had left far behind. Many a time during those first few weeks did I think wistfully of the eastern tribes, where men and women still had some respect for the wisdom of their forebears. Here, if I wanted folk tales, I found myself confronted with salesmanship;

demand created the supply, and a self-styled specialist in folklore, mythology and local information
offered his services confidently at $25 per day. He
could make that by manual labor; why should he
use his brains for less? And as soon as it was noised
abroad that we were interested in ethnographical
specimens, unblushing "dealers" grew up in a twinkling on every side, asking up to $50 for any trifling
ornament.

I felt hopelessly out of my element in all this.
But fortunately, all this outward "civilization" was
but skin-deep, and it was not long before I managed
to arouse the people to some interest in their own
past. I talked to them for hours—free of charge—
of all that we had seen and learned on our journey
hitherto, of their kinsfolk to the eastward who knew
their history; and after a while, awoke some response
in themselves. Indeed, before leaving western Canada, I had acquired a great amount of new and valuable information myself. But this will be set out
in another place. For the present, we must continue our journey.

We held straight on our course towards Herschel
Island, halting, however, at any settlements by the
way that offered anything of interest. In Liverpool
Bay, for instance, I visited a first rate story-teller
named Apagkaq. He began by scornful criticism of
my interest in such an unremunerative occupation;
but when I promised him $50 for five days' work, he
grew more interested himself. The work went but
slowly to begin with; art and bargaining do not go
well together. But after a while the bargain part

of it was forgotten, and we worked as brothers. He was unquestionably a magnificent artist, the finest I have met outside East Greenland. He came originally from the region of Noatak River and Kotzebue Sound, and several of his stories bear traces of Indian influence. One of them, "The Wise Raven" is a whole creation myth in itself, and bears notable points of difference as compared with other Eskimo versions. I filled many pages with Apagkaq's stories, and when we parted I could hardly see out of my eyes. I slept on my sledge most of the first two days after. Looking back, I have a faint misty remembrance of meeting a jolly old fellow named Ularpat, the first in these regions to catch white whale in nets. Dried whale meat and blubber was served, the meat was a trifle mildewed, and when this was commented on apologetically, I answered with a Greenland catchword to the effect that mildew was good for the system. Ularpat's retort stuck in my mind. "Yes," he said with a laugh, "we say the same thing in our country; probably to save the trouble of washing the meat clean. Laziness often makes things 'good for you' in that way."

On again to the west. We decide to cut across Liverpool Bay and make for Nuvoraq (Atkinson Point). In the evening we reached the house of a hospitable American, Mr. Williams, where we also met the chaplain, Mr. Hester, with whom we afterwards travelled for some weeks; an earnest and untiring worker, with the welfare of the Eskimos ever at heart. He had formerly been working over in the region of Coronation Gulf, but had been obliged to move in nearer to civilization, as the missionary society which sent him out could not afford to keep him so far afield. Having in mind the sums spent on punishing criminals here in the wilds, it seems a pity that it should be necessary to economize in a field of work which more than all else helps to prevent the growth of criminal tendencies.

On the 5th of April we visited the chief Mangilaluk, whose residence might well be the envy of many a town-dweller dreaming of a country house. It was a log hut built of very heavy timber, the principal apartment measuring 7 metres by 5½, and something over 3 metres high. This, however, was eclipsed by another house of the same type where we spent the night on the eastern bank of the Mackenzie River, where the living room was 7 x 10 metres, and 3½ metres high. The walls here were lined with beaver board, the floor covered with linoleum, and in place of the old-fashioned Eskimo sleeping bench I found a bedroom with two iron bedsteads, spring mattresses and all!

During the past few days, the country has changed altogether; the soil is grassy, and all the valleys thick with water willows.

At Kitikarjuit, formerly inhabited by some 800 Eskimos, and famous for white whale, we found no Eskimos at all, but only the manager of the Hudson's Bay Company's station, and an inspector. The manager, John Gruben, was remarkably well acquainted with the Eskimos of this district.

On the 10th of April we again passed the house of a fellow countryman, Niels Holm, on the eastern

bank of the Mackenzie Delta. Here also we found
the site of a former Eskimo village, with many ruined
houses and graves, especially graves of chiefs, in
which the property of the deceased had been in-
terred with the corpse; umiaks, kayaks and sledges.

We were now anxious to get on to a place where
we could finish off our work in Canada before entering Alaska. Herschel Island would be the best for
this purpose. The delta, however, is difficult country to travel through without a guide, owing to the
many tributary streams all looking alike. To avoid
losing our way and precious time, we persuaded
Niels Holm to accompany us to Herschel Island,
where we arrived on the 17th of April.

Herschel Island has an excellent natural harbor,
the only real harbor on the whole range between
Teller and the Arctic coast; it was first discovered
in 1848, and at once became the centre of the whaling industry from Mackenzie River to Baillie Island
and even farthest east. The whaling has now altogether ceased, but the harbor remains as a main
centre of supply for the east arctic districts, which
may at times be completely blocked by ice.

The Hudson's Bay Company has for many years
past carried on trade in the Mackenzie Delta. In
former times, supplies were only brought down by
river. The formation of the many new stations to
the eastward, however, necessitated direct communication by sea from Vancouver, and these voyages
were accomplished with great skill, often with serious risk. The considerable quantities of goods thus
poured in upon a coast where the inhabitants are

YOUNG WOMAN AND CHILD FROM BAILLIE ISLAND

In the great days of the whaling industry, Herschel Island was a favorite winter harbor, and mixed types are not infrequent among the Eskimo of the Mackenzie Delta.

INSPECTOR WOOD OF HERSCHEL ISLAND, CHIEF OF THE ROYAL CANADIAN MOUNTED
POLICE IN THE NORTHWEST TERRITORY

still in a primitive state has of course its dangers, and it must be admitted that the great trading concern has, despite its mercantile interests, realized its responsibility as the most powerful organization in the district. Throughout the North-west Passage I invariably found the traders on the best of terms with the Eskimos near.

There are wide regions where the Hudson's Bay Company is the only link between the native population and the outer world. The Hudson's Bay Company stands for civilization, and its outposts in these desolate lands represent the life and work of men who bear the white man's burden, the white man's great responsibility.

At the headquarters of the Mounted Police on Herschel Island I had the pleasure of meeting Inspector Wood, who was in charge of the police administration along the whole of the Arctic coast; a keen and capable man, fully alive to the difficulties of maintaining law and order throughout a country extending from Demarcation Point to the Magnetic Pole. To him had fallen the task of hanging the two poor devils from Kent Peninsula the February before, and there were several Eskimo families from the east still at the station, either as witnesses or accused of complicity in cases of homicide. Witnesses and accused alike lived on the best of terms with the police and the local Eskimos, and save for some homesickness, might have been enjoying an innocent holiday, with all expenses paid. The only ones who seemed at all serious about it were the few who might find it their last journey on earth.

The Mackenzie Eskimos were once a great people by native standards; it is estimated that about the middle of the 19th century they numbered about 2000, of which about half lived at Kitigarssuit— various epidemics, however, have seriously reduced the population since then, and it now amounts to only some 400 souls. Of these again some two hundred are recent immigrants from Alaska, more especially from the region of Noatak and Colville River. In the old days before the Hudson's Bay Company had set up stations in the delta itself, the regular yearly trading trips extended up the Mackenzie River as far as Fort McPherson, or at times even beyond, and though one can now purchase everything needed on the coast, there are still some families that go up to the Arctic Red River, attracted by the rich prospects of trapping in that region, and the fine salmon fishery.

These inland journeys brought them from very early times into contact with the Indians; and here for the first time throughout the expedition I learned that cases of intermarriage between Indians and Eskimos had formerly been common; true, it was marriage by capture, but both Indians and Eskimos agree as to its having taken place. I have often in the foregoing referred to the Indians in the terms used by the Eskimos in describing them; the old stories in particular represent them as cruel, bloodthirsty and treacherous. At Single Point, I met a young Indian woman, the wife of the Hudson's Bay Company's Manager; she had been born and brought up among the Takudh Indians. She explained that there had always been a great deal of intercourse between the Eskimos and the Indians, especially before the trading stations were established. Every summer, the Eskimos used to come up to Fort McPherson and camp on a great plain near the hill where the Indians had their tents. They played football on the plain, but on one occasion, trouble arose owing to the rough and unsportsmanlike behavior of the Eskimos; the Indians retired from the game and the Eskimos struck camp and went off in anger. Next year they came again in great numbers, ready for battle, but the Indians, not wishing to give any occasion for bloodshed, moved into the bush with their tents and loosed their dogs. These dogs were very fierce, and the Eskimos were greatly afraid of them. My informant was then only six or seven years old, but she remembers being driven in with her little companions farther into the bush, in case there should be fighting. She had taken an axe with her, hoping to kill an Eskimo herself. No one was afraid, for such scenes were of frequent occurrence. But the dogs, which also appeared to hate the Eskimos, kept guard so well that nothing came of the attack. The Eskimos made peace, and that was doubtless the last feud between the two peoples. Now they are good friends, but in former times, "the hoskies" were noted for their treacherous attacks, and the Indians feared them, more especially for their habit of carrying off their womenfolk; hence the many half-breed types, of Eskimo and Indian blood.

This account, given by an Indian woman, is interesting as showing how the Indians regard the Eskimos; and one cannot say that any great affection exists between them.

Our first meeting with the Western Eskimos thus took place at the close of our three years' exploration in Canada, just before we left the country. We found a people that had changed their ways in most essential respects. Skin boats had given place to schooners, sealing to trapping and fur trading on modern lines; earth-and-stone huts lined with driftwood were now replaced by something approaching modern bungalows or villas; and in addition to all these external changes, their ancient faith had given place to Christianity. One would hardly think that all these changes would be favorable to any continuance of the fellow-feeling between them and their kinsfolk to the eastward; we found, however, that racial traditions lived on unimpaired in their stories and legends. I wrote down over a hundred such, and found a surprising number of old acquaintances among them, both from eastern Canada and from Greenland.

The journey through these sparsely populated wastes was now at an end, and our route henceforward lay through richer and more civilized regions. I was glad, however, to have had the opportunity of studying these people before they had quite given up their ancient ways of life. As it was, I had an abundance of material, and was now more than ever filled with admiration for the Eskimos themselves.

I cannot leave this part of the country without saying that I got a strong impression of the way in which the Canadian Government evidences its feeling of responsibility toward the Eskimos. Admittedly the supervision is difficult, because the people are scattered far along inaccessible shores. Nothing can be done without great expense.

The plan of allotting reservations to the Eskimos is undoubtedly the only right one, for it shields them somewhat in those first meetings with civilization which are always the most dangerous for a primitive people.

Yet in one thing I believe progress is still in order. Now the Government has all of its contacts with the Eskimos through the Mounted Police. With all the admiration I hold for the Mounted, for the way they carry out all usual police duties, and many others, I do not feel that they can justly be expected to substitute for all of the agencies of civilization. Some educational department must be established to deal with the Eskimo on the gentler side. There can be no step back to the Stone Age for any people that has once had contact with the white man. Canada cannot afford to be behindhand in attempting the educational paternalism that has done so much in Greenland and in Alaska to fit the Eskimo to meet the cruder contacts with the white man, in the person of the trader, the competing trapper, and the policeman.

CHAPTER XXIII

ON the 5th of May, early in the morning, we entered Alaska. Near Demarcation Point we passed the line of stakes that marks the frontier; we were in the land of which so many adventurers had dreamed.

We had now a run of 800 kilometres along this barren coast before we could halt for any length of time; the land is now flat tundra, stretching away as far as Point Barrow almost in a straight line, broken only here and there by small indentations of the coastline. Just offshore are narrow sandy reefs, forming the so-called lagoons, where we find fine smooth ice just inside the barrier, very different from the tumbled pressure ridges beyond. The dogs moved at a steady trot, and we ourselves were growing accustomed to trotting alongside.

The Eskimos are scattered about in little encampments all along this coast; we find, too, a few white men, Scandinavians for the most part, some with small schooners, others with nothing but their bare hands and their traps. The distance between dwellings depends on the chances of a good haul.

At last, on the 23rd of May, we found ourselves on the high road, as it might well be called, to Point Barrow, the most northerly settlement in America.

This was our first real town since leaving Godthaab in Greenland, in 1921. Our arrival aroused quite a sensation among the inhabitants, when it was known that we had come from so far east; all had sufficient book learning to form some idea of the distance involved. Consequently, I was invited to give a lecture on Greenland and the other countries we had passed through, which I did, in the local school house, on the following day. My Greenland accent and idiom occasioned no difficulty among the natives here; a fact which promised well for future work.

The population consists of some 250 natives and a few white men. There are big shops with stores and warehouses, but what mostly struck us is the presence of a school, a hospital and a church. We had not seen a school for three years, and it looked quite imposing. The schoolmaster in charge was a young Dutchman, Peter van der Sterre, who very hospitably received us as his guests.

I had not expected to find anything of interest on this part of my journey, and really considered my collections at an end on leaving Canada; I soon found, however, that this was not the case. Men and women here were less sophisticated than those of the Mackenzie Delta, and there was a store of folklore and mythology ready to hand. I decided therefore to take advantage of the opportunity, and make some stay here, despite the advice of experts who declared that if I did not push on at once, I should have to wait until August and go on by sea. We were just at the most exciting part of the annual whaling season. Only a few kilometres out from land was the open sea, rocking the loose icefloes; the sea birds had gathered in dense flocks, and their cries could be heard right up over the land. Nearly all the men lived out at the edge of the ice in rough hunting camps; only the women and children were at home. All were excited, and no one ever seemed to go to sleep. When we ourselves went to rest, at four in the morning, and opened the windows, we heard on all sides the chatter of women, the cries of children and the howling of dogs. But on all the highest points of the clay cliffs were watchful outposts, waiting for the moment when they could with a deafening shout, announce to these careless night-birds that a whale had been harpooned.

Alaska was discovered in 1741 by the Danish explorer Vitus Bering, then in the service of Russia and voyaging up through the Strait which bears his name. Little more was known of it however, for many years after. In 1826, an English expedition under Beechy visited Point Barrow and opened the way for others. The Eskimos who lived between Norton Sound and the Arctic Ocean appear to have been a warlike people, their young men being regularly trained for war, hardening themselves by all manner of athletic exercises, dieting themselves, and often obliged to fast in order to habituate themselves to great hardships, or making journeys on foot for many days in succession as a test of endurance. Not only were the different tribes constantly at feud among themselves; they did not hesitate to enter upon combats with Indians or white

WOMAN FROM POINT BARROW

POINT BARROW, THE MOST NORTHERLY SETTLEMENT IN AMERICA

The reindeer seen in the foreground are tame animals, driven in to be branded; in the background, the Government School and Presbyterian Church.

men when these ventured into their territory. Fighting was carried on as a rule with bow and arrow, but they had also special inventions of their own; among the most notable were breastplates of walrus tusk, proof against arrows, or great saw-toothed clubs designed to crush the skull of an enemy.

This period, moreover, was not so far distant but that I was able to obtain my information from the elders, men and women, whose fathers had themselves taken part in such fights. Russian trading methods proved of little advantage to the natives; indeed, they were well on the way to extermination when the United States, in 1867, bought the whole territory for a sum of $7,200,000; probably the best deal of its kind on record. In 1890, the Bureau of Education set to work to improve the conditions of the native population, and now, after 35 years, we find them industrious, ambitious and independent, a wonderful testimony to the value of systematic educational methods. A point of great importance in material respects was the introduction of tame reindeer from Siberia. Dr. Jackson, the Alaskan Eskimos' greatest benefactor, succeeded in getting some 1280 animals brought over, and there are now close on half a million, with every prospect of running into millions before long.

All the young people of the present day speak English as well as any American, and have thus the first qualification for entering into competition with immigrant whites. That this should be possible is due to the fact that the school was from the first made the centre of everything.

But there was also another form of education which was of importance, and that was the establishment of the so-called co-operative stores. The population contributed themselves towards the funds for starting these, but state assistance was also needed, and the government vessels which inspect the schools and medical service bring up goods for a freight which just covers expenses; the Eskimos thus obtain cheap wares, and can themselves take part in determining the prices of all necessaries. They manage these businesses themselves, under supervision of the two local school-teachers, and it is generally considered that they thus gain experience greatly conducive to the development of their own independence.

During my stay at Point Barrow, I gained a lively impression of the contact between the native population and the white men, who had come into the country to deal with cultural tasks. At the hospital, there was a medical missionary in charge, a Dr. Greist, with his wife, both keenly occupied in social work. Mrs. Greist devoted almost the whole of her time to "The Mothers' and Babies' Club," the principal objects of which were hygiene and care of children. The three nurses at the hospital had also their special tasks, carrying on schools in their leisure time for practical and religious instruction especially for women and children. And through the comfortable school rooms passed a constant stream of men and women, who were invariably received by Peter van der Sterre with tireless and patient helpfulness. I learned, of course later on, that conditions are not equally ideal everywhere; the great difficulty is to get the right kind of workers. But Point Barrow at least was a place where all, from the youngest to the oldest, worked sensibly according to the principles of the Board of Education, and I was glad to obtain the best introduction here at once.

Of great importance to me and my work at Point Barrow was my meeting with a man named Charles Brower, who had lived among the Eskimos for forty years. Mr. Brower was a personality who had with lively interest followed the fate of the Eskimos through all these years, and very thoroughly made himself acquainted with their past history. He had married a native woman from the locality, and spoke the Eskimo tongue excellently. He was rightly called the King of Point Barrow; for there is hardly a man all along the coast who enjoys such respect and veneration both among white men and Eskimos. Mr. Brower and I soon made friends, and thanks to his advice, I was able at once to hit on the spots where there was work to be done, and get into touch with the people who knew what I wanted to learn. My numerous conversations with Mr. Brower are among the most pleasant and most instructive I have ever had.

In Alaska, natural conditions and animal life have necessitated a development of industry on two definite lines: the caribou hunters on the one hand, the whalers on the other. Hunting by sea had its definite seasons, precluding any very nomadic form of life, while the immense areas through which the caribou had to be followed on the other hand made it impossible to keep to the coast in the whaling season. Consequently, some of the natives sailed up the rivers and settled more or less inland, though coming down once a year to the coast for sealskin and blubber, bringing caribou skin and furs in exchange.

Point Barrow has always been one of the main centres for the Eskimo whaling industry. The whales begin to arrive in numbers about the beginning of April, and continue to come in until the first week in June; the whaling was carried on from skin boats out at the edge of the firm winter ice. During the months the whaling lasted, all the men lived uninterruptedly out at the edge of the ice, despite much inconvenience arising from the tabu system. Tents were forbidden, and they had therefore to be content with storm-shelters made of skins, or seek some protection from the elements under the boat. It was also forbidden to dry clothes, and raw food was tabu; all meat had to be boiled. Meantime, the women and children spent an anxious time up in the winter houses. As soon as a whale was captured, they drove out and fetched the meat, which was stored in great subterranean larders, dug so deep down that the meat remained frozen throughout the summer.

The edge of the ice was not so far from land but that it was easy to follow the progress of the hunting from on shore. The skin boats and their crews were posted at spots where the clean straight line of the ice-edge was indented by small creeks cut by the storms. The whales, following the margin of the ice, invariably moved up into these creeks, where

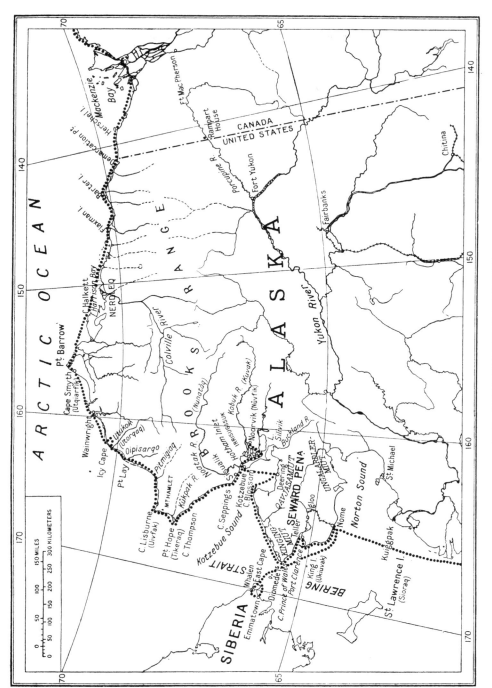

MAP: MACKENZIE BAY TO EAST CAPE

THE NALUKATAQ

At the close of the spring whaling season, the Alaskan Eskimos hold a great festival, with singing, dancing and games. The principal item on this part of the programme is the Nalukataq, in which men and women are tossed in a blanket of walrus hide.

they were easily harpooned. The harpoons were pointed with slate or flint, which it was not difficult to thrust through the thick layer of blubber; the harpoon lines were as a rule 20–25 fathoms long, with three bladder floats, one at the end of the line and two others tied together about 5 fathoms from the head of the harpoon.

The tradition of many generations, and years of practice, had given steersmen and harpooners great skill in calculating the movements of the whale. All the boats lay on the ice ready to be tipped off at a moment's notice, and the whale, as a rule, passed so close that it could be harpooned from the ice itself. At the same moment, all the boats put out, scattering over several kilometres round, and waiting for the whale to come up again, when it would be given a few more harpoons, with lines and bladder floats, to drag along; these checked its pace, and enabled the hunters to come to close quarters with their great lances, which were thrust in at a spot where the flint head could be sure of penetrating. The next thrust would be directed towards one of the great arteries in the neck; or an attempt would be made to sever the tail fin; the whale could then no longer dive, and was easily killed.

Only occasionally was a whale attacked in open sea; this being a far more difficult matter. When it was done, the hunters could, however, reckon with the fact that a whale approached from the front sees badly but hears fairly well, while if approached from behind, it cannot see, and hears but poorly. Anything coming from either side, however, it can both see and hear a considerable distance off. The first time a whale was harpooned it would come up some 3–4 kilometres from the spot where it went down; but as the boats always lay spread out along the edge of the ice, it would not be long before the lances got to work and the whale was despatched.

With these primitive implements of the stone age type, the hunters could, in a single spring season, account for up to 22 whales at Point Barrow alone. Considering what this means in meat and blubber and hide, it is not hard to understand that in this district in particular there was the possibility of a flourishing period of culture.

An Eskimo who is a practised whaler is called "Umialik," a word which, originally meaning merely the owner of a boat, has come to have the significance of "chieftain," as the great boat-owners, the more daring whalers, had unrestricted authority over their crews, and held the position of chieftains in their own communities.

Whaling implements were only allowed to be used for one season; this applies to the skins of the boats, and all gear and equipment. In earlier times, all the harpoons were burned with the other implements in a great bonfire during the festivals held at the conclusion of the season; later, it became the custom simply to hang up the harpoon heads on a frame, where they were left until the chieftain died, when they were placed with him in his grave.

When a man had got his first whale, it was his duty, at the great whaling festival, to throw away all that he owned of furs and other things; his fellow-villagers had then to fight for a share, the costly furs being cut into fragments that as many as possible might have a part. Altogether, there were many remarkable and amusing customs associated with the whaling. As a rule the greatest weight was attached to meaningless magic songs that had to be declaimed immediately before harpooning was to take place; there were, however, also other important points to be observed before setting out, customs originating in the belief that the whale, in the earliest days of the world, had been a human being, just as had other animals.

The whale is dangerous to hunt, but is also amenable to advances from human beings, especially women. Thus, for instance, a chief's wife, on learning that her husband's crew has harpooned a whale must at once take off one boot and remain quietly in her house. This preliminary step towards undressing was supposed to affect the soul of the whale and draw it towards the house. When then the boat neared the land, she must fill her water-vessel with fresh water and go down to the dead whale in order to refresh its thirsting soul with cool water.

The chieftain himself mostly took the part of steersman; it is reckoned a great art to calculate the movements of the whale. He would choose for his harpooner a young and powerful man, whose duty was to drive the harpoon into the whale as soon as he gave the signal. On the day before going down to the ice edge to begin the whaling, the young harpooner had to sleep in the forepart of the boat, and would be visited there in the course of the night by the chief's wife. A chief had as a rule several wives, and it was the harpooner's right to be visited by the youngest and prettiest. This meeting with a woman put the young man into high spirits, and the soul of the whale also was supposed to be attracted by the idea of being killed by a man coming straight from a woman.

That is the way whaling was carried on in the olden days. Now, the old harpoons with their ingeniously worked flint and slate heads are long since relegated to the category of antiques, and instead, a modern "darting gun," with explosive bombs, is used. Only the skin boat still remains; it is considered the most practical form of craft, as it has often to be carried long distances over the ice.

I had learned that there was a considerable encampment of inland folk on the Utorqaq river, and decided to go up, with Miteq and Anarulunguaq, and visit them, Leo Hansen remaining behind to get some pictures of the festival which the natives celebrate on the conclusion of the whaling season. He would then come on by sea when navigation opened, and bring our collections through to Nome.

On the 8th of June we reached the mouth of the Utorqaq at Icy Cape, or as the Eskimos call it Qajaerserfik, "the place where kayaks are lost." The name is probably due to the fact that the settlement is built on a sandbank so low that it is sometimes flooded when the wind blows hard on shore. It was spring, but the blizzards were by no means over; the trading station at Wainwright was so com-

pletely buried in show that it was hard to get into
the houses at all. The inhabitants here, with a veteran whaler named Jim Allan, had been working
hard since April without getting so much as a walrus.
At Icy Cape, however, they had been more fortunate, and had got a whale, in honor of which
event, the place was full of visitors from a reindeer
camp near by—the very one I was on my way to
visit. The festival must come first of course. It
was on the 10th, and fortunately the weather was
magnificent. Men, women and children were dressed
in new garments specially made for the occasion, and
gathered in the course of the forenoon at the qagsse,
or dance hall.

Certain parts of the whale meat—the tail, dorsal
fin and the skin from the jaws—are set aside as
delicacies for the feast. There are games, including a
glorified form of tossing in a blanket, two walrus
hides sewn together being held out by as many
hands as can find a hold, and the victim then shot
up into the air, endeavoring to come down upright
and feet foremost. Roars of laughter greet those who
fail; and not infrequently broken bones may result.
When this has gone on for some hours, the feasting
begins, and lasts for the rest of that day and the
night, with intervals of singing and dancing. Ten
performers with drums sit in a row, with a chorus of
male and female voices gathered round; the dancers,
generally two women and one man, came in by turns.
I was rather disappointed in the songs, which were
little more than refrains as an accompaniment to the
dance, with no text to speak of; certainly nothing to

compare with the lyrics I had found among the North-west Passage Eskimos.

On the following morning we set off for the mainland, to the village where I proposed to stay for the present.   Besides the old men and women I had specially wished to see, there were some young reindeer herdsmen, rounding up a herd of some 800 head. The season's calves had to be branded, which is done by marking the ears with the owner's particular sign.

CHAPTER XXIV

THE GIFT OF SONG AND DANCE

THE north and north-west corner of Alaska, comprising all that vast plain to the north of the Endicott Mountains, is watered by great rivers, which have played a great part as channels of communication during the period before the arrival of the white men. Three rivers rising close together gave rise to the many villages in the interior, and served as waterways through the country, in which all the Eskimos formed one community, with winter quarters close together. The three rivers are the Noatak, flowing into Kotzebue Sound, the Utorqaq, debouching into great lagoons between Icy Cape and Point Lay, and finally, Colville River, with its great delta meeting the Arctic Ocean near Cape Halkett.

The Eskimos call the Colville River Kugpik, or the Great River, but the dwellers on its banks are called Kangianermiut, after one of its tributary streams. It is quite near the source of the Utorqaq, only separated by a range of hills, the Qimeq, the distance between them being so slight that skin boats can easily be carried from one river to the other.

The Kangianermiut sailed down the Colville River in the spring, when the channel was clear of ice; often fifty boats at a time, or something like 500 souls. Little wonder that the Indians feared them! The journey up river took longer, and the boats had to be towed by men and dogs together over the many reaches where the current was too strong for paddling. A great camp was formed in the delta, and in the course of the summer, salmon were caught in great numbers for winter use, the implements used being nets made of caribou sinew. Caribou hunting was also carried on at the same time for present needs. The object of the visit, however, was to procure blubber from the natives round Point Barrow, who came out here to trade. Encounters with the Indians were not infrequent, and every man who had slain an Indian was tattooed at the corners of the mouth as a mark of distinction.

All these people loved their inland life and the merry journeys up and down the river in parties. In summer they lived in tents of caribou skin, built to a special pattern, on a wooden framework of some twenty branches interwoven so as to form a kind of beehive dwelling, easy to heat. A tent of this kind is called Qalorvik. Winter houses were built on the same principle, but with a stronger framework, and covered, first with peat or moss, and then with earth stamped down to form a hard crust. The inside was then lined with a thick layer of branches to prevent the earth from crumbling down. The whole was then built over with snow blocks, resembling an ordinary snow hut; indeed, it was probably modelled on this. Large stones set in the middle of the floor formed a fireplace, and a hole was left in the roof above to let out the smoke.

The natives of the Noatak River moved down in the spring to Cape Seppings and Kotzebue Sound, while those of the Utorqaq, the Utorqarmiut, as they are called, made for the whalers' quarters at Icy Cape. The Utorqarmiut are also called the wolf people, on account of their following the caribou like wolves, instead of staying at one place throughout the winter. These migrations took place between October and March, along the frozen rivers, which with their many tributaries form a network of paths through the hills and wooded valleys. Owing to the scarcity of food for the dogs, teams were generally reduced to two, and men and women hauled at the sledges themselves.

Thus, roughly, was the round of life among the dwellers on the great rivers. Generally speaking, they lived at peace among themselves, and also with the coast folk with whom they traded. But with those living farther off, they were constantly at war, and constant watchfulness was necessary, as their enemies might at any time swoop down upon any party that could be taken unawares. The men always lay down with their weapons ready to hand.

After the primitive methods in use among the Caribou Eskimos of the Barren Grounds, it was interesting to see the degree of skill and ingenuity which these people had developed in their methods of hunting, apart from the spiritual culture. I noted no fewer than twenty such methods of capturing or killing various kinds of game, and took down, from the lips of my informant, Sagdluaq, details of the most important.

As regards their religious ideas, I found here, despite the difference in conditions of life as compared with the eastern tribes, the same fundamental principles as I have already noted. Their spiritual culture, like their material, was on a higher level, but based on the same ideas of tabu, of spells and charms and propitiation of evil spirits, with the angakoq as mediators between them and the supernatural powers. It has hitherto been generally believed that incipient totemism existed in these regions, and the marks found on implements have been adduced as evidence of this. Were this the case, it would mean a breach of continuity between the eastern and the western tribes. I therefore devoted particular attention to the study of this question, and came to the conclusion that the marks found on harpoons, knives, and implements generally, which had formerly been regarded as totem marks, were purely personal, a means whereby the owner could readily identify his property, as we might use initials or a crest.

Here also we find the dominant principle of rites and prohibitions in connection with the different animals hunted; skins of caribou must not be worked on near the sea, nor those of the seal within sight of the river; certain work must only be done at certain seasons, and the like. Particular rules obtained in regard to caribou caught in traps; such animals must never be cut up with iron knives, but only with flint or slate; and the meat had to be cooked in special pots.

Wolf and wolverine are more or less of a luxury,

SAGPLUAQ, FROM COLVILLE RIVER

He was young in the days when caribou were still hunted with bow and arrow.

WOMEN FROM POINT BARROW

A half-breed and a pure Eskimo, both wearing the picturesque dresses made from the white-spotted skin of tame animals trimmed with fur of wolf and wolverine.

inasmuch as their flesh is not eaten, and they are only sought for as providing a finer sort of fur for trimmings. The hunter who aspires to the pursuit of these must not cut his hair, or drink hot soup, for a whole winter, and no hammer of any sort must be used in his house. On returning home with the skin of a wolf, intricate ceremonies have to be observed, in which the neighbors also take part.

The hunter must first walk round his own house, following the sun. For a male wolf, he strikes his heel four times against the wall of the house, five times for a female, indicating the four and five days' tabu for male and female respectively. At the same time, the women inside the house must bow their heads and turn their faces away from the entrance, while a man runs out and informs all the men in the other houses of the kill. Then all go out with their knives, in the hope that the soul of the wolf, supposed to be still present in the skin, might "like" their knives and let itself be caught by them next time. The hunter then carries the skin to the drying frame and hangs it up; a young man runs up with a piece of caribou skin which he hands to the hunter. The latter then strips, and standing naked in the snow, rubs himself all over with a piece of caribou skin, after which a fire is lit, and he further cleanses his body by standing in the smoke. His knives, bows and arrows are hung up beside the wolf's skin and all present cry aloud: "Now it sleeps with us"—"it" being the soul of the wolf.

The hunter then enters his own hut and sits down beside his wife, all the women still sitting with heads

bowed and faces averted. The hut is then decorated with all the most valuable possessions: knives
and axes, often of flint or jade, are hung up, bead
ornaments, tools, anything a wolf might be supposed to like, or that the family specially value.
Then all the men of the village come in, and the
hunter tells stories, not to amuse his guests, but to
entertain the soul of the wolf.   It is strictly forbidden
to laugh or even smile; the wolf might then become
suspicious and take it for gritting of teeth.   Two
stories must always be told, as one "cannot stand
alone."   Then the visitors leave, and all can retire
to rest.

But the ceremonial is not yet done with.   On the
following morning, the soul of the wolf has to be sent
on its way.   The hunter falls on one knee by the
fire place, with a white stone hammer in his hand,
and sings a magic song, and then howls: "Uhu!"
four times for a male, five times for a female wolf,
and raps four or five times on the floor of the hut.
He then runs out and clambers up on to the roof,
listening at the window, while another man takes his
post by the fireplace and cries out, "How many?"
The hunter outside answers "Four" or "Five" according to the sex of the wolf, and the man within
howls accordingly.   This ceremony has to be repeated in all the other houses.   Then all the men
walk up to the place where the skin is hung up, and
the same formality is gone through once more, all
crying at last:

"Leave us now as a good soul, as a strong soul!"

And now, but not before, a great banquet is held

in the hunter's house, the feast symbolizing the dead wolf's provision for the journey. All the meat has to be cut up beforehand into mouthfuls, for though each guest brings his knife, no knives are allowed to be used, nor may the meat be served on an ordinary dish, but must be set out on a caribou skin. All available delicacies are served up with the greatest care. Nothing must be left, and anything not eaten must at once be given to the dogs.

No hunter may kill more than five wolves and five foxes in one season; as soon as this number is reached, all his traps have to be taken in. Neglect of this precaution involves either loss of the animals already caught, or the risk of being bitten to death.

This cult of the beast-soul, or the continuation of life after death, reappears in numerous myths designed to instruct the inexperienced. A point repeatedly emphasized is the slight difference between human and animal life, and we find constant reference to the times when beasts could turn into men and men often lived as beasts. I give one of these myths as told me by Sagdluaq, of Colville River.

How Song and Dance and the Holy Gift of Festival First Came to Mankind

"There were once a man and a woman who lived near the sea. The man was a great hunter, sometimes hunting game far inland, and sometimes seal in his kayak.

"Then a son was born to these two lonely ones, and when the boy grew up, his father made for him a little bow for shooting birds, and in time he grew to be very skilful with this. Then his father taught him to hunt caribou, and the son grew to be as great a hunter as his father. And so they divided the hunting between them, the son hunting caribou in the hills while his father went out to sea hunting seal in his kayak.

"But one day the son did not come back from his hunting. In vain they waited for his return; in vain they searched for him after; no trace could be found. Their son had strangely disappeared.

"Then they had another son. And he grew up, and became strong and skilful like his brother, but he too disappeared one day in the same mysterious manner.

"The man and the woman then lived alone, knowing nothing of any others, and mourning greatly the loss of their two sons. Then a third son was born to them; and he grew up like his brothers, fond of all manly sports, and even from childhood eager to go out hunting. He was given his brothers' weapons, first the little bird bow, then the great strong bows for reindeer, and it was not long before he grew as skilful as his father. And between them they brought home much meat, the father from the sea, and the son from the land, and had to build many store frames for all the game they killed.

"One day the son was hunting inland as was his wont, when he caught sight of a mighty eagle, a great young eagle circling in the air above him. He soon drew forth his arrows, but the eagle came down and settled on the ground close to him, thrust back its hood and appeared as a human being. And the eagle spoke to the hunter and said:

"'It is I who killed your two brothers. And I will kill you too unless you promise me that song festivals shall be held on your return. Will you or will you not?'"

"'I will do as you say, but I do not understand it. What is song? and what is festival?'

"'Will you or will you not?'

"'I am willing enough, but I do not understand.'

"'Then come with me, and my mother shall teach you. Your two brothers would not learn, they despised the gifts of song and festival, and therefore I killed them. Now you shall go with me, and as soon as you have learned to join words together in a song, and learned to sing it, and learned to dance for joy, then you shall be free to return to your home.'

"So they went up over the high mountains. The eagle was now no longer a bird, but a young and powerful man in a wonderful dress of eagle skin. Far and far they went, through many valleys and passes far into the mountains, till they came to a house high up on the top of a mighty cliff, from where they could see out over the plain where men were wont to hunt the caribou. And as they neared the house there was a strange beating sound, like mighty hammers, that rang in the hunter's ears.

"'Can you hear anything?' asked the eagle.

"'Yes, a deafening sound as of hammering.'

"'That is my mother's heart you hear beating!'

"Then they came to the house, and the eagle said:

"'Wait here; I must tell my mother you are coming.' And he went in.

"In a moment he came out again and took the hunter into the house with him. It was built like an ordinary human dwelling, and within sat the eagle's mother, aged, weak and sad. But her son spoke aloud and said:

"'This young man has promised to hold a song festival when he comes home; but he does not know how to put words together and make songs, nor how to sing a song, nor how to beat a drum and dance for joy. O Mother, human beings have no festivals, and here is this young man come to learn!'

"At these words the eagle's old mother was glad and wakened more to life. And she thanked him and said: 'But first you must build a big house where all the people can gather together.'

"So the two young men built a Qagsse bigger and finer than any ordinary house. And then the old eagle mother taught them to make drums, and to set words together making songs, and then to beat time and sing together, and last of all to dance. And when the young hunter had learned all that was needful, the eagle took him back to the place where they had first met, and from there he went back alone to his own place. And coming home, he told his father and mother all that had passed, and how he had promised the eagles that festivals should be held among men.

"Then father and son together built a great qagsse for the festival, and gathered great stores of meat, and made drums and made songs ready for the feast; and when all was ready, the young man went out over great far ways seeking for others to join in the feast, for they lived alone and knew of no others near. And the young man met others coming two and two, some in dresses made of wolfskin, others in fox skins, or skins of wolverine; all in different dresses. And he asked them all to the festival.

"And then the feasting began, first with great dishes of meat, and when all had eaten, gifts were given them of other things. Then came the singing and dancing, and the guests learned all the songs and could soon take part in the singing themselves. So they sang and danced all night, and the old man beat the drum, that sounded like great hammers; like the heart of the old eagle mother beating. But when it was over, and the guests went away, it was seen that those guests in the skins of different beasts were beasts themselves, in human form. For the old eagle had sent them; and so great is the power of festival that even animals can turn into human beings.

"And some time after this, the young man was out hunting, and again met the young eagle, who took him as before to the house where his mother lived. And lo, the old and weakly mother eagle was grown young again; for when men hold festival, all the old eagles regain their youth; and therefore the eagle is the sacred bird of song and dance and festival."

CHAPTER XXV

I HAD now to bid farewell to some of my faithful dogs. It was impossible to take them all the way back with me, and I was anxious to leave them somewhere where they would be well cared for. I therefore handed over the majority to Ugpersaun, the trader at Icy Cape, keeping only four in case we might have need of them later on.

I had been warned that it would be impossible to travel along the coast of Alaska at this season, and was prepared for the worst. Sledging was dangerous, as the ice was already adrift in many places; we therefore decided to sail through the lagoons. Part of the way we were towed by the dogs, where the coastline admitted of this; the animals trotted along on shore, with the boat at the end of a long towline out in the water; often at such a pace as to send up a fountain of spray from the bows. At times we ran aground in the shallows, and had to turn out and wade about looking for some passable channel. After three days of this we reached Point Lay, where there was an Eskimo village.

The natives here were too well off for words. My host, Torina, had a store of coffee, tea, sugar, flour, tobacco, petroleum almost enough for a year, with a quantity of cloth and other material; he was also the owner of a splendid new whaleboat, that had cost $1000 the year before, besides a skin boat and two smaller craft. We had still some distance to the end of the lagoons, and needed help to get through; I offered $75 for two men and a boat for two days, but had to go up to $105 before I could get what I wanted. This brought us to the end of the lagoons, after which we had to revert to the old toilsome fashion of sharing our baggage between men and dogs on pack saddles, and trotting along side by side.

On reaching the Pitmigiaq River we found some Eskimos with a rotten old skin boat who undertook to get us through to Point Hope. That boat was a marvel. The skins were so rotten that they were past patching; we stuffed the holes with scraps of reindeer skins and woollen comforters that trailed their ends in the water after us. And in this crazy coffin ship we rounded the dreaded Cape Lisburne.

On the 16th of July we entered the great lagoon at Point Hope, and here encountered the local missionary, Mr. Wm. A. Thomas, out in his motor boat with his wife and son. They took us in tow, and a few hours later we were in their comfortable home, hospitably invited to stay as long as we pleased.

Point Hope, or Tikeraq, "the pointing finger," is one of the most interesting Eskimo settlements on the whole coast of Alaska, and has doubtless the largest collection of ruins. The old village, now deserted, consists of 122 very large houses, but as the sea is constantly washing away parts of the land

and carrying off more houses, it is impossible to say what may have been the original number. Probably, the village here and its immediate neighborhood had at one time something like 2000 souls, or as many as are now to be found throughout the whole of the North-west Passage between the Magnetic Pole and Herschel Island. Human bones are scattered about everywhere, and Mr. Thomas informed me that he had himself during his short term of residence seen to the interment of 4000 skulls!

The whaling here is still excellent, and there was abundance of everything, with no fear for the coming winter. I arranged with a couple of storytellers to work with me, and thanks to the kindness of my host, Mr. Thomas, was able to spend my time to the best advantage. Qalajaoq, a notable authority on local affairs, gave me the following account of the origin of the place:

"In long forgotten times, there were no lowlands here at the foot of the mountains, and men lived on the summit of the great mount Irrisugssuk, south east of Kotzebue Sound; that was the only land which rose from the sea; and on its top may still be found the skeletons of whales, from those first men's hunting. And that was in the time when men still walked on their hands, head downwards; so long ago it was.

"But then one day the Raven—he who created heaven and earth—rowed out to sea in his kayak far out to sea, and there he saw something dark moving and squelching on the surface of the water. He rowed out and harpooned it; blood flowed from the wound he had made. The raven thought it must be a whale, but then saw that it was a huge dead mass without beginning or end. Slowly the life ebbed from it, and he fastened his towline to it and towed it in to the foot of the hills south of Uivfaq. Here he made it fast, and on the following day, when he went down to look at it, he saw it was stiff; it had turned into land. And there among the old ruins of houses may still be seen a strange hole in the ground; that is the spot where the raven harpooned Tikitaq. And that is how this land came."

The Tikerarmiut were once a mighty people, and there is a legend of a great battle fought by them on land and sea against the Nunatarmiut, somewhere near Cape Seppings; the Tikerarmiut were badly defeated, and never regained their former power. Then in 1887 came the establishment of the whaling station at Point Hope. The chief of that period, Arangaussaq, endeavored to oppose the progress of the white men, but without avail, and on his death the natives made peace with the whites, who thence forward assumed the mastery.

Point Hope is most interesting as a centre and repository of the ancient Eskimo culture, with much that is not found elsewhere. I gained some considerable knowledge of their more particular mysteries from Qalajaoq. A notable feature is the use of masks and figures in their festivals, which is carried to an extraordinary degree.

The angakoq, after a visit to the spirit world, endeavors to give a record of what he has seen by carving masks to represent the different faces he

has seen, the spirits also being present. He further
calls in the aid of others, who carve according to his
instructions, producing a great number of remarkably fantastic masks. Special songs and dances are
composed, and used in conjunction with the masks
at the great feasts, which are held at different seasons in honor of the different animals forming the
staple of food.

Greatest of all is the Great Thanksgiving Festival
to the souls of dead whales. This is held in the
qagsse, which serves ordinarily as a place of assembly for all the men of the place, but on special occasions as a temple or banqueting hall. The upper
part of the interior at the back is painted to represent a starlit sky, much trouble being taken to procure colored stones to serve for pigments. A
carved wooden image of a bird hangs from the roof,
its wings being made to move and beat four drums
placed round it. On the floor is a spinning top stuck
about with feathers; close by is a doll, or rather the
upper half of one, and on a frame some distance from
the floor is a model skin boat, complete with crew
and requisites for whaling.

The proceedings open with the singing of a hymn;
then a man springs forward and commences to dance;
this, however, is merely the signal for mechanical
marvels to begin. The bird flaps its wings and
beats its drums with a steady rhythmic beat. The
top is set spinning, throwing out the feathers in
all directions as it goes; the crew of the boat get to
work with their paddles; the doll without legs nods
and bows in all directions; and most wonderful of

ANARULUNGUAQ WITH TWO OF OUR DOGS

Between Point Lay and Point Hope all navigation was barred by the ice, and we had therefore to proceed on foot along the coast. Dogs as well as men had to bear their share of the load.

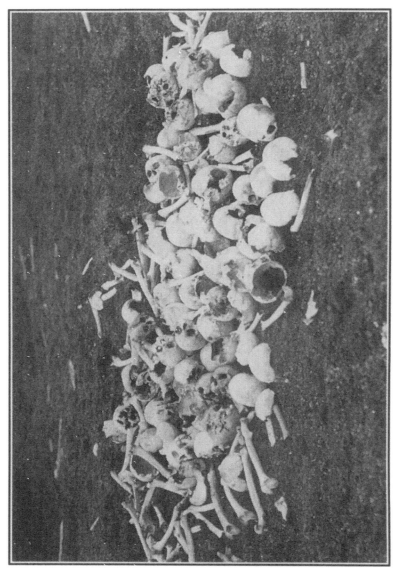

BATTLEFIELDS OF FORMER DAYS

The Eskimos of Alaska were a very warlike people, and battles between the tribes were often fought with bow and arrows. Many such battlefields are still to be seen, with piles of bones and skulls marking the site.

all, a little ermine sticks out its head from its hole in the wall, pops back again and then looks out, and finally runs across to the other side to vanish into another hole, snapping up a rattle with a bladder attached as it goes. All hold their breath, for should the creature fail to enter the hole with rattle and bladder behind it, one of those present must die within the year. But all goes well, and the company gasp in relief. Then follows a general distribution of gifts, edible delicacies mostly, to all present, and the guests depart.

On the 31st of July, having collected a great store of folklore, and finding the weather more favorable, I decided to push on. We travelled now in a little dinghy with motor attached, keeping close in to shore and visiting natives here and there. We met Elektuna, the first of the Eskimos to own tame reindeer; he has now a herd of 800 head, tended by himself and two sons. On the 3rd of August we came to a camp of young people from Noataq River, with a herd of 3000 reindeer, of which 1000 were the property of a single man. These people were cleanly, intelligent, well to do, and contented, retaining many of their sound Eskimo qualities, but speaking English fluently, and living as traders, in direct communication with Seattle.

At last, on the 7th of August, we crossed Kotzebue Sound; the water was shallow, and perfectly fresh, as three rivers, the Noatak, Kuvak and Silivik, flow out into the sea just here. We had to make a wide sweep round, following different channels, and landed late in the evening among gold-diggers, traders and Eskimo salmon fishers.

Kotzebue was an outstanding point on our long journey; for here it was that I could get into touch once more with the outer world, after three years of exile; here at last I should find a telegraph station—the most northerly in America. Naturally then, my first errand on landing was to send a message home announcing the successful completion of our long sledge trip.   We had pitched our camp among the Eskimo tents, and the telegraph station lay in the opposite end of the town.   And my mind was very busy as I strode down to the office, mentally writing out my message on the way.

I was not a little disappointed then to learn that the telegraph, newly installed, was not in working order at the moment; the operator, whom I had looked to electrify with my news, listened stolidly, and suggested at last that I might try to get through from *The Boxer*, a vessel lying some ten miles to the south.   This meant waiting till next day with a sleepless night between, and this too failed.   I had perforce to return to the office in Kotzebue again, and it was two days—the longest on the whole expedition—before the operator succeeded in getting through to Nome.   The same evening I had the reply from Copenhagen.   All was well at home, and my comrades had got through successfully.

The good news affected me to such an extent that for the first time in months I put aside all thought of work, and treated myself to an unlimited rest.

I slept for twenty-four hours, to the great astonishment of those about me. Thus refreshed, I could look about for the best means of utilizing our stay here until the mailboat from Nome could take us on.

Kotzebue (Qeqertarsuk) was the biggest town we had visited as yet, with a school, postoffice, the aforementioned telegraph station, and five or six big shops. Then there were gold diggers of various nationalities; and a camp of about a thousand Eskimos.

In the white traders' quarter, I came upon an enterprising young native, Peter Sheldon, who owned a small motor boat, a neat and swift little craft with cabin and skylights; the very thing for a trip up the river and a glance at the country round. I arranged with him to go up the Kuvak as far as Noorvik, of which I had heard a great deal already.

Noorvik is a remarkable place, a township built to order, for the Bureau of Education. It had been found difficult to work with the numerous scattered little Eskimo villages with a few children in each, and arrangements were therefore made to shift them up inland where they could be taught together, and at the same time removed from the danger of demoralizing influences on the coast. The result was a model town of 300 inhabitants.

At six in the morning we sailed across Hotham Inlet and entered the Kuvak. It was wonderful weather. The sun had come out after a long spell of rain and mist; and we, who had been blockaded by ice throughout the summer, revelled in the sight of this new country, unlike any Eskimo territory we had ever seen. Here were wooded hills, fringing the fertile delta, rich grass land and soft warm breezes laden with the scent of trees and flowers.

Hotham Inlet (Imarsuk) is a big sheet of water, looking bigger than it is from the fact that the low shores are invisible until one is close upon them. Here, as throughout the whole bay, the water is so shallow that navigation is only possible by following the channels of the rivers. In rough weather, the crossing is impossible, as the water simply boils over the shallows, and parts are left high and dry.

In the course of the morning, we reached the Kuvak Delta, a big plain cut through by numerous channels, forming a maze which it would be impossible to negotiate with safety were it not for the marks set up at intervals along the fairway. The landscape seems altogether tropical to us, after the desolation of the Arctic coast. Bushes, low trees and tall grass run right out into the water, and ducks, geese and other waterfowl rise noisily as we near them. At noon we land at a little "road house" or travellers' shelter, open to any who happen to pass. It is designed more especially for winter use, and comprises, in addition to the house itself, a kennel with room for 15 dogs, a store of hay and a stack of firewood. We got a fire going in the stove, and had a meal ready in a twinkling. This disposed of, we went off up river once more. The vegetation grows richer and taller as we advance, and a couple of hours after leaving the road house we have fir trees on either side. Only a few at first, looking like forgotten Christmas trees, solitary strangers among the native birch and willow, but they soon

NASUK, FROM KOTZEBUE SOUND

An old wiseacre, well up in the ancient traditions of his people and an excellent teller of folk tales.

VIEW OF THE BEACH AT NOORVIK

The Bureau of Education has established an Eskimo township some distance up the Kopuk River, with sawmills and electric generating station.

grow bigger and more numerous as we go on, until there are whole woods, running down to the water's edge. Farther on again, the banks are tangled forest where axes would be needed to cut a way through. Here and there we come upon a deserted village; the natives have forsaken their fathers' hunting grounds and gathered about the modern wonders of Noorvik.

We reached there late that evening, and found the place well worth a visit. Three schoolmasters, an inspector, a doctor and two nurses attend to the various departments, and all are earnestly interested in the work. Everything is arranged on the most modern lines. There is a fine hospital with an operating theatre excellently equipped, and 40 beds, the whole in a two-storied building. Medical attendance and medicines are free, but patients admitted to hospital pay 75 cents per day if they can afford it. I found natives of all ages here; convalescents were admitted to the doctors' rooms and were given books, magazines and illustrated papers, besides being entertained with gramophone concerts. They seemed to be having a thoroughly good time altogether.

The Eskimos live in neat wooden houses, with electric light installed; for this, a charge of a dollar per month per house is made, the proceeds serving to pay the wages of the engineer in charge of the power station. The Eskimos have themselves defrayed the cost of the generator, the remainder being provided by the state. The place being in good timber country, a sawmill has been set up and the natives can have any quantity cut on payment in kind, a sixth of the load being the usual cost. The doctor's wife, who is herself a nurse, acts as a kind of sanitary inspector and looks after hygienic conditions in the homes.   Last winter, a flag with the Stars and Stripes was offered as a prize to the housewife who kept her home in finest order.   Visits of inspection were made at all hours throughout the winter in the different homes, but the lady inspector found them invariably so thoroughly washed and scoured and clean and neat that no white woman could have done better.   At the end of the term, the question as to who should have the flag became a problem indeed, for all seemed equally to have deserved it.   And the ingenious solution ultimately arrived at was, that it should go to the one who had most children and *yet* had kept her house as clean as the rest.

The white men seem to be thoroughly well in contact with the natives all round.   The Inspector often goes out felling timber with them, and lives in camp among them.   His wife helps the girls with their needlework, in addition to her missionary work. The doctor takes an active part in the affairs of the community apart from his own special task.

Much could be said for and against such an arrangement.   Theoretically, it looks excellent, as an experiment in systematic popular education.   But it is always risky to interfere overmuch in the private life of grown men and women.   The Eskimos appear content with their life here so far, though they do not greatly like the automatic "lights out" at 9

P.M. or the prohibition of smoking. These of course are trifles, though undoubtedly constituting interference with the liberty of the subject. More serious is the increase in competition owing to numbers. In consequence of this, the hunters, in the trapping season, have to leave the settlement and scatter in distant camps throughout the forest, while women and children are left behind out of regard to the schooling. The same applies to the fishing season in spring and autumn. It is perhaps doubtful whether this splitting up of families can go on for long; at present, owing to the confidence inspired by the Bureau of Education among the natives, it seems to work well enough.

We spent a day at Noorvik, and were most hospitably entertained in all the houses we visited. On the following evening we were back in Kotzebue, once more.

On the 21st of August the mailboat from Nome, a little schooner named the *Silver Wave*, arrived. We went on board, and found the Captain was a Norwegian, John Hegness. After a stormy voyage, we reached Nome on the 31st of August.

CHAPTER XXVI

CLIFF-DWELLERS OF THE ARCTIC

NOME lies on a moist grassy plain with a fine range of fertile hills in the background, making an imposing picture to those coming from the wastes of ice and snow. My two Greenlanders gazed wide-eyed at the spectacle, impressed by the white men's power of forming great settlements far from their own country.

Thirty years ago, the population consisted of a few Eskimo families, winning a bare existence from the sea. Then, in 1900, gold was found, and as if by magic a town sprang up, with room for ten thousand souls. The haste with which it was constructed shows even now in the lack of regard for beauty or comfort. Gold was the one idea. It is said that in Nome, there is gold underfoot wherever you tread; and during the last twenty years, the district has produced over eighty million dollars. Methods at first were of the most primitive sort; men dug with spades in the sand wherever they could get at it, or stood in lines along the shore trying to wash out gold dust from the sand. Mighty machines have superseded all this, and men now prefer the certainty of a high wage regularly paid to the chance of a fortune that may never come.

The season at Nome is but short; in the first half of June the ice disappears and navigation begins; by the end of October, or early in November, the last vessel has left for the south. The summer population now is about 2000; in winter barely 900, chiefly whites; of the permanent residents hardly more than a hundred are Eskimos. The town is a sort of capital for North-west Alaska, a centre for equipment of trading expeditions, and the constant stream of people passing through in summer provides a means of existence for stores, agencies and trades of various kinds.

My companions were naturally interested in the sights of the place; the streets with their curious wood paving, and the shops with all manner of wares they had never seen before. Anarulunguaq in particular could hardly believe it was all real. After a first look round, we went into a restaurant to get something to eat. To my astonishment, we were turned out! I had forgotten that we were now in regions where people are judged by their outward appearance, and had not given a thought to our old, worn clothes. We took the hint, however, and at once set about to procure the garments of respectability; took rooms at an hotel, and arranged our mode of life on modern lines.

I had reached Nome at a fortunate time for my work. Here were assembled Eskimos from all parts of Alaska; the entire population of King Island, the so-called Ukiuvangmiut, the inland Eskimos from Seward Peninsula, the Qavjasamiut, the Kingingmiut from Cape Prince of Wales, the Ungalardler-

miut from Norton Sound and the mouth of the
Yukon, the Siorarmiut from St. Lawrence Island, and
finally, natives from Nunivak Island. They had
come in for the tourist season. Some lived in gold-
diggers' cabins, but most of them in tents, and great
camps had sprung up at either end of the town,
where the Eskimos worked away making "curios,"
quaint carvings in walrus tusk, a form of industry
which might bring in three to four hundred dollars
in the course of one summer, enough to purchase
necessaries for the winter with which to return home.
The streets were full of Eskimos trotting about on
business; they rarely, if ever, offered their wares
direct for sale in the streets, but sold them to shop-
keepers who retailed them. All were cleanly and
decently dressed, kindly and respectful when spoken
to, without the least sign of having become demoral-
ized by life in town.

It was a festive time from first to last at Nome; an
ugly little town, but a town that quickly won one's
heart. It is the threshold of Alaska out towards
the great adventure of the north, and the people one
meets are inspired with the same love as we ourselves
for that Nature which calls and enthralls. No wonder that one finds friends here. I shall always
remember with especial gratitude the members of the
"Lomen dynasty," who, with the splendid old Judge
and his wife at their head, threw open their charm-
ing home to all the members of the Expedition, white
man and Eskimo alike.

I calculated that I could afford to spend a month
here, even allowing for a visit to East Cape, as the

vessel which was to take us down to Seattle would not leave until the end of October. I had thus an excellent opportunity of studying the various Alaskan types without having to travel in search of them, since they were all assembled here. I have here selected two of the most distinctive, namely, the King Islanders of Bering Strait, and the natives of Nunivak Island, south of the Yukon delta.

The native myth regarding the origin of King Island is as follows:

A man from the neighborhood of Igdlo came rowing down the river in his kayak. Near Teller he sighted a giant fish, which he harpooned with a bird dart. The great fish splashed about so violently that the river overflowed its banks, forming the sheet of water now known as Imarsuk. It then swam on again, and the man pursuing harpooned it once again, when the creature in its further struggles gave rise to a new inundation, forming the bay at Port Clarence. It then swam far out to sea, the hunter followed, and at last killed it. He then cut a hole through the snout, in order to fasten a towline, but a great storm came on, and he was obliged to leave it. And there it stayed, and turned to stone, and became the island of Ukiuvak (King Island). There is a hole at one end of the island, cut right through the rock; and that is the hole which the man cut in the fish's snout.

The Qavjasamiut lived in the interior, some way inland from Teller. In one of their villages there was a girl who, being scolded by her mother, ran away, and leaping on to an ice floe, was carried out to sea, and landed on King Island. She was the first human being to land there, and kept herself alive by magic; afterwards, others came over from the mainland, and a great village was formed. But the island was steep, and there were no valleys where houses could be built in the ordinary way; they had therefore to be set up on wooden supports on the steep rocky slopes. It was very cold here, with a constant wind, and the houses were built with three walls all round; first of driftwood, then a covering of hay, and over all a thick outer layer of walrus hides.

Thus the native account of King Island, its origin and colonization.

It is beyond question the most inhospitable island I have ever seen; some 3–4 km. long by 2–3 across, with steep rocky sides all round. In calm weather it is generally wrapped in fog; and when clear, harried by fierce winds, with a heavy swell that makes landing difficult among the broken rocks and churning waters at the foot of the cliffs. For a great part of the winter the place is cut off from the mainland altogether. When I visited the island, it was deserted for the time being, the entire population having gone in to Nome. We managed to land, in a small boat; and certainly it was worth a visit. It was like climbing up a bird cliff. The houses stood on piles leaning over the precipice; here and there, in the more exposed parts, the buildings were "moored" to the rock itself with ropes of plaited walrus hide. Ropes were fastened also from points on the shore up to the houses, as an aid to the ascent. Here and there one saw flat spaces under the houses themselves, where the rock had been levelled to make a playground for the children.

KING ISLAND, A SMALL ISLAND IN THE BERING STRAITS

The Eskimos have built their dwellings on a steep rocky slope. This is an excellent spot for hunting, but not for building; the houses are set on strong supports made from driftwood.

IN BERING STRAITS

The Eskimo hunt seal and walrus in small short kayaks which, despite their insignificant size, are excellent sea boats.

There was a notice board on the island, stuck up between a couple of boulders, with the following announcement in a flourishing hand:

NOTICE

All property on this Island belongs to the Eskimo. Do not take or disturb anything. Failure to comply will result in arrest and prosecution.

AVLAQANA,
Chief, King Island.

The King Islanders are zealous Catholics, and generally visit the Catholic Mission station at Nome during the summer. They are not only regular church-goers, but send their children to school as far as they are able, while the little ones themselves are keenly interested in their lessons. Unfortunately, there is not a single spot on the island where a school could be built. The Board of Education therefore proposed, some years back, to shift the entire population to St. Lawrence Island, where there is level ground and fertile soil; and as an inducement, each family was offered a two-years' supply of provisions, with special facilities for acquiring tame reindeer. They were invited to hold a meeting, presided over by their chief, and were given time to consider the matter. It took them very little time, however, to decide; not a single family would leave the naked rock they called their home; to them, it was the finest spot in the world.

These King Islanders are for the most part tall and well built according to Eskimo standards; they are, moreover, particularly neat and orderly with their gear. Their skin boats, kayaks, harpoons, and implements generally are the most handsomely worked in Alaska, and they have nearly always a full store of meat in reserve for the winter. Close to the village is a cave thirty metres deep, where meat will keep frozen all through the summer; it is entered through a narrow passage, and great torches have to be carried, as it is perfectly dark inside. Joints and carcases are marked with their owner's mark, the one store-chamber serving for all.

Their names for the different months of the year give an idea as to their manner of life.

October is the month of thin ice. Winter is approaching, and those who have been over to the mainland hurry back to set their house in order. The weather is unreliable, and it is dangerous to venture far out to sea. There is little hunting of seal or walrus, but fishing is carried on, mostly for small cod.

November is the hill-climbing month. The houses are built on the south side of the island, where there is now open water and very rough seas. The prevalent north wind, however, drives the ice in on the north shore; seal and walrus assemble there, and the villagers "climb the hill" to descend and go hunting on the opposite side. The yield, however, is but poor at this season.

December is the dance month. Weather stormy, and days too short for much to be done in the way of hunting; there is, however, generally a plentiful supply of meat in reserve, and the dark stormy days are passed in feasting.

January is the turning month, when the sun turns on its journey and begins to rise again. Light returns, the Strait is filled with ice and hunting commences on the north side of the island.

February is young-seal month. The seal are now heavy with young and are caught at the breathing holes and patches of open water. Sometimes the ice is firm enough for the islanders to cross to the mainland.

March is preparation month. Larger spaces of open water appear, the ice breaks adrift and kayaks and implements are made ready for use.

April is the month of getting out kayaks again. Winter hunting has now ceased altogether, the ice scatters, and the walrus begin to make their appearance. Seal and ribbon seal are harpooned from the kayak. This is the commencement of the spring season.

May is the month of flowing streams. The ground is now clear of snow and the earth "comes alive." Hunting in kayaks is continued among the drifting ice.

June is the month of light nights; game is abundant, and hunting is carried on by night and day.

July is the month of sleeping walrus, when the animals gather in great numbers on the ice and sleep in the sun, being then easily harpooned. During this and the following month most of the winter's store of meat is procured.

August is the month of fledglings. Seabirds are now caught in great numbers; many of the islanders, however, prefer to go farther afield, catching marmots for fur or gathering berries.

September is skin-forming month,—i.e., when the velvet begins to form on the antlers of the reindeer. In earlier times, the islanders went over at this season to the mainland, hunting caribou; now, however, they buy skins of tame reindeer from the owners of herds, and sell carvings and curios made during winter to the tourists at Nome.

The King Islanders are remarkably adapted to the harsh conditions under which they live, on a barren rock in the middle of the Bering Strait. They are hardy and always in training, frugal and industrious, obstinate and independent in character, and holding fast, despite their conversion to the Roman Catholic faith, to many of their ancient festivals, stories and songs. In their isolated position, with the monotony of winter on their little island, they naturally seek such diversion as can be found. Occasionally, in summer, several villages will hold great song festivals just as in the old days; and the King Islanders are famous for their dancing. There are a couple of dance houses in their village which appear to be of very ancient date. They are altogether overgrown with grass, which is so astonishingly luxuriant that it has almost filled up the chasm in which these two buildings are stuck like fantastic birds' nests. I clambered up into one of them and wormed my way through the six metres of entrance tunnel built of stones and earth; the place was hung about with tambourines and weird, staring masks—more like a temple of the spirits than a dance house. Unfortunately, there was no one on the island at the time of my visit, and I had to be content with making the acquaintance of the islanders in the picture-drome at Nome, where I found them wondering at the coldly impersonal manner in which white men go to their "festivals."

The Eskimos from the south and west of the Yukon spoke a dialect differing so considerably from the others that I found it, contrary to all previous experience, impossible to discuss difficult questions such as matters of faith and ceremonial, without the aid of an interpreter. I was fortunate in finding an excellent helper in the person of one Paul Ivanoff, a half-bred Eskimo, from St. Michael, who had also lived several years on Nunivak Island. I understood his speech without the slightest difficulty, while he also spoke the southern dialect, which is more or less the same throughout the whole range of country down to Kuskokwim and Bristol Bay.

One might expect to find the Eskimos more civilized farther to the south; this however is not the case. The Nunivak Islanders occupy a poor and barren country with clay soil, round the deltas of the great rivers; there is nothing here to attract the white man. No gold, no furs to speak of; the natives live mainly on seal and fish. Navigation is difficult along the coast here, owing to frequent storms, shallow water and lack of harbors, so that the people here have remained practically cut off from the development of the rest of Alaska. Only recently has the Bureau of Education begun to set up schools in this region, but in most places the natives are still heathen, cannot read, or even speak

English.   They were thus peculiarly interesting from my point of view, and I was able to procure a great deal of information as to their customs and ceremonies, in which a marked Indian influence is apparent.   A notable feature in this respect is their use of masks, in which the spirit element is developed to a degree far exceeding that noted under Point Hope. There is still a belief in the very slight distinction between the animals and man, and the power of animals to take human form; hence many of the masks represent seal, or birds, or beasts of prey, with human faces.   Each type is credited with some particular power, and serves to assist the angakoq in his invocation of helping spirits which here as elsewhere are the mediators between life and the supernatural.

Despite the miserable country and climate in which they live, the natives here have by no means lost their capacity for festival entertainments; on the contrary, we find here some of the prettiest ceremonies in use.   When a child is born, the parents give a great feast to all those from some distance round, and old men and women are given gifts by the mother, according to her wealth and position. Every husband is expected to lay in a store of costly furs, garments and finely worked weapons and implements, to be given away at the birth feast; the birth of a child is considered so great a blessing that a man may well give away all he possesses.

Similar feasts are held for the dead, with a view to preparing the way for them and making them happy in the world beyond.   The ceremonies here last a week, with various rites each day, and costly gifts to all present. As a rule several families combine in a festival for their respective dead, but even then the proceedings may be so expensive that several years of saving may be required to defray the cost of a feast worthy of the standing of the deceased.

The frail kayak to which the hunter trusts himself on the sea is built with great ceremony, special rites being designed to ensure safety and good hunting. The kayak is generally renewed each year, as it is considered unpropitious to enter on a new hunting season with old gear of any sort. During the time when a man is engaged on the building of a kayak he does not enter the women's house, but remains isolated in the dance house, which is also the men's workshop. Work must be done fasting, no food being taken until the evening, when the day's work is done. All has to be done slowly and carefully, with the observance of various forms of tabu. When it is finished, the kayak is consecrated on the first fine day when the sea is calm. The whole family will appear in new clothes, man, wife and boys—girls are considered unclean. The kayak is set on the ground with all the new implements decoratively arranged in place. The ceremony takes place at dawn; the man walks in front holding a lighted lamp, and all step round the kayak, the idea being that the flame scares away all evil spirits. The man then utters these words:

"May we never neglect an opportunity of work, of procuring food."

Then he goes out hunting, and the day he brings

home his first seal, with the new kayak, his wife loads up a little sledge with good food, fish, game and seal meat, and drives from house to house, giving gifts to all widows and fatherless children.

Thus gratitude should be shown for the blessing of daily food.

Every autumn a great festival is held in honor of the ribbon seal, which is an important factor in their life. The strange ceremonies here in use reveal the fundamental elements of that religious belief which we find among the Eskimos far to the east, in connection with preparation for winter work and the making of new clothes for the coming year, where strict rules of tabu must be observed.

The preparations for the festival begin in November and last a whole month. During this time the men must live apart from the women, remaining in the dance house, which their wives are only allowed to enter when bringing their food. The women, who are regarded as unclean in connection with all animals hunted, must take a bath every morning before carrying food to their husbands, and when so visiting them, must wear the waterproof garments used in stormy weather.

Every festival begins with new songs composed by the men, a kind of hymns invoking the spirits, men and women singing and dancing together. While the men are composing these hymns, all lamps must be put out, and all must be silent in the dance house, with nothing to disturb them. All males must be present, even the smallest boys, so long as they are old enough to talk. This is called the Qarrtsiluni, or time of waiting for something to break; for it is held that in the silence and darkness, when all are striving to think only noble thoughts. the songs are born in the minds of men as bubbles rising from the depths of the sea to break on the surface. The song is a sacred thing, and silence is needed for its birth.

Here is one of the songs:

The autumn comes blowing;
Ah, I tremble, I tremble at the harsh northern wind
That strikes me pitilessly in its might
While the waves threaten to upset my kayak.
The autumn comes blowing;
Ah, I tremble, I tremble lest the storm and the seas
Send me down to the clammy ooze in the depths of the
     waters.
Rarely I see the water calm,
The waves cast me about;
And I tremble, I tremble at thought of the hour
When the gulls shall hack at my dead body.

As soon as a song has been made it must be sung, and the women are called in to learn it with the rest. The making of songs, and dancing, must only be done in the evening; in the daytime, all are busy with other things; the women sewing, the men carving selected pieces of driftwood into various implements and utensils for the winter; large handsome vessels for water, drinking bowls and ladles, meat dishes and the like, so that each family has its own new set of requisites. When the men and women have finished their respective tasks, the angakoq is invited to call upon his helping spirits.   He appears in new winter boots and creaking waterproof skins, and sits down in the middle of the floor.   A line is brought out and a noose laid round his neck, four men hauling at each end of the rope, yet he utters his warnings and prophecies in a clear voice, despite the fact that he is apparently being strangled. Thus, almost hanging by the neck from the rope, he invokes the various animals, and informs the company when the winter hunting can begin.

As soon as this is over, the floor boards are moved away from the dance house, and a fire is lit in the space beneath.   All vessels, marked with the owners' respective marks, must now be exposed to the heat of the fire, the men at the same time purifying themselves by a perspiration cure.   The window in the roof is removed, the smoke escaping from the opening, yet so fierce is the heat that the men are dripping with sweat.   Finally, they wash in còld water.   This concludes the preparations for the great feast.

The feast itself lasts eight days.   During the past year, the bladders of all ribbon seals caught have been carefully preserved, and these are now brought in to the dance house, hung up with bundles of herbs under the roof, where a harpoon and line are also fixed, with a small lamp lighted beneath them. Then with great solemnity the new clothes are put on, and the new utensils handed round to their respective owners.   The women are called in, and feasts are held every day, ending with song and dance. At last, the seals' bladders are dropped into the sea through a hole in the ice, while the angakoqs implore the animals to be generous to men. On the eighth evening, men and women exchange gifts, and promise to try their best in the coming winter to be better in conduct and in their respective tasks.

The festival ends, as it began, in deep silence, the silence of good wishes and good resolutions.

And then the winter hunting can begin.

Here I conclude this description of the Alaskan Eskimos. . . . They number a little more than the Greenlanders, or about 14,000. The total number of the Eskimos is thus distributed approximately as follows: Greenland about 13,000, Canada about 5,000, Siberia about 1200—total thus about 34,000.

In material respects, the culture of the Alaskan Eskimos resembles more or less that of the natives of Point Barrow, Point Hope and on the great rivers up inland, as already described. There were of course adaptations to local conditions, but in the main, the old principles were followed throughout. Hunting on the ice is in these regions, as in the greater part of Greenland, relegated to a secondary place, and we naturally find it most highly developed in the neighborhood of the North-west Passage, where it remains the only form of seal hunting. The netting of seal, however, unknown farther to the east, is an important feature; even to this day nets are made from thin strips of sealskin and placed in narrow openings of the level ice near open water. But hunting at sea is the staple form, and is carried to a high degree of perfection. The Eskimo methods were doubtless developed on the shores of the Bering Sea, but whether this was due to the natives alone or aided by alien influence, cannot be determined with certainty.

The southern territorial limit of the Eskimos at present is on the east coast of Bristol Bay and at Kodiak in the Pacific, formerly, however, they extended as far as Prince of Wales' Sound and the coasts immediately to the southeast. Here lived also the northernmost tribes of the North-west Indians, the Tlingit, and the Eskimos here encountered a highly developed culture based on the same forms of hunting as their own. It is always possible that they may have learned something from their neighbors. This is certainly the case as regards some of their legends, especially the raven myths; also the cult of masks and the complicated ceremonial at their festivals. It is at any rate characteristic that these particular customs should have attained their highest development in these southern regions.

It is a consolation to every explorer that even the most comprehensive expedition never comes to an end, but by its researches opens the way for further work. It lies then with the future to investigate more closely the problems thus raised.

DANCING AT THE NATIVE FESTIVALS IN ALASKA

Men and women dance to the accompaniment of songs and tambourines. The men's dancing is designed to display manly qualities such as strength, ability and humor, while the women seek rather by suitable movements to exhibit beauty and grace.

EAST CAPE, SIBERIA, THE WESTERN BOUNDARY OF ESKIMO OCCUPATION

CHAPTER XXVII

THE BOLSHEVIK CONTRAST

WHILE flying before the gale on board the *Silver Wave*, just off Cape Prince of Wales, we sighted a little flotilla of quaint looking skin boats that came dancing over the choppy waters of the Bering Strait. The sails were so close-reefed that the wind had but the merest rags to catch hold of, but the boats were heavy laden, and tore through the waves like so many flapping seabirds.

It was a party of Siberian Eskimos from East Cape, on their way home from Teller, where they had been to trade. It was a hurried meeting, but thrilling in its way, and left me more than ever keen to visit these people on their own ground. In the extreme eastern corner of Siberia live the most westerly of all the Eskimos, and here surely was the most fitting point at which to end the Expedition.

Before landing anywhere in Siberia, it was necessary, I knew, to have a passport issued by the Central Office of the Soviet Government in Moscow. I had no such pass, for reasons which will appear later on. I was therefore prepared to meet with some difficulty, but my own keen interest in the task led me to imagine that my reasons must appear sound enough to anyone. The obstacles to be reck-

357

oned with arose from causes which had nothing whatever to do with my own work and aims. In the first place, relations between the Soviet Republic and America were generally strained, and secondly there was a particular cause of dispute just now in the matter of certain small schooners which had for generations past traded with Siberia under the United States flag, and now wished to continue without paying for the license which the new government not unreasonably demanded.

There were two ways of crossing Bering Strait. I could go in an Eskimo boat. This would be, to me, the easiest and simplest way of accomplishing my errand; but there was this disadvantage attached to it, that the native skin boats can only cross with a certain wind, and I might have to wait some time for it. And I had no time to spare. Also, in the event of any collision with the authorities on the other side, I should be alone, and at the mercy of any arbitrary official.

The other way was to charter a schooner. I should then have the advantage of being in company with other white men; on the other hand, it might prejudice my case if I were to arrive in one of those very vessels which were the subject of dispute.

Anyhow, the crossing must be made somehow. Ultimately, I chartered a small schooner, the *Teddy Bear*, captain and owner Joe Bernard, a well known and respected personality in these waters. I had at once, on getting into touch with the wireless at Kotzebue, sent off a message asking for permission to land from the Soviet Government, but after waiting three weeks I was forced to start without it, as otherwise the season would have been too far advanced to cross at all.

Bering Strait is one of the most treacherous waters in the world, gale follows gale almost incessantly, and in this part of Alaska there are practically no harbors in which one can seek refuge. We started on the 8th of September, and had a stormy week to start with, which forced us to seek the shelter of small islands and headlands here and there, shifting our refuges from time to time as the wind changed about, and in daily peril of being carried out into the still more dreaded Bering Sea. At last, on the 16th, about noon, the weather began to clear, and that evening, in the dark, we passed Cape Prince of Wales. From here, our course lay past Diomede Island over to East Cape itself. We came from Teller, and rounded the steep black cliffs in fine weather; the summits stood right up among the clouds, and there was a mighty wash of breakers at the foot. At the extreme limit of the land, on a piece of level ground, was an Eskimo encampment. We heard women laughing, dogs barking, and children at play, but saw only a cluster of lighted gutskin windows, the only visible sign of human habitation.

I was tired out after the restless threshing about of those stormy days, and turned in early that night, but next morning at dawn, Captain Bernard came in and roused me; we were nearing Diomede Island. I turned out at once; it was still barely light and I could just make out a great dark mass rising sheer and inhospitable from the sea, with thousands of seabirds wheeling and screaming over the cliffs, while the water broke in a scurry of foam on the rocks below. And this was fair weather—what would it look like in a storm? Yet the place was inhabited, though it looked like a bird cliff and nothing more. We made in towards the headland, intending to anchor, but just then a mass of fog came up, and the island vanished as suddenly as it had appeared. We gave up the idea of a visit for the time being, and made straight for East Cape.

Towards noon the fog lifted, and we sighted a forbidding rocky coast with snowclad hills rising from the sea. There was a desperate loneliness in the bare look of that land; a fitting aspect for the utmost verge of a continent. Masses of drift ice lay spread along the shore; the place looked desolate and far from any recognized route to anywhere. It was almost a shock to perceive a big steamer making straight towards us. The vessel was a patrol boat, and we were soon aware that the Soviet was keeping guard over its farthest frontiers. We hoisted the Danish flag, and the big boat seemed to peer inquisitively, only to turn its back on us next moment as if disdaining to approach anything so insignificant.

The ice almost hides the Eskimo village from view, and we can barely make it out. Anyhow, there is no shelter here, so we shape our course for Emmatown, some miles farther south. Captain Bernard, an experienced navigator, knows that the coast there will be clear of ice with this wind, and give us anchorage under shelter of a spit of land. There is a small township there consisting of a few Tchukchi families, some traders, and the Soviet representative. We are not particularly anxious to run right into the arms of the frontier police, but we shall have to meet them sooner or later.

We came sailing in with the Danish flag flying, and at once the red flags of the Republic were hoisted on shore. I am not sure that they had seen the white cross in ours. Captain Bernard and I were both pretty certain we were in for a trying day, and accordingly, had a good meal before going on shore. At last we got the dinghy out, and rowed to land, where we were met by a well known trader named Charley Carpendale, who has lived here for a generation. He at once introduced us to a giant of a man, whose height was further accentuated by a tall fur cap; this is the frontier guard, Allayeff. We shook hands, and I found myself looking into a pair of very friendly eyes; but there was a hint of obstinacy about the mouth that I feared might mean trouble. We found here also a Russian-English interpreter named Leo, and some traders from the recently established Soviet store.

We had hardly got our boat hauled up on shore before Allayeff requested us to accompany him to the police station. Here, with the energetic assistance of Bernard, I endeavored to explain my errand, and the reason for my having no passport, at the same time requesting permission to stay for a month among the Eskimos of East Cape. I promised, of course, that no trading should take place with the natives.

Allayeff declared that he had no authority to give

me any such permission, and that if we did not put
to sea again at once he would be obliged to send me
under escort to the Governor at Wahlen. I recognized that this would at least prolong my stay in the
country, and add to my chance of obtaining what I
wanted; accordingly, I declared my willingness to
make the journey.

I was then led over to the Tchukchi village, where
a team of twelve dogs was in readiness. I had barely
time to glance at the place. It was at once evident
that these were people of a different type from the
cheery, noisy Eskimos. These men looked serious, and from their expression, appeared to regard
me as some dangerous criminal. Curious types
there were among them, but all looked poor and ill
cared for. Women came out from the big dome-
shaped walrus hide tents and stared curiously at
our party; they were not unaccustomed to seeing
people carried off never to return. A few dirty
children clustered round the sledge.

All my papers had been taken from me and handed
to the Tchukchi who is to take me to the Governor.
The dogs are started—a miserable team—and we
move slowly over the sodden, melancholy tundra.
Not a trace of snow here, only swamp and water-
course and marsh. The only enlivening feature of
the landscape is the neck of East Cape rising strongly
in the east; there, the first snow has already fallen
on the heights, and gleams encouragingly; but for
the rest there is nothing but flat marshland, mud and
mire and wet; and as if this were not enough, the
sky sends down a steady soaking drizzle.

My driver had his own way of urging on his team. He carried a special kind of harpoon, with a sharp-pointed nail at one end, which he threw from time to time out among the dogs. At first they stopped dead; then, with howls of pain, they put on the pace for a few minutes. It was a pitiful proceeding for an experienced driver to watch; but the man was my jailer at present, and all my papers were in his charge, so it would hardly be wise to interfere. Moreover, there was no means of making oneself understood.

The dog-harpoon, or flying whip, is furnished at the kindlier end with a bunch of steel rings that rattle when shaken, and the sound also serves to urge on the team to fresh effort; evidently, the poor beasts have learned by experience what to expect if they fail to answer this hint. The dogs were harnessed in pairs, and I will in justice admit that despite their slowness, doubtless due to a summer on short commons, they were most obedient. After a couple of hours' energetic persuasion, they seemed to think it as well to make an end of the business, and went on at such a pace that we had to take it in turns to sit on the sledge.

I had always wanted to visit Russia, but the atmosphere of this monotonous tundra, the endless unchanging expanse of cheerless waste, was hardly what I had looked forward to. Moreover, I was not altogether free from anxiety as to the outcome of the interview awaiting me. Nevertheless, I was convinced that I had done the right thing so far.

Some distance out we encountered another sledge coming from the opposite direction; it proved to be a

Tchukchi, who spoke a few words of English, and we halted for a few minutes' talk. It was an awkward sort of conversation, standing there in the drizzling rain, shifting our feet continually to keep from sinking into the mud. I could not make out my fellow-traveller's name; it sounded rather like the chatter of a seagull as he pronounced it. He was very interested in my doings. Was I a trader? Had we any sort of goods on board our ship, and would we trade with him, somewhere out of sight along the shore?

I explained that I wished to conform to the law of the land, at which he protested, urging that the shops were all empty, and one could not even purchase ammunition. To make my own position clearer, I told him a little story I had heard myself regarding one of the American traders a few weeks before our arrival at East Cape. He had been informed, through one of the Eskimos on Diomede Island, that the Russian authorities had no objection to his landing at East Cape and trading with the natives there. Trusting to this safe conduct, he went across, and started bartering, only to find himself immediately seized and accused of illicit trading. All the ready cash on board his vessel, some $2000, was confiscated; the trader himself got away, thankful that they had not taken his ship as well. But when the Eskimo intermediary on Diomede Island heard what had happened to his friend, he crossed to the mainland himself to complain of having been made the instrument of a plot in defiance of good faith. All he got for his pains was a fine of $25 for insulting the authorities, and the fine being doubled each time he renewed his protest, he was at last obliged to give in.

My Tchukchi friend nodded sadly, as one who understood only too well. And we agreed that it would not be wise to risk any cause of conflict under present conditions. We shook hands heartily, and parted. I could see his team winding through the long grass like a serpent till it dwindled and finally disappeared.

The mist gave place to a magnificent rainbow arched across the heights; the weather cleared, and we arrived at Wahlen in a golden sunset, we ourselves, however, covered in mud from head to foot.

Wahlen is prettily situated on a low spit of land with the native yarrangs strung out like beads on a string. In the midst of these primitive, but picturesque walrus hide dwellings stood a big brand-new building, the residence of the Governor, looking perhaps a trifle self-assertive against the rest. Out at sea, the ice was packed as close as in winter, but in shore was a broad lagoon with smooth water reflecting houses and hills. It was perfectly calm, and the smoke from the cooking fires hung over the place in a fluffy white cloud.

As we drove up, a crowd of loose dogs came running out and entered into a lively battle with our team. At the same time, the men of the place crowded in from all sides and surrounded us; heedless of the dogs which tore at their skin clothing, they plied my companion with questions in a tongue of which I could not understand a word.

In front of the yarrangs stood women in their

curious combination garments of reindeer skin, worn
as a rule with one arm out of the sleeve, leaving half
the body naked. They were not without a certain
simple grace, rather reserved, and trying not to
appear inquisitive. I had not time to study them
closely, however; an elderly man, broad-shouldered
and of stern countenance, stepped forward and I
braced myself to meet the Governor. As it turned
out, however, this was only a bankrupt trader—one
of the victims of the new monopoly. A moment
later another Russian appeared, dressed from head
to foot in sealskin; he introduced himself in excellent
English as Peter Cossigan, trader and interpreter.

Authoritatively he waved the crowd aside, got my
papers from the driver, and led the way up to
Government House, where my fate was to be decided.
On the way, I managed hurriedly to explain who I
was and what I wanted. As a sufferer under the present régime, he seemed inclined to sympathize with
my position.

Despite the commotion occasioned by our arrival
among the natives, none of the Government officials
appeared, and we made our way in to the office. Here
all was wild disorder, with papers and documents
strewn about everywhere, and a medley of people
dodging about and getting in one another's way.

"Datskaya Ekspeditiya" is all that I could make out
of what is said in the course of an eloquent speech
introducing me to the Governor, one Nikolaus Losseff. He wore a ragged old sweater, and his manners
were as informal as his dress. Losseff appeared to
be a kindly soul, personally most willing to oblige,

and was deeply distressed on hearing what is the matter. I was introduced to the other officials present:
Vassili Dimitrievitch Kouslmin, Chief of Police,
newly arrived from Leningrad; Peter Bodroff, Inspector of Finances for the Chukotsk Peninsula, and
Police-Constable Maxim Penkin, a giant of a man,
who smiled with the simple kindliness of giants as a
race.

The Chief of Police at once took over all my
papers, including a passport issued from Montreal,
a letter of recommendation from the Danish Lega-
tion at Washington, a letter from the Danish Con-
sul at Seattle, and one from the American Minister
of the Interior, strongly emphasizing the purely scientific aims of the Expedition. Unfortunately, it soon
appeared that the Chief of Police could not read our
alphabet, and the Governor, who is in no better case,
strides up and down the office, to all appearance
much perturbed. All these people have treated me
with the greatest courtesy, altogether different from
what I had expected of the new Soviet type; and
after the exaggerated informality of Canadian and
American manners, it was quite refreshing to see a man
bow, actually bow politely, when one is introduced.
A chair was placed for me, and Russian cigarettes
were offered. Then the negotiations commenced.
I was no longer conscious of my wet clothes; my
one thought now was for the Expedition. With the
aid of an excellent interpreter, I endeavored to make
clear to them that my object in visiting East Cape was
strictly and exclusively scientific, and that this was
abundantly evident from the papers I had shown

them. With all the energy at my command I urged that my having no passport was due to the fact that there was no Government of Siberia in existence at the time when I started from Denmark, and that the Governorship of Wahlen was not established until a year after. Also that I had endeavored, through the nearest Danish consulate, to get into communication with Moscow, but in vain. And finally, that after three years of travelling from one Eskimo settlement to another, I had arrived at East Cape in order to study the Eskimos there, and begged the Soviet authorities to accord me the same facilities as I had received in Canada and America, where an Expedition coming from the Arctic regions is regarded as exempt from passport formalities.

In vain the Governor tugged at his hair, went out and came in and went out of the room again, all the time hugging the one solid fact which he seemed unable to get over, namely, that I had no passport from the Supreme Government in Moscow, and that his instructions left no margin for acting at his own discretion. I was further informed that the great concentration of officials was due to the strained relations existing between the Soviet and the rest of the world, and not least the formal conflict regarding the possession of Wrangel Island, to which place a warship had been despatched that summer.

Scientists do not appear to be popular after Vilhjalmur Stefansson's exploit in planting the British flag on Wrangel Island, which the Russians regard as Russian territory. England refused to recognize the annexation, and Stefansson established a trading concern on the island by himself, but later ceded the rights to a syndicate at Nome, which brought over Alaskan Eskimos to the disputed colony.

All unsuspecting, I had tumbled innocently into a political wasps' nest, and made the best use of such arguments as I could find, pointing out, for instance, that it would hardly be wise to turn away a scientific expedition from Russian territory after it has been received with interest and encouragement everywhere else—especially just now, when the Soviet should be keen on showing the world that Russia under the new régime appreciates the value of culture and science generally. All, however, apparently to no purpose.

All at once the Governor seemed to recollect that I had been travelling for some time; and appeared also to notice that I was covered with mud.

"Are you hungry?" he asked suddenly.

I admitted the fact. Whereupon he dashed out into the kitchen, to return a moment later and drag me through with him. Two smiling Russian girls were busy preparing a meal, and I passed them with a bow, finding time to notice their peculiar beauty, the dazzling white skin, and their eyes with long dark lashes that seemed like an expression of all unspoken melancholy in the world. We entered the dining room, the Governor sat down at table with me, and the women followed. One of them was his wife, the other a young schoolmistress from Irkutsk. I made an attempt at conversation, trying three languages, but in vain. We turned energetically to the dishes before us; oversweetened cocoa and some hot, sweet preserve eaten with bread; famished as I was, it went down as meat with a hungry Eskimo.

The dining room was an apartment with bare walls devoid of ornament, perhaps in order to focus attention the more directly upon the Constitution of the Soviet Republic, a copy of which covered the whole of one wall. And also—I had almost forgotten it—in one corner a picture of Lenin, dressed as a simple street scavenger. I gazed at him, not without bitter reproach at the thought of his having given this otherwise amiable Governor instructions leaving no room for the slightest deviation: the letter of the law, or off with his head!

A moment later the Chief of Police came in and informed me that I might stay the night in the Governor's house, but must return to my ship the following day and leave Siberia at once. Very sorry, but . . .

It was goodbye to East Cape.

I had thus one evening and part of the following day to work in, and hoped that after all I might be able to make some use of my time. East Cape was out of reach, but there were a few old Eskimos at Wahlen and at Emmatown whom I could talk to. There were also the Tchukchis; and I had here an excellent interpreter in the person of Peter Cossigan, who spoke their language and English with equal fluency. The police imposed no further restrictions on my liberty; I was free to go where I pleased and speak with whom I pleased during the eighteen hours or so that I was still suffered to remain in Soviet territory.

I began by calling on the traders, who were assembled in a small house, and discussed with them the situation generally. They were all Russians, but in spite of this, their position was worse than my own. The Soviet monopoly forbade them to trade on their own account, while at the same time, the government offered them no other means of making a living, and no opportunity of getting out of the country. One of these unfortunates, whose name I will not mention, fumbled in an old chest full of oddments, and pulled out a huge bundle of notes—paper roubles from the time of the Czars. These were his savings; rouble on rouble hoarded up by years of economy; and now, he declared, worth less than so much cigarette paper.

I asked how many there were.

"What does it matter?" he answered. "I used to know the whole sum to a kopek, but now, I cannot say. Thirty thousand, a hundred thousand roubles, it makes no difference either way."

One old trader named Gobrinoff, who had suffered the same fate, burst out suddenly into a foolish mirthless laugh, and the rest of us fell silent.

These bankrupt traders speak no ill of the Soviet, in spite of the fact that they, like everyone else in the district, have to look forward to a winter without tea or coffee, perhaps without tobacco, though, as they explain almost apologetically, there will be plenty of walrus meat and blubber. It is something of a degradation in their old age; they were wealthy merchants once, men of distinction in the place, and are now reduced to eating the blubber of charity and seeking the warmth of the native yarrangs as soon as the winter drives them from their own wooden huts, which they have no fuel to make habitable.

It was not a cheerful party, and I was glad to take my leave and go visiting with Peter Cossigan among the natives. The information I acquired in the course of these visits, and subsequently, may be summarized as follows:

Save for the Governor's residence and a couple of stores, Wahlen consists exclusively of yarrangs—huts of the Tchukchi type—inhabited by a couple of hundred people, who get their living solely from the sea. The Tchukchis, and also the Eskimos of East Cape, still live exactly in the same fashion as before any white men came to their country. No attempt at spiritual influence has ever been made. It was thus a magnificent field for ethnographical research, and one in which I might well have spent some months. As it was, I had only a few hours, and can only give one or two of the main features.

Peter Cossigan, who had himself married a Tchukchi woman, led me first of all into one of the largest yarrangs. It was a curious structure, half hut, half tent, consisting of a heavy wooden framework built to the shape of a dome, and covered with walrus hide. We found ourselves at first in a sort of front room which occupied about half the entire space, with a fireplace in the middle of the floor, on which some walrus meat was cooking at the time. Despite a couple of ventilation holes in the roof, the place was so full of smoke that it was some little time before I made out the figure of a woman kneeling by

REPRESENTATIVE OF THE RUSSIAN SOVIET FROM EMMATOWN

He refused us permission to land at East Cape in Siberia.

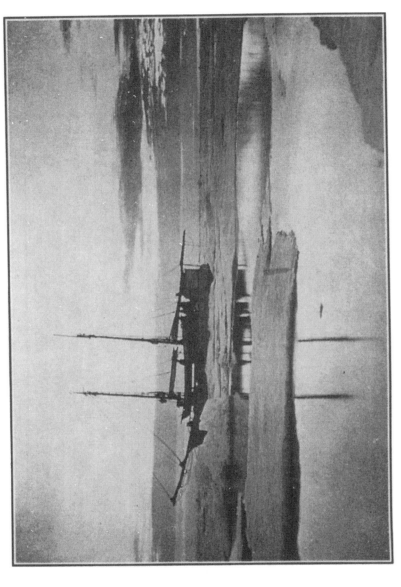

THE "TEDDY BEAR"

The voyage from Nome to East Cape was made on board the little schooner *Teddy Bear*, Capt. Joe Bernard. The vessel is here seen ice-bound off East Cape.

the fire and tending her pot. She rose to her feet
with a little laugh, and invited us to enter. I now
perceived that there was a small tent of reindeer
skin hung up in the interior of the hut, being fastened
by thongs to the wooden framework, but without
tent holes of its own; this was just large enough to
enclose what would have been the raised sleeping
place in an Eskimo hut. There was no particular
entrance to this tent; we simply crawled in anywhere under the sides, which were made of heavy,
thick-haired winter skins. In this inner apartment
sat a young woman perfectly naked, busy preparing some sealskin. The temperature indeed did not
call for any excess of clothing, for though the sun
was blazing down outside on the walrus hide, and
making the place intolerably hot already, there were
two blubber lamps burning in addition. There
was no raised platform or couch to serve as a bed-
place, but the floor itself in this apartment was made
of wood covered with layers of walrus hide. The
place served as a workroom for the women during
the day, and a bedroom for the whole family at
night. Looking about me, I realized that all the
implements in sight, knives and other tools, even
the drums, were of exactly the same type as those
I had found among the Eskimos. It was therefore
the more remarkable to find that I understood not a
single word of the language. The young woman
greeted us with a friendly smile, and went on with
her work, and my companion now informed me that
only women were generally to be found in the
houses during the daytime; they did their cooking

and needlework here, while the men were out in the open air practically all day long. When not actually out hunting, they would be outside somewhere, whatever the weather was like. We should therefore find no men anywhere indoors at this time of the day, and therefore found it best to invite a couple of Cossigan's Tchukchi friends in to the little hut, where his native wife, a gentle and kindly soul, at once made tea for us.

The one thing most prominent in my mind at the moment was to find out what the Tchukchis and the East Cape Eskimos respectively thought of each other, and get their views as to relations generally between the races. One old man whom we questioned was well up in this subject, and began by pointing out emphatically that his people were the original inhabitants of the country, and nothing to do with the Eskimos. In which connection he gave us the following story:

"In a strange land, among a strange people, there lived a little girl whose mother was always displeased whatever she did. No matter what trouble she took with the tasks assigned to her, she was continually being scolded. At last she could bear it no longer, and ran away from home, taking with her all her dolls. She walked and walked for ever so far, till she came to a land she did not know. And here she built herself a shelter from the wind, and decided to live there. But one night she woke up and found that all her dolls had come alive; had turned into real men and women. And from these, it is said, sprang the race of the Tchukchis."

Originally, all the Tchukchis were hunters, but some learned in course of time to tame the wild reindeer, and grew rich; others, who could not attain to the ownership of a herd, moved down to the coast in the hope of finding better fortune there. When the Tchukchis first came down to the coast, there were no Eskimos there. They found all manner of beasts in the sea; seal, whale and walrus, but it was long before they learned how to hunt them; they tried to make boats so as to follow them out at sea, but their hunting implements were poor, and they were often hungry, despite the wealth offered them by the sea. At last they took to making long sea voyages, along the coast and far out to sea, where they could perceive land in the farthest distance. This was Diomede Island. Here they met a strange people whose tongue they could not understand; a people who called themselves Eskimos, and lived likewise on the beasts of the sea. But they had fine weapons for their hunting, and many curious ways of killing seal and whale and walrus; they had harpoons furnished with lines and bladders; they had big skin boats for long voyages and little swift kayaks. But they were a hostile people, with whom it was not wise to live for any length of time, and there was often war between the two peoples. Once a whole boatload of Tchukchis was attacked and slain to the last man. This was too much. All the men from many villages assembled and sailed across the sea; and when the Eskimos saw this great number approaching, they made ready for a battle. But the Tchukchis had not come to fight; they only proposed that an agreement should be made between them, so that they could live in peace and trade with one another thereafter.   They then laid out all the trade goods they had brought with them; skins of the caribou, and handsome white spotted skins of the tame reindeer; skins of wolf and wolverine they laid out on the rocks by the strangers' village, and the Eskimos saw all these skins, which they themselves needed but could not get, because they lived on a little island in the midst of the sea.   Thus the Tchukchis offered to make peace, and peace was made between them, and has never since been broken. And it was not long before the Eskimos in turn began to make trading voyages to the coast of the mainland, and finding excellent hunting in the neighborhood of East Cape, they determined to build a great village of their own there.   Thus the two peoples became neighbors, and the Tchukchis learned all the Eskimo methods of hunting; they built skin boats and made lances, harpoons and bird arrows, and lived as the Eskimos did.   The Eskimos in their turn wished to dress as the Tchukchis did, and copied also the manner of their houses, which are built of wood and walrus hide.   They also learned to cut their hair in the same way.   So the one people learned of the other, but each retained its own language, and only very rarely did those of one race intermarry with the other.

The Eskimos, however, were from the first superior on the sea, and so they remained.   The East Cape Eskimos, who hunted with the American whalers, became famous for their skill in managing a boat;

and in a mixed crew of Eskimos and Tchukchis, it will always be the Eskimos who take command. When hunting on the ice in winter, if difficulties arise, it is invarably an Eskimo who is chosen to lead the way.

All this I had from the mouth of the old Tchukchi himself.

According to the Tchukchi tradition, then, the Eskimos are a new people who came into Asia from Alaska and the islands of the Bering Sea. This tradition accords entirely with the Eskimos' own recollections of the manner in which the islands in question, and East Cape itself, became inhabited.

All the old myths agree that the first men came to King Island, from the interior east of Tellar, while Diomede Island was inhabited by people coming from King Island and Schismareff; from here again they found their way to East Cape, and thence further along the coast of Siberia both north and southwest. Ruins of Eskimo houses are also found in both directions. I was naturally unable to make excavations here, but I did manage to examine a number of old houses at Wahlen, which were indubitably of Eskimo origin. The only island in the Bering Sea colonized by Eskimos from the Asiatic side is St. Lawrence Island, called by the Eskimos Sioraq; this, however, is due to the geographical situation, the island lying close to the Siberian shore, so that adventurers from East Cape would reach it by way of Indian Point.

I managed during my short stay to note down a list of native words showing that the East Cape dialect is very like the language spoken at St. Lawrence; and oddly enough, both resemble mostly that spoken south of Norton Sound and over the Yukon right down to Bristol Bay, differing considerably from the form current in the rest of Alaska.

Until the American Bureau of Education commenced work in Alaska, the Siberian Eskimos were greatly superior to the American, both in conditions of life and in general estimation; now, however, the reverse is the case, and those Siberian natives who have been to Nome for trading purposes marvel at the enormous progress made by their fellows on that side, while they themselves live in a country whose government seems to take no interest in them whatever beyond getting their furs at the lowest possible price.

This then was the result of my visit to Wahlen and my encounter with the Soviet.

On the following day I was taken back across the same dreary tundra, and escorted on board the *Teddy Bear* by the Chief of Police and the kindly giant of a constable, Penkin. I was shown out; requested to leave and that forthwith; but it was some consolation to reflect that my visit had not been altogether fruitless. The information I had gathered fitted in admirably with the previous results of the expedition, and confirmed the correctness of what we had already learned.

We hoisted sail and got under way. The ice lay close in to shore, and we were forced to lie for a little while off the Eskimo village at East Cape. It was

like looking into the promised land that one was not
fated to enter. Novoqaq is a big village with some
400 souls. The jaws and ribs of whales were used
for building material, as we could see, not only for
the houses but for platforms and drying frames outside. The houses themselves were built on a slope
of the steep hillside, wall to wall; down on the beach
were skin boats and whale boats ready to put out
the moment an animal was sighted. It was in the
height of the walrus hunting season, and one had
not long to look with a good glass before one perceived the great heavy bodies on the ice-floes as
they surged along close together to the northward.
The walrus were dozing; as if well aware that the
boats could not put out because of the ice between.

Young men and children came running down, out
on the ice itself, and right up to the ship. A few
came on board and stayed with us for an hour;
they knew I was not allowed to stay, and the situation called forth expressions of regret on both
sides. Needless to say I should have been glad to
see more of them, and I could see that they would
have welcomed me among themselves.

However, there it was. A few days later we were
back in Nome. And the Fifth Thule Expedition
was at an end.

As I rowed on shore in the dinghy, I saw a man
running backward and forward on the beach, waving something in his hand. It was a telegram,
addressed to myself, and I opened it not without
some excitement, as to its contents. It proved to
be from the Danish Foreign Ministry, stating briefly

that permission had been obtained from the Soviet Republic for me to land at East Cape.

Only, as fate would have it, the information arrived six weeks too late.

CHAPTER XXVIII

SILA

"All true wisdom is only to be found far from the dwellings of men, in the great solitudes; and it can only be attained through suffering. Suffering and privation are the only things that can open the mind of man to that which is hidden from his fellows."— IGJUGARJUK, of the Caribou Eskimos.

ONE morning at the end of October, 1924, I awoke for the last time in the little wooden dwelling on the outskirts of Nome, where I had been living for the past month. By noon that day I must be on board the big tourist steamer bound for Seattle, and these years of life among the Eskimos would be at an end.

I was delighted at the work I had been able to accomplish during that time, and my thoughts naturally turned once more to a last survey of the vast regions which we had traversed and the people we had met. One could not but feel some regret that it was all over and done; a happy spell of work that would never come again, and now must give place to the hurry of returning to civilization, and the monotonous toil of trying to give out again something of all I had received.

Alas, what are words compared with life itself!

I went out into the morning sunlight and felt the

cool breeze in my face. The lakes were already frozen over, and the first sledges were driving over the snowy plains. The town itself was getting ready for the coming winter; white men were writing their letters for the last mail before the port was closed by ice, and the Eskimos were making preparations for return to their scattered villages far around.

As fate would have it, this very morning I received a visit from an angakoq; one of the few still remaining in these parts. And as he was the last of all I met, it seems fitting to conclude with him.

His name was Najagneq, and I met him for the first time in the streets of Nome, as a fugitive in a strange place. His appearance alone was enough to create a sensation; among the well-dressed people, with fashionable shops on either hand, and motor cars hurrying past, he looked like a being from another world. His little piercing eyes glared wildly around, his lower jaw hung down, swathed in a bandage half undone; a man had recently tried to kill him, and wounded him badly in the face.

Strange things were told of him. He had turned his house into a fort and waged war single-handed against the rest of his tribe. And against all white men as well. He had already killed several people, when he was captured by a ruse and brought in to Nome. Here he was kept in prison for a year, and had just been released for lack of evidence to convict him. Opinions were divided as to the rights of the case; some declared he was simply half-mad, and a danger to the community; others regarded him as fighting on behalf of his people against the whites,

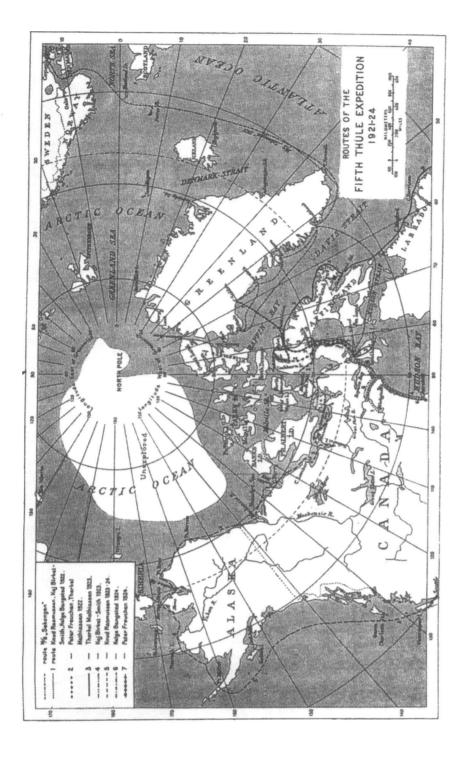

and against those misguided natives who supported them. He was forbidden to speak his own language in prison, and as he could not speak any other, he did not speak at all for a whole year. By the end of that time, ten witnesses from his own village had been brought in to give evidence against him; but when confronted with the accused, all without exception declared they had nothing to say. He was known to be a powerful wizard, and no one dared to give evidence against him. In face of this, there was nothing to be done but release him, and send him back to his own place, on Nunivak Island.

I managed to get into touch with him just before his release, and as I happened to be working among his fellow countrymen at the time, I had ample opportunities for observation. He was never tired of telling stories of his life in prison, and by no means disinclined to triumph a little over those of his own people who had tried to rid themselves of his eccentricity by alliance with the whites, yet had not dared to say a word when brought face to face with him in court.

He had found fresh food for thought in this great town. Though accustomed only to earthen huts, sledges and kayaks, he was not impressed by the great houses, the steamers or the cars; but a white horse pulling a heavy cart had set his imagination working. And he solemnly informed his wondering fellow-tribesmen that the white men in Nome had killed him ten times during the past winter; but he had had *ten white horses* for his helping spirits, and by sacrificing one on each occasion he had managed

to save his life! For the rest, his confinement in a
solitary cell had not crushed his spirit. He, the great
hunter, had learned to talk to the darkness, had vanquished solitude itself, and now, released at last, had
accustomed himself to the lack of open air life, of
speech and humankind.

This 10 HP wizard was an oldish man, with fiery
eyes, a power of words and a forceful utterance
that impressed those with whom he spoke. He was
curiously gentle and friendly toward me, and when
we were alone, was not afraid of confessing that he
had been playing on the credulity of his native
friends. He was not a humbug really, but a man
accustomed to finding himself alone against a crowd,
and with his own little tricks of self-defense. Whenever the talk turned on his early visions and the faith
of his fathers, he spoke firmly, clearly, and in the
plainest earnest. His words were brief and to the
point; and I suited myself to his manner as far as I
could. So that a conversation between us would
be something like this:

"What does man consist of?"

"Of the body; that which you see; the name,
which is inherited from one dead; and then of something more, a mysterious power that we call *yutir*—
the soul, which gives life, shape and appearance
to all that lives."

"What do you think of the way men live?"

"They live brokenly, mingling all things together;
weakly, because they cannot do one thing at a
time. A great hunter must not be a great lover of
women. But no one can help it. Animals are as

unfathomable in their nature; and it behooves us who live on them to act with care. But men bolster themselves up with amulets and become solitary in their lack of power. In any village there must be as many different amulets as possible. Uniformity divides the forces; equality makes for worthlessness."

"How did you learn all this?"

"I have searched in the darkness, being silent in the great lonely stillness of the dark. So I became an angakoq, through visions and dreams and encounters with flying spirits. In our forefathers' day, the angakoqs were solitary men; but now, they are all priests or doctors, weather prophets or conjurers producing game, or clever merchants, selling their skill for pay. The ancients devoted their lives to maintaining the balance of the universe; to great things, immense, unfathomable things."

"Do you believe in any of these powers yourself?"

"Yes; a power that we call Sila, which is not to be explained in simple words. A great spirit, supporting the world and the weather and all life on earth, a spirit so mighty that his utterance to mankind is not through common words, but by storm and snow and rain and the fury of the sea; all the forces of nature that men fear. But he has also another way of utterance, by sunlight, and calm of the sea, and little children innocently at play, themselves understanding nothing. Children hear a soft and gentle voice, almost like that of a woman. It comes to them in a mysterious way, but so gently that they are not afraid; they only hear that some danger threatens. And the children mention it as it were casually when they come home, and it is then the business of the angakoq to take such measures as shall guard against the peril. When all is well, Sila sends no message to mankind, but withdraws into his own endless nothingness, apart. So he remains as long as men do not abuse life, but act with reverence towards their daily food.

"No one has seen Sila; his place of being is a mystery, in that he is at once among us and unspeakably far away."

These mighty words form a fitting close to the sketch I have tried to give throughout this book of Eskimo life and thought. Before many years are past, their religion will be extinct, and the white man will have conquered all, the country and its people; their thoughts, their visions and their faith.

I am glad to have had the good fortune to visit these people while they were still unchanged; to have found, throughout the great expanse of territory from Greenland to the Pacific, a people not only one in race and language, but also in their form of culture; a witness in itself to the strength and endurance and wild beauty of human life.

Najagneq's words come as an echo of the wisdom we admired in the angakoq we met at every stage of the journey; in the inhospitable regions of King William's Land, in Aua's snow-palace at Hudson Bay or in the circle of the Caribou Eskimo Igjugarjuk, whose words are quoted at the head of this chapter.

A month later, I stood on the roof of a skyscraper looking out over the stony desert of New York. Miteq and Anarulunguaq stood beside me, impressed, as I was myself, by the marvels we saw about us.

"Ah," sighed Anarulunguaq, "and we used to think Nature was the greatest and most wonderful of all! Yet here we are among mountains and great gulfs and precipices, all made by the work of human hands. Nature is great; Sila, as we call it at home; nature, the world, the universe, all that is Sila; which our wise men declared they could hold in poise. And I could never believe it; but I see it now. Nature is great; but are not men greater? Those tiny beings we can see down there far below, hurrying this way and that. They live among these stone walls; on a great plain of stones made with hands. Stone and stone and stone—there is no game to be seen anywhere, and yet they manage to live and find their daily food. Have they then learned of the animals, since they can dig down under the earth like marmots, hang in the air like spiders, fly like the birds and dive under water like the fishes; seemingly masters of all that we struggled against ourselves?

"I see things more than my mind can grasp; and the only way to save oneself from madness is to suppose that we have all died suddenly before we knew, and that this is part of another life."

The Expedition was at an end. The years which to us white men had been full of strange happenings and experiences, were just everyday life to our two Greenlanders. It was their turn now; their expedition was beginning.   But as I showed them the marvels of this new world, my thoughts were constantly returning to the people we had left, to the men and women who had spoken so simply and yet so powerfully of the greatest and the smallest things.   Hunger and feasting, happiness and adversity, the daily round and the great moments of life—they spoke of all with true and simple feeling.   So here; face to face with a chaos and confusion of marvels, Anarulunguaq found the very words for all it meant:

Nature is great; but man is greater still.

INDEX

A

Aberdeen Lake, 76

Adelaide Peninsula, 168, 201, 240–241

    Native populations, 218, 234

Admiralty Inlet, 140, 145

afterlife beliefs. *See* death; soul

Agdlilugtoq, 171

Aggjartoq, 85–86

Agiaq, 269

the Agiarmiut, 269–278

the Ahiarmiut, 244–245

Ahongahungaoq, 283

the Ahongahungarmiut, 283–284

Ailanaluk, 235

the Aivilik, 8, 115–117

Akilineq, 76, 169, 245

the Akilinermiut, 5

Akjartoq, 93

    Akjartoq's Song, 94

Alaska

    Eskimo ethnology, 116–117

    Eskimo immigrants from, 289, 300

    monetary influence in, 289, 293

    Native populations (western Eskimos), 222, 268, 284, 304–340

Albert Edward Bay, Native populations, 245

Alekamiaq, 279–280

Allan, Jim, 315

Allayeff, 361

Alorneq, 180–182, 184, 210

Amitsoq, 205, 206

amulets, 84, 126, 134, 136, 180, 198, 224–225, 272, 385

    acquisition of, 180, 182–187

    charms, 136–138, 145, 183, 188, 198

    described, 135–137

    spirit belts, 13, 84

    See also religion; spirits; tabu

Amundsen, Roald, 178, 201, 217

Anarnigtoq, 90

Anarqaoq, 121–122

Anarulunguaq, 35, 52, 156, 158, 189, 204, 206, 209–211, 247, 269, 314, 341, 387

Anderson, Dr. Martin, 283, 285